W9-ATE-656

Correction of a
Correctional Psychologist
in
Treatment of the Criminal Offender

Publication Number 859

AMERICAN LECTURE SERIES®

A Monograph in

The BANNERSTONE DIVISION *of*
AMERICAN LECTURES IN BEHAVIORAL SCIENCE AND LAW

Edited by

RALPH SLOVENKO, B.E., LL.B., M.A., Ph.D.
Wayne State University
Law School
Detroit, Michigan

Correction of a
Correctional Psychologist
in
Treatment of the Criminal Offender

By

HAROLD F. UEHLING

*Formerly Senior Staff Psychologist
Division of Corrections, Wisconsin
Department of Health and
Social Services*

CHARLES C THOMAS • PUBLISHER
Springfield • Illinois • U.S.A.

Published and Distributed Throughout the World by
CHARLES C THOMAS · PUBLISHER
BANNERSTONE HOUSE
301-327 East Lawrence Avenue, Springfield, Illinois, U.S.A.

© *1973, by* CHARLES C THOMAS · PUBLISHER
ISBN 0-398-02615-7
Library of Congress Catalog Card Number: 72-81721

With THOMAS BOOKS *careful attention is given to all details of
manufacturing and design. It is the Publisher's desire to present books
that are satisfactory as to their physical qualities and artistic possibilities
and appropriate for their particular use.* THOMAS BOOKS *will be true
to those laws of quality that assure a good name and good will.*

Printed in the United States of America
Y-2

This book is dedicated to the memory of Dr. Frank C. Richmond, *psychiatrist, lawyer, and first director of the mobile Psychiatric Field Service "circuit" of the Wisconsin State Board of Control during the years 1924 to 1935.*

FOREWORD

THIS book is a frank exposé of the embryonic struggles and eventual metamorphosis of a prison psychologist. It begins with early institutionalized psychometry which was spawned in the impoverished economy and penologically congested aftermath of the 1929 stock market crash. In scope, it embraces both clinical and custodial shortcomings over a period of almost four decades. It uncovers a tenuously inconsistent and uncoordinated effort which, up to and including the wave of social unrest and criminal violence associated with the 1960's, has to a large extent resulted in an abortive benefit to the criminal offender.

The book is written from the standpoint of a recently retired senior staff psychologist who served 37 continuous years as a correctional psychologist in a penal setting. The subject matter covers the repressing rigidity of the early psychometric evaluations which emphasized statistical incentives at the expense of the criminal offender's capacity for emotional expressiveness. It takes the reader on an excitingly hopeful, but frustratingly inadequate, "swing of the pendulum" from one extreme of rehabilitative endeavor to another. Each "swing" fortifies the ultimate impression of an insensitive neglect of the criminal offender's own self-evaluation, the depressing effects of which provide no inner incentives for change.

Since the revelations of the clinical psychologist in a correctional setting are governed by his own "security needs" under traditionally regulated supervisory restraints, his retired status permits a more open appraisal at both ends of the treatment continuum. The purpose of this book, therefore, is to provide an overall perspective of the mood-saturated "ups and downs" in a prison-oriented treatment program, culminating finally in a contrasting awareness of the colossal tragedy involved in a rejecting waste of individual potential behind unexpressed emotional needs.

Surprisingly, these needs are now recognized as most responsive to an appropriate group interaction of criminal offenders on a time scale and priority level geared to fit the unique requirements of each individual situation. Representative case illustrations of the emotional conflicts and subsequent rehabilitative progress of some of the most difficult treatment prospects are offered, together with a revealing example of the coming treatment emphasis in the all important context of family therapy. The aim of this time-tempered, analytical study is toward the ultimate acceptance of personal responsibility on the part of the criminal offender.

During his career, Harold F. Uehling initiated or participated in a number of firsts for Wisconsin Corrections. In 1943, he pioneered the use of the Rorschach Test at the Wisconsin State Prison. In 1948-49, he directed a program of aptitude analysis at the prison which was intended to serve as the basis for recommendations for jobs and training to the classification committee. In 1951, he was instrumental in establishing the first therapy group at the prison. Initially, the groups consisted of Criminal Code offenders who had presented disciplinary problems to the institution staff. In 1956, this technique was begun with those sentenced under the Sex Crimes Law and today is a treatment of choice for many individuals committed to correctional institutions.

In addition to his clinical activities, Harold F. Uehling has prepared 12 professional papers beginning with an article coauthored with Dr. Harry Harlow and Dr. Abraham Maslow. He is recognized as an expert in the use of psychodrama as a treatment technique and has modified this approach for use with offenders. He was certified to practice psychology by the Board of Examiners of the Wisconsin Psychological Association. He received his bachelor's degree in Psychology in 1931 from the University of Wisconsin.

In 1969, Harold F. Uehling retired as senior staff psychologist in the Bureau of Clinical Services at the Wisconsin State Prison. The writing of this history of clinical services was completed during his retirement.

RALPH SLOVENKO, *Editor*

PREFACE

Psychotherapist: "Actually, you are a prisoner of feelings which you have chained to the past."

Inmate Offender: "So? How can I get rid of them?"

Psychotherapist: "You need to dredge out all of the hate and fear you have locked up in the miserable childhood which you are so reluctant to tell me about. Surface all of your early unpleasant experiences no matter how much it hurts to talk about them. Expose these feelings to the light of the present. That will give you more depth—a new perspective concerning your own involvement. Then you will be able to accept your feelings for what they really are."

Inmate (six months later): "I can't face it. All of this digging into the past makes me morbid and depressed. Sometimes I feel so low I want to kill myself. I need tranquilizers. I can't get along without medication. If I were on the outside I'd get drunk. I just can't describe how miserable I feel. But maybe you can help me. The fellows say you're different, that you try to understand. I'm desperate. What can I do?"

Second Psychotherapist: "You've got the wrong attitude. It isn't good for you to brood. You must not dwell on these morbid thoughts. I want you to look to the future with new hope, and a new faith in your ability to succeed. That means you will have to get outside of yourself. Think only for today. Become involved. Lose yourself in an interesting activity or hobby of some sort. In the meantime, I shall refer you to Dr. X for a new prescription to ease your tension and help you to concentrate."

Inmate (three months later): "This medication is getting me down. When I'm relaxed I am also tired and sleepy. Then I lose interest and don't want to do anything. Otherwise, I feel as tight as a drum —like I'm hanging onto a limb that is about to break. At times I have a sensation like I'm floating and not quite able to touch down with my feet. Will you ask Dr. X to call me in? I'd like him to give me some new kind of pill. Either that or take me off the stuff he's got me on."

Third Psychotherapist: "You shouldn't be taking any kind of pill if it affects you in that manner. Anyway, it isn't good for you to become too dependent upon tranquilizers. They are only meant to tide you over the rough spots."

Inmate: "So, what can I do?"

Psychotherapist: "Now, I've got something new I'd like you to try. We call it counter conditioning. Actually, it is a form of re-learning—a desensitization of wrong attitudes and troubled feelings. It goes something like this: I'm going to do something that will help you to relax while you are in the act of calling up mental images of your deepest anxieties. We have pictures and slides which we will use for this purpose. I shall gradually lead you into situations which we have found to be most painful and threatening for you. But, with your cooperation, we'll move you into a state of mental and emotional relaxation while you are in the act of facing these unpleasant issues. Then, after a time, you'll discover that your tensions are a thing of the past, or at least subject to your own ability to live with and control."

Inmate (meekly acquiescent): "I'll try."

Psychotherapist: "All of this, of course, is somewhat experimental, and to a large extent dependent upon your own effort and application. But the success of this venture does not call for tranquilizing medication, nor does it ask you to understand your feelings or to probe deeply into your past. It simply asks that you have some belief in your capacity to change, and that you have faith in me and what I am trying to do for you."

Inmate (subserviently agreeable, but obviously not convinced): "Whatever you say, Doc."

I am sure that I, as well as many well-meaning and otherwise dedicated psychotherapists, have conveyed the inconsistency, ambiguity, and confused irony of these thoughts many times to the continued exasperation and bewilderment of our clients. It is impossible for anyone to unravel the paradoxical, double-binded entanglements of so much clinical advice. Least of all, is it possible for any intelligent offender to have faith in the examiner who contradicts his own contention of integrity and sincerity of purpose?

We have yet to place ourselves unequivocally in that very unique, and so often, untenable situation in which the criminal offender finds himself. My own position, however, is one in which I have a need—a compulsion, if you will—to put 37 years of clinical practice in its proper perspective. From this somewhat transcendental, but none-theless, empirically based viewpoint, I might, hopefully, be of some help in alleviating the trials and accumulative frustrations of an emo-tionally conflicted and long-suffering group of penal commitments.

Happiness for everyone, including the correctional psychologist, depends on a sense of fulfillment. Much too often, however, the grasping impulse associated with an attempted realization of this elu-sive need is the product of an artificially toned, ego-oriented motiva-tion. The self-centered needs of the psychotherapist, immersed as they are in an atmosphere of professional jealousy and competitive selfishness, become, on too many occasions, a primary aim at the expense of any well-integrated or wholesome fulfillment on the part of the criminal offender.

Our particular experience, going back to post World War I years and gathering momentum in 1930 on the eve of the general depres-sion preceding our involvement in World War II, parallels the eco-nomic and spiritual frustrations of the entire population. So-called situational pressures on the overall economic plane were often the criminal's most acceptable rationalizations for a generalized impover-ishment of the spirit. The real deprivation, quite apart from the more tangible material advantages, hinged on the presence or absence of a sense of inner worth or drive toward achievement.

The ups and downs of our professional attempts at reversing a half-century of progressively involved criminal activity have crystal-lized a new awareness of a common affectional urgency and what is technically known as empathy with the unique characteristics and underlying needs of our clients.

The pendulous oscillations associated with two generations of clinical practice in the correctional field reflect a persistent theme of continuous effort despite the painful catharsis of so many unpredict-able failures. Equally disheartening, from the standpoint of scientific integrity, was the grossly misunderstood accumulation of unexpected successes which provoked the statement that time and circumstances provide the only real and necessary form of treatment.

The spontaneous interest and hopeful purpose of the pioneering clinical spirit in an attempted reshaping of the lives of a long line of criminal offenders is, nonetheless, deserving of our most profound and thoughtful consideration.

This book is devoted to the constructive goal of providing a detailed and analytical account of the sequence of events which attempted to check and control the tide of criminal behavior presently sweeping into the spotlight of national importance. In retrospect, and through a comparative weighing of pertinent pressures and circumstances on a time scale of almost four decades of correctional experience, a much more effective and coordinated approach to the all-encroaching specter of criminal behavior is bound to emerge.

It should be noted that while the content is real, the names and other identifying features of the case illustrations in this book have been altered so as to protect those involved. Care has been taken, furthermore, to provide anonymity with respect to certain overt characteristics, geographic location, or recency in the events of the personalities described.

HAROLD F. UEHLING

ACKNOWLEDGMENTS

THE author is happy to convey, through this channel, his deep appreciation for the freedom of movement, as well as the faith in his integrity and sense of personal responsibility, which had been extended to him over the past decade. He is especially grateful for the interest and understanding concern of Dr. Asher R. Pacht, Dr. H. T. Bassett, and Dr. Seymour L. Halleck who provided much of the flexibility which made staff discussions and sensitivity training so productive. The author is also indebted to Dr. Raymond J. Corsini whose earlier enthusiastic interest in research and group psychotherapy promoted incentives for creative effort which might otherwise never have been tapped.

Finally, I am most intimately indebted to my wife for her patient support of my moods during the most frustrating years of my career, as well as her later receptive attitude toward my need for a spontaneous discussion of the contents of this book. The incentive to achieve, and to continue achieving, is an asset with which not many of us are blessed, and for the continuing opportunity to exercise this need, I am extremely grateful to all of my professional colleagues, particularly those whom it has been my privilege to know in recent years.

H. F. U.

CONTENTS

Correction of a
Correctional Psychologist
in
Treatment of the Criminal Offender

Chapter 1

THE REGIMENTED YEARS

Few people are aware of the deadening effects of an exacting and subservient prison routine on the minds and ambitions of inmates whose behavior we supposedly strive to correct. An atmosphere wherein silent conformity and apathetic compliance to the authoritarian will are encouraged is also the best possible medium for an accumulative anger which defies expression through normal channels. Least of all does it provide the necessary incentives for maintaining an alert and inquiring mind, without which a sense of personal worth and consequent emotional health are all but impossible.

Add overcrowded conditions to the stifling void of a repressive prison system and you have fertile soil for perpetuating criminal or aggressively hostile behavior against an ill-informed and affectionally aloof society.

You have an administrative staff which relies on punitive measures and fear of punishment as the only means of control. You have a prison warden and custodial staff whose primary concern is a smooth-operating institution through restrictive practices not possible in a free society. You have power-conscious authoritarian figures who idolize the tight-fisted masculine concept, while denying the right to any healthy expression of masculine assertiveness among members of the inmate body.

In essence, the line between master and servant, privileged and underprivileged, is sharply drawn, and love and understanding on either side degenerates into a perverted form which allows no areas of agreement in the projected void of "right" and "wrong" concepts wedging the two opposing worlds.

It was into this morally biased and spiritually impoverished atmosphere that the first correctional psychologist was introduced with

3

his armor of tests and measurements. The rising crime rate, then as now, was a headache to the legislators and their tax-paying constituents, and the psychologist was brought in to help uncover some of the unknown specifics relating to crime and delinquency. He came in at a time when psychiatrists were respected as holding the key to asocial behavior, and when the need for examining the criminal as an individual was at its peak.

It was a time when primary emphasis on the physical abnormalities or measurable characteristics of a "criminal brain" had been abandoned, and the hereditary theory of criminality had given way to a consideration of the total human being and his functioning under pressure of social and environmental influences.[54]

There was, nonetheless, a persistent and continual attempt to link some form of mental defect with criminal behavior. The need for isolating specific determinants as a cause or adjunct to criminality lingers on, and the history of criminal psychiatry is fraught with controversy over the intangibles of varied medical-legal approaches to the problem of crime.

It soon became apparent that the correctional psychologist was expected to discover some common relationship between mental deficiency, or mental defect, and the tendency toward crime. And this is what he proceeded to do, utilizing the Revised Stanford-Binet Intelligence Scale. Employing a mental age concept comparable to that noted in American school children of a particular chronological age, it was technically a very precise, and at that time, a highly respected instrument in the measure of "global" intelligence.[105, 110]

In our particular setting, all new penal commitments, as well as all parole applicants in five adult correctional institutions, were routinely and painstakingly examined. Pertinent historical data, along with a psychoneurotic index and an intelligence quotient, were obtained on each.[88, 109]

Since a minimum of eight inmates were individually examined each day, a half hour was allotted for the administration of the abbreviated intelligence test. The other half of the hour involved rapid-fire questions calling for yes or no responses to a 116 item personal data sheet,[108] along with the longhand recording of significant facts relating to family background, marital status, military history, social history, history of offense, and institutional adjustment.

This was obviously a big order which allowed little or no time for rapport, and which naturally promoted tension and resistances on the part of the inmate. These resistances, in turn, precipitated an equal measure of frustration on the part of the rule-strapped examiner whose conscientious attendance to duty emphasized a highly concentrated form of psychometric notation. The resultant pressures, under the circumstances, drained any semblance of personal warmth from the interview.

The entire mental set was geared toward the recording of factual information. The psychometrist was making a hard drive for facts—sharp, isolated facts, pinpointed and pigeonholed for the purpose of future scrutiny under the cold, white light of the statistician's lamp. The scoring of test results, and the consolidation of individual case findings, together with any reflective concern for the inmate as a person, was necessarily reserved for an extra two to three hours of the examiner's "free" time in the evenings.

All of the mental strain and emotional drain on the examiner, however, seemed well worth the effort when, after several years of tedious psychometric application, a statistical analysis was made. Along with the evidence of broken homes and a grossly inferior educational level, came the startling disclosure of feeble-mindedness or borderline mental deficiency for at least 50 percent of our adult penal population.

This finding was "scientific" proof of an inherent mental defect which gave the institution administrative head, as well as the psychiatrist, a factual basis for future prognostications about crime. A liaison function was established between the psychiatric services and the institution school, a numerical rating in the form of an intelligence quotient was forwarded to the deputy warden and to the parole board, and an elaborate scheme of mental classification was devised. All of this had a tangible appeal from administrative and legal points of view, as well as from the standpoint of an orderly and well-disciplined medical mind.

The classification system placed great stress on the intelligence quotient, the overworked IQ, as the index of an inmate's mental potential. These now archaic numerical designations included the authoritatively labelled extremes of idiot, imbecile, low and high grade moron, subnormal, normal, superior, and very superior categories. The various types of offenders were otherwise listed in accordance with the nature of their crimes and the severity of their criminal records.

A fourth offender with an IQ of 68, for example, was referred to as a high grade moron, habitual criminal type, whereas a first offender with an IQ of 95 and an average term commitment for a relatively innocuous offense was described as a character defect type. A second or third offense, however, would classify the latter offender as a recidivistic character defect with indications of morbid impulsiveness.

Still another example might be that of an inmate with superior intelligence and a second or third conviction of rape, sodomy, incest, or murder who was described under the morbid impulses class as sexually perverted or mentally depraved.

According to mental status, age level, present offense, and past criminal record, the criminally delinquent population was generally ordered under one of six main categories: (1) *Mentally Deficient*, (2) *Mentally Defective*, (3) *Mentally Diseased*, (4) *Mentally Deviate*, (5) *Mentally Distorted*, and (6) *Mentally Delayed*.

The *Mentally Deficient* group was subdivided into "morally defective" types comprising first and second offenders, whereas the "morbid impulses" type under this heading referred to third and subsequent commitments, as well as those convicted of offenses indicative of a "depraved mind."

Under the second, *Mentally Defective* grouping, the so-called "simplex defectives" were regarded as responsible individuals, many of whom were considered to be "self-regenerate" and possessing the necessary potential for social readjustment. The recidivistic type in this group referred specifically to second and third offenders, while the habitual type included the fourth and subsequent convictions.

The more severely involved, or "mentally depraved" type of offender within this *Mentally Defective* classification, included those who were found guilty of rape, incest, first and second degree murder, and other offenses which in the eyes of the examiner were regarded as distinctly morbid or vicious in quality.*

Those categorized as *Mentally Diseased* at the time of diagnosis were so obviously incapacitated and out of touch with reality that

---

*The *Mentally Defective* category, in this instance, applies to the earlier medico-legal concept of social defect in contrast to the later, statistical designation of this term as a quantitative index of mental deficiency.

even the layman recognized the need for commitment to a psycho-pathic ward pending transfer to a hospital for the criminally insane. There were, in those days, no "shades of gray"; an inmate who created a disturbance because of bizarre and/or antisocial thought processes was either crazy or punishable as fully responsible for whatever vicious tendencies his behavior might indicate. If there were doubt, a week or two of "silent treatment" under intensive observation in a bare, padded cell would usually tip the balance.

Under the fourth group, designated as *Mentally Deviate*, it was noted that the regeneration and welfare of these borderline cases was largely, if not entirely, a problem of clinical psychiatry. Those in this group were characterized as social misfits, being seldom "self-regenerate," and often socially adaptable only as a consequence of intensive medical care and psychiatric attention.

Under group five, referred to as those who were *Mentally Distorted*, it was noted that there was a need for a category in which personality disorganization, rather than defect, was the outstanding feature. This disorganization was regarded as an acquired characteristic, being more or less superficial and amenable to treatment.

It was indicated that those who were included in this group, while legally responsible, were "self-regenerate," and practically all were cases in which the contributory factors might be corrected, removed, or remedied. The social rehabilitation of these individuals was regarded as affording an inviting field for physicians, sociologists, economists, lawyers, legislators, and others who might be interested in the problem of delinquency

Within the sixth group, characterized as *Mentally Delayed*, there was a subgroup classified as "subject to retarded general mental development," which included those juveniles and minors whose psychometric test results revealed an IQ above 69 and less than 87. The phrase, "without indication of mental defect," referred to those who were simply disobedient or incorrigible, whereas, "with indications of mental defect," was a direct reference to those boys who steal, and to those girls who were sexually delinquent.*

*It should be noted that this classification system, as applied in penal and correctional diagnosis, was introduced, along with his own adaptation of a psychoneurotic index and a psychotic questionnaire, by the first director of the Wisconsin Psychiatric Field Services. It was adopted in the post World War I era, and put into practice over a period of more than 20 years up to the conclusion of World War II.

The institution disciplinarian was delighted with a system of classification which relieved him of the responsibility of making difficult decisions on disciplinary matters of a threatening or unknown context. The school principal was intrigued with the challenge of boosting the educational level of one who had been diagnosed as mentally deficient, and the parole board members were equally stimulated with ideas as to the adjustment possibilities of a particular level of mental classification.

It was a time when the psychiatrist and psychologist, working in close harmony, yet individually and alone in their respective disciplines, were held in reverent esteem by administrative personnel. No behavioral problem seemed insurmountable, and there was an apt classification and a believable disposition for each incompetent felon and for each aberrant finding or vicious act.

It wasn't until much later, just prior to the advent of World War II, that serious doubts began to creep in. Our entire system of classifying criminal offenders was much too rigid; too air-tight, and too intent on simplifying a very complex and multifarious overlap of criminal activities. And we gradually began to realize several important aspects in our testing procedure which, despite all of the conscientious effort and thoroughness of our application, tended to invalidate our test results.

For a time, we staunchly resisted and defended the testing routine to which we had grown accustomed over so many years. The Revised Stanford-Binet test manual had been our Bible—one to which we had literally adhered as letter-perfect and beyond reproach. It was almost like giving up the early instilled convictions of an ancestral religion.

Our procedural blind spots, however, could not be denied. Our first inkling of this came from the institution school and the critical manipulations of our academically oriented, University Extension Division field contacts. The University field representative, striving with all of the initiative and power at his command to inaugurate university extension courses into the prison school system, responded with great favor to all inmates who expressed an interest. These included the psychologically determined mentally deficient, as well as those who had been classified as intellectually normal. And each academically motivated inmate was subsequently graded in accordance with an achievement score which in many cases failed to match, or even approximate, the stereotyped IQ designations of the institution psychologist.

As a consequence of this unwanted "interference," we discovered that a particular group of inmates whom we had rated as possessed of borderline intelligence were actually doing average work in school. We had, of course, already noted that the borderline and low average groups were capable of some measure of change in a positive direction upon retest with the same measuring instrument. This we attributed to practice effects, but there was also the question of better rapport, of probable language difficulties, and of a mental set which unknowingly induced underachieving resistances on the part of the inmate undergoing the examination.

All of this became much more understandable when we began looking behind our clinical utopia, and into the negative aspects of a prison environment.

Chapter 2

AN IMPASSIONED GLIMPSE OF THE PERSON
BEHIND THE OFFENSE

Any serious self-doubt for most of us involves a painfully unwelcome ordeal of inner tension and self-recrimination which interferes with our working efficiency and peace of mind. The resultant emotional stress, however, tends to uncork a rare quality of empathy in those who make a conscious effort in the direction of tolerance and understanding. In the conscientious and more sincerely committed therapist, it calls for a willingness to become imbued, at least partially, with the feelings of the convicted offender who makes his first appearance at the prison gate.

In order that we might better appreciate his point of view, let us attempt to infiltrate the new inmate's feelings as the heavy, barred door clangs behind him. The sheriff escort, whose main concerns are those of secure handling and effective detention under adequate physical controls, now shakes out his keys, and unlocks the prisoner's cuffs with the swift assurance of a practiced hand.

Without delay, and with the sweeping motion of one who is well acquainted with the needs of this particular situation, he relinquishes his gun holster to the cynically observant, main-gate turnkey. Then, in a condescendingly casual, easygoing manner, he delivers his prisoner to a second turnkey in the main lobby. It is quite natural at this point that the prisoner is ignored while a few trite pleasantries are exchanged during the intermediation of necessary papers in this very routine and commonplace transaction.

The new inmate, who is emotionally torn to a raw edge inside with abrasive thoughts about his mother's white-faced suffering, his father's hostile attitude, and his wife's martyr-like rejection of his sensitive inner core, tries to match this impersonal reception with a bland indifference of his own. His forced grin, and somewhat flippant attitude, is a necessary defense against an intolerable anguish which might otherwise drive him to the brink of despair.

So, here begins a vicious circle of nonaccepting attitudes which invite further rejection, an absence of emotional warmth, and an ever-widening barrier to any understandable verbal communication.

At least three more smoothly operating, but coldly unyielding iron gates jar the inmate's nerves with their unrelenting mechanical insertions before his first of many seemingly endless days is spent. Now he has been fingerprinted, photographed, and "suitably" garmented during the course of a long-established routine which deprives him of all remaining vestiges of his former individuality.

He finds himself wishing for the special attention which he might have gotten from some unusual physical defect, rare, communicable disease, unique offense, newspaper publicity, or special reputation as a hardened offender or "wheeler-dealer." In lieu of any of these "assets" at a time like this, an uninhibited burp or an abrupt, noncommittal response to a direct question was always of some help in firming up a sense of inner strength, however misunderstood he might continue to be as a result of this false, outer veneer.

The quick anger and red-faced frustration which a subtle piece of mimicry, monosyllabic acquiescence, or sullen indifference provoked in the interviewer, was sometimes well worth the sharp reproof and warning threats of an otherwise deadpan exchange. It at least stimulated a genuine emotional response which had a temporary, but nonetheless, ego-satisfying effect on what he perceived as an immense phoniness in the shadows of his formidable surroundings.

In his mind, the only alternative would be that of a passively harmless, altogether subservient nonentity who blindly followed all of the rules (oftentimes conflicting directions) like a loyally naive automaton. Certainly, this kind of inmate offered nothing which might serve to merit any personal respect. If he were at all normal, he would be yearning for some special attention in exchange for his submissive attitudes and altogether obedient performance.

Perhaps a "trusty's" job, or maybe a quick parole? But easy time? Hardly ever, except insofar as he was able to hide and control his true feelings. All of which was bad, very bad, when it came time for his ultimate release and the sudden unshackling of feeling which he had grown so dependent upon through outer restraints for control.

To the institution authorities, this submissive inmate might be regarded as a model prisoner in the dependable execution of otherwise distasteful but necessary chores. He might even be accepted as a necessary and desirable "fixture" in the mechanics of institution management and control. Experience had shown that he was not a security risk, and to the rule-conscious disciplinarian, any change in the quality of his conforming suggestibility might provide a thermostatic index of the violent potential of many of his inmate associations.

But to his peers, and to the inmate body as a whole, he became a pliable weakling—one who couldn't be trusted with personal or confidential matters, especially when subjected to the agitating pressures of an inmate probe or official investigation. At best, he was one who must be shunned as a probable informer. At the worst, he had laid himself wide open as a mollycoddle for perverts who used him under threat of exposure for their own sordid purposes.

The ultimate degradation of the inmate's self-concept followed the routine shaving of his skull prior to any regular indoctrination into the institution program. It was only after this supposedly humbling, but severely humiliating experience that he was deemed ready for a number of overlapping, and what was then regarded as a very necessary cross check of security-oriented interviews.

The first interview, following his impersonal, but positively identifying record office experience, was with the deputy warden who shouted threats of dire punishments in supposedly alert anticipation of the inmate's unspoken rebellion against institution rules.

Then came the medical interview by the prison physician's knowlegable inmate assistant who sought out the doctor's favor with advanced hospital correspondence studies commensurate with his high IQ. This protégé of prison hospital adaptability took precise notes of the physician's cursory utterances, while quietly shelving his own observations of certain physical assets and quirks in the mass of helpless nakedness parading before him.

Next came the achievement tests in the institution school; the determination of a score which invariably fell one or two grade levels beneath his claimed attainment, and which revealed a particularly low capacity for concentrated effort and thought control. Naturally, the inmate's achievement scores in arithmetical reasoning and the mechanics of grammar suffered the most, although emotional blocking at that time was not taken into consideration as a probable cause.

Other interviews, not so precise, included those of the social worker, or institution parole officer as he was then called, the shop foreman to whom he was temporarily assigned on the basis of institution needs, and the prison chaplain who too often expressed an intensely biased and overly solicitous concern for the impossibly narrow and literal aspects of the inmate's spiritual needs.

The institutional parole officer, in line with his particular interest and training experience, was engrossed in the inmate's family contacts and general environmental needs. He sat with the three-member parole board during their bimonthly institutional visits, and a neatly compiled dossier of general information was his primary concern.

The shop foreman was, of course, motivated in the direction of the inmate's production capacity and related manual skills, while the prison chaplain turned every ingratiating spiritual maneuver in the direction of a tangible church registry.

All interviewers, in fact, had one common responsibility with a primary emphasis on the needs of the institution. The administrative pressure for material advantage and institutional self-sufficiency necessitated a justification of each particular function in a generally misunderstood and colossally abused "rehabilitative" process.

Eventually, after each interviewer had, in effect, implicitly drilled the inmate on his inferior status and gross incompetence in association with "normal" people, he appeared for a final analysis by the visiting psychiatric unit. This unit had a mobile function which took it on a rigidly planned schedule from one institution to the next.

Unlike the other departments, members of this pioneering traveling clinic were responsible only to the overall Psychiatric Field Service director, and therefore not subject to policy restrictions in accordance with a particular institutional need.[88] Recommendations were, nonetheless, limited to the earlier indicated medico-legal classification framework encompassing what was then a very ineffectual assessment of individual needs (see pp. 5-7).

The mobile psychiatric unit consisted of the psychiatric director, who in those early years had both a medical and a law degree, a general medical practitioner who supplemented the institution physician's report with additional data pertinent to the psychiatric appraisal, and the junior psychologist whose duties were primarily those of a psychometrist.

The psychologist was hired with a twofold purpose which included the accumulation and sifting of psychologically oriented data for a statistical analysis of the criminal offender, while he was at the same time acquiring as much clinical knowledge as possible preparatory to entering medical school.

The director was, thereby, utilizing an altruistic need to provide appropriate services for the downtrodden as the most practical step toward encouraging a personally guided selection of correctionally minded, clinical neophytes into the medical profession. Although the sincerity of his objectives was beyond question, there were the ever pressing appropriation needs which, then as now, called for a certain amount of deceptive political manipulation. This only added to the reality of the authority conflicts, and associated individual disadvantages, with which the criminal offender was faced.

The antiquated prison hospital, in itself, exuded a morbidly repressive atmosphere which gave the final touches to a conditioning process focusing on mental incompetence and gross personality deficiencies. The severe, steeply designed hospital building with its long, narrow corridors, unusually high ceilings, closely barred windows, and restricted room space, was, first of all, a fire trap. The potential danger of a holocaust in those cramped, iron sealed quarters was forever present, despite the massive, limestone exterior which rose in sharp angled solidity over a three story reach of its two floor occupancy.*

The single flight of stairs amounted to almost a two story climb of steep risers and deeply worn oak treads which tempted the less hardy to pause for a new breath, while a suspicious guard looked down from halfway up the long, straight assent. The building, originally designed according to the penal needs of the civil war era, combined

*In the mid-sixties, this ungainly, thick walled structure was torn down with understandably energetic inmate help. Once the necessary appropriations had been made, a spiritually uplifting and much needed chapel was erected on the same site, not far from a new hospital, and directly across from a newly constructed institution treatment center.

a horse equipment and storage center with solitary confinement cells on the ground floor. Throughout a viable century of drastic social change, the solid rudiments of an old, bale-hoisting pulley attachment were still visible in the roof apex just above the 1858 stone-chiseled insert marking the construction date.

After the long, hard climb, inmates were forced to stand in line facing the wall with arms folded across their chests, awaiting their turn for an interview. Considering that there was a prison dentist, an institution physician, and a three-member psychiatric team, all of whom were scheduling interviews and examinations in the crowded space of their own small quarters, there was little room for chairs in the hallway. Even so, however, it would have been a rather exceptional guard who, in that early day, was inclined to alleviate the inmates' many apprehensions in this manner.

There were times each day when an inmate, who had been forced to wait an hour or more silently facing the wall, was sent back to his cell, or to his working location, because there was no longer time for him to be seen in an interview. Here again, no allowance was made for the abysmal tension and frustrations which one would normally expect to build up in a pending examination of this sort.

"A pass to see the nut doctor," was the commonly voiced expletive on the part of the cell keeper or prison guard who sent the inmate on his way for an interview with a member of the psychiatric team. Or, if he were called for more than two follow-up tests or examinations: "The nut doctor's got your number. He's really fixing to put you away!" And on the fourth or fifth call up: "The next step will be the nut house; once more and you're headed across the tracks for sure."

Even the interview passes, which the inmate was directed to carry fully exposed in his hand, were colored white, pink, blue, or yellow so as to alert members of the custodial staff at a glance regarding the nature of his pass. A bright yellow was the color designation reserved for the psychiatric unit, and the spinelessly unstable connotation of this underhanded emotional brand seldom failed to sear its insidious impressions on the more alertly sensitive members of the inmate body.

Throughout the 50-foot length of the narrow hospital corridor, a weird mixture of discordant noises, savory food smells, and intermingling, nauseating odors prevailed. This was a second floor hospital adaptation which attempted to provide space for the hospital kitchen and inmate quarters, as well as a tubercular ward and two claustrophobic observation cells opposite the physician's high-windowed examination and operating rooms.

On the top stair landing, one was greeted by the dentist's octopus-like equipment suspended from the ceiling and almost bulging through the open door. Opposite this contortus display was the psychiatrist's swivel-chaired interview room of solid oak, and dark, old, schoolroom appearance. This formidable enclosure doubled as the prison doctor's office on less congested, visit-free occasions.

Oh yes, there was also a prisoner's cramped "water closet," and a somewhat larger staff employe's toilet. Almost inconceivable in the light of present-day needs, the latter served an additional function as the dentist's makeshift laboratory, as well as being the most ideal place to grab a quick, and otherwise strictly forbidden, drag on a cigarette.

Two of the attendants alternated on call for 24-hour-duty, and two others had a chef and assistant chef's responsibility for the hospital patient's meals, as well as their own and that of two hospital guards. The guard's freedom of movement, like that of the inmates, was at the time grossly restricted on 12 hour shifts, with the former earning less than $100 a month plus two meals per day. The junior psychologist, by comparison, earned $150 per month plus full expenses while on institution visits and away from home.

Among other things, the psychologist was handicapped by the need for arranging his voluminous papers, manuals, and testing materials on the coarse, gray blanket of a sagging cot in order that the rough-hewn, paint-chipped table would be free of unessential cluttering at the time that the inmate's mental age test clearances were assiduously checked off. In doing so, however, a certain narrow space had to be allowed between the table edge and the other double-decked cot to permit an attendant to pass by should certain articles of laundry or linen in the back closet be necessary up front on a more or less frequent emergency call.

Since the psychologist's working space adjoined the hospital kitchen, the permeating odors were the most pleasant aspects of his otherwise oppressively congested surroundings. The inmate attendants were deceivingly friendly and continually courting the psychologist's favor with offers of coffee and choice pieces of pie through the adjoining door to the kitchen. They also begged, or attempted to arrange, for the otherwise forbidden acquisition of "misplaced" cigarettes, a trap which invited more favors from the uninitiated or unwary civilian.

Apart from the sporadic request for favors, there was a continual sparring for special information, along with a childish testing of an overworked psychologist's patience and limits of endurance. The night attendant, for example, would on occasion be lying "asleep" on the upper deck of a cot, hoping that his presence would be overlooked, and that he might unobtrusively listen to the testing procedure on an unsuspecting fellow inmate.

Needless to say, this form of interference was quickly discouraged, as were also any special favors which the inmate might tender as a means of promoting some personal advantage in line with his own psychopathic needs. When told that it was not possible to carry out a testing program while he was sleeping on the cot, the inmate murmured somewhat acidly: "If it were me doing the testing, I'd throw out one or two quick ones and then guess at the IQ. All of this questioning won't get you the right answers anyway."

As it developed, this particular inmate, no matter how psychopathic his makeup might have been, was quite right in his deductions. It was true that much less attention should have been paid to the literal directions so explicitly set forth in the intelligence test manual. Despite the admonition as to uniformity of approach, much more emphasis should have been placed on a more relaxed, emotionally toned interview which permitted a meeting of the minds and a capacity for sensing the special needs behind the other's apparently prejudiced or distorted point of view.

Let us indulge ourselves for the moment with the feeling, quite apart from the intellectual understanding, with which the inmate is imbued at the time of his dejected, head-shaven appearance for a mental examination. It is important that we keep in mind the fact that he had already experienced a minimum of 15 to 20 minutes of arm-folding surveillance in a foot-shuffling, low-whispering, "standing room only" corridor of conflicting tensions and frustrated desires.

He was, first of all, offered a straight-backed, hard, oak chair, which in that congested setting matched the equally plain seat occupied by the psychologist. He was then quickly informed of the fact that he was about to be tested, and the authoritative expectation of a pertinently concise and honest response was implied in the examiner's direct manner and practiced approach to the interview. Actually, lying, under these conditions, was more acceptable than the stammering truth, so long as it provided a direct sweep of the cobwebby uncertainties which threatened to clutter the examiner's mind.[53, 68]

The psychometrist, with rare exceptions reserved for those of known high school graduate standing, launched into the mechanics of administering subtests covering elementary mental age levels in order to establish a basic mental age in which all of the important test categories were passed by the examinee.

At the eighth grade level of mental growth, for example, he was expected to give a useful definition for at least eight common words out of a list of 45, ranging from the simplest and most widely used to those of less concrete and more abstract connotation. Another of the "starred" tests on the abbreviated scale of this particular age level called for a verbalized awareness of three out of four verbal absurdities, an example of which was: "I read in the paper that the police fired two shots at a man. The first shot killed him, but the second did not hurt him much."

One of two other "starred" tests at this particular age level called for a satisfactory expression of similarities and differences in three out of four situations, an example of which was: "In what way are an airplane and kite alike and how are they different?" The other was a test of general comprehension, which at this stage of mental growth required two correct answers out of three in response to questions such as: "What would you do if you found on the streets of a city a three-year-old baby that was lost from its parents?"

In the event that all of the subtests on this particular mental age level were passed, the examiner moved on to the nine-year-level, and then on to the tenth, eleventh, or twelfth, or until total failures for all of the tests in a particular mental age grouping were encountered. It was then assumed that the subject's ceiling of innate intellectual capabilities had been reached, and that no further upper range testing was indicated.

During the course of his mental age journey to this level of complete failure, the subject had theoretically been tested on several vocabulary age levels, each calling for a higher degree of word symbol proficiency. The same was true of his word associations and memory retentive powers, his capacity for detecting absurdities on a more socially sophisticated plane, and his ability to note similarities of a more subtly refined and abstract nature than those indicated in his earlier recognition of simple differences.

Interspersed throughout the length of this mental age scale, also, was a gradually advancing exercise in the subject's capacity for visual and auditory memory retentive powers, together with a measure of related judgment and reasoning ability through the medium of pencil and paper tests involving visual-motor coordinative skills.

As indicated earlier, there was no question regarding the scientific proficiency and overall developmental considerations with which this measurement of intellectual capacity had been standardized in the school setting for which it was originally intended. But, after long years of conscientious application to an educationally inferior and culturally impoverished adult penal population, there were very serious doubts as to the effect this particular approach had on intellectual motivation as we normally perceive it.*

What, for example, did a methodical recording of pluses and minuses, to the point of total failure at a particular mental age level, do to the inmate's emotional incentives for greater achievement? What might it have done to encourage his need to rebel in the form of passive resistance at a time when his intellectual energies were faced with their greatest challenge? What, instead, might it have done to promote a defeatist attitude as opposed to the spontaneous effort and enthusiasm which we know to be a very necessary ingredient in any wholesomely integrated performance?

Or, let us consider the emotional effects of going in the opposite

*To the writer, an "experienced" psychometrist in a typically overcrowded penal setting during the "depressing thirties," this realization came in slow waves of indirect criticism and frustrating controversy which at first had nothing better to offer. In the end, however, he could hardly deny that he had been blinding himself to the very elements of his own capacity for self-criticism and potential for change which he presumed to measure in his routine application of an inappropriate and inadequate testing instrument.

direction in order to determine a basic mental age as a starting point in the measurement of adult penal commitments on a mental age scale. It would seem that here, too, the very recognition of a need for reversion to a more elementary, or "schoolboy" approach, would tend to provoke an inhibiting emotional barrier to any effective intellectual response.

For example, suppose a particular test, like the one focusing on the penciled reproduction of a diamond at the seven-year-mental-age level, were failed. Even though all of the other subtests were passed, the test rules called for a performance demonstration of the subject's ability to pass all of the tests at the next lowest six-year-mental-age level. Here, however, he was confronted with a visual-memory test which called for the stringing, and appropriate grouping, of colored, kindergarten-shaped beads in a manner which might easily provoke a disgusted "kid-stuff" rejection of the entire proceedings.

Obviously, any suggestion of ridicule, no matter how seriously presented on a scientifically determined scale of mental abilities, is going to have an adverse effect on the incentives of what we know to be a hypersensitive inmate population. This inherent sensitivity, and the many false faces behind which it is disguised, is still the big stumbling block to any true rapport with the criminal offender's underlying motivation toward a socially constructive form of self-lifting behavior.

In retrospect, at this point one can only reflect on a most amazing set of circumstances in all of this conscientious effort and exacting testing procedure. That is to say that, from this distant point in time, a correctional psychologist finds it possible to recognize, with considerable humility, a large measure of his own transient shortcomings. It should now be apparent to everyone that there is an insidious quality about the manner in which institution disciplinary needs, together with professional statistical incentives, have apparently conspired to so great an extent, and over so long a period, to promote so much blind disregard of the criminal offender's basic needs.

Chapter 3

PSYCHOANALYTIC ARC OF THE PROJECTIVE EVALUATION PENDULUM

THE transition from an arbitrary, numerically stereotyped classification system to a more relaxed and less conforming appraisal of the criminal offender's total personality was, as our experience testifies, far from a painless one. The massive resistance to this change becomes more apparent when we consider the conflicting needs of the individual as opposed to the repressive influences of what public policy dictates as minimal protection under maximum security conditions.

The maximum security institution is, of course, geared toward repressive control of chaotic emotions which it is feared might get out of hand if permitted the freedom of a more relaxed approach. In the early years, punitive preoccupations fostered the rigid entrenchment of a tightly linked chain of tradition-steeped, institution administrators. It was not possible at that time even to summon a listener to the need for a coordinated effort in the direction of a safe emotional release of conflicting feelings. Much less was it possible to advise institution administrators on the psychological and psychiatric implications of an accumulative hostility which was being perpetuated by the policing methods of a rigidly immobile authoritative system.

The one exception was that which involved a certain amount of subterfuge wherein feelings were sublimated in objective form through tangible, easily perceived outlets. Examples were in the arts and crafts and related hobby activities, talent shows and competitive athletic exhibitions, and various achievement scores or rating scales, all of which allowed for the exercise of an authoritatively satisfying, "institutionalized" ego.

The fulfillment of a tightly controlled, authoritarian ego was also the reason why the IQ, and all of its associated rigidity in mental classification, had been so acceptable. It, likewise, provides an explanation as to why the more abstract and intangible analysis of the criminal offender's inner needs met with so much authoritative mistrust.

On the whole, and except for those instances wherein a prison riot or change in administration gave it a special push, the transition continued to be a discouragingly gradual and individually uncertain one. In the light of an occasional back step, or reaction in the opposite direction, the change was, in fact, almost imperceptible.

There was, for example, the continued rigid adherence to the Revised Stanford-Binet Intelligence Test Scale despite the long-accepted awareness of its inadequacy as a measuring instrument for an adult population. As indicated earlier, this was especially true of its attempted adaptation to criminal offenders in a prison environment. But, along with the opportunity for activating a pioneering research project, the psychologist had his own need for authoritative recognition and respect, and an obsolete and ill-adapted intelligence test scale was maintained simply because no better measuring device was at that time available.

The need for a return to timeworn, security dictated practices, however, was at times forced to run the gauntlet of a refreshing forward spurt. This was true of the sudden confrontation with a completely new adult intelligence test scale.[119]

The individually unique qualities of the Wechsler Adult Intelligence Test Scale, by comparison with the older Terman model,[105] promoted a relatively open acceptance of an otherwise radical psychological change which gained momentum in adult penal settings from the time that it first became available in 1939. The mental age concept, as well as the childish, schoolboy connotation of the earlier test scale, was thereby eliminated, and the psychologist was intrigued with the unaccustomed flexibility and individual qualitative distinctions which he was now enabled to make.

Among other changes, a performance scale had been introduced which took away much of the earlier handicap involved in academic proficiency and language comprehension. A rigid adherence to tests focusing on speed and accuracy under grossly inhibiting circumstances, was no longer a primary issue. There was, furthermore, an allowance made for a normal deterioration of mental alertness and abstract reasoning power with advancing age, so that one might be compared on the intellectual scale with those of his own age group. Formerly, the overall standard of comparison was that of a prime functioning, academically oriented age group at the height of their innate mental development.

In the new adult intelligence test scale, an efficiency quotient analogous to the original intelligence quotient, was devised along with a deterioration index based on a comparison of "hold" and "don't hold" tests in relation to age. The overall effect was one which promoted increased testing incentives on the part of both examiner and subject, as well as offering the examinee a much greater latitude in both verbal and manual expression of his particular skills.

In addition to the increase in scope and quantitative advancement which this test provided was the qualitative discernment which the medium afforded through observation of emotional blocking and general behavioral reactions. The clinically minded psychologist, for example, was now able to offer some conclusions as to the subject's innate mental potential in relation to his actual functioning level.

He was, likewise, enabled to make deductions regarding basic skills, special aptitudes, and the extent of emotional interference in the intellectual functioning. He was, in other words, becoming increasingly cognizant of related values within a given context, the projection of feelings, and the marked contrast between the offender's outer veneer and the actual makeup which he had so "successfully" concealed underneath.

This change of approach in Wisconsin accompanied what the traveling psychiatric unit, or Psychiatric Field Service, would paradoxically recall as the "dark ages" of clinical application in correctional institutions. This was because it paralleled a sudden, irreversible loss in advanced psychiatric team work which, in the late depression years, was supplying the psychiatric needs of interested county judges, as well as those of the state institutions.

For a "golden age" period of almost two years between 1937 and 1939, there was a climactic interest and demand for psychological and psychiatric services on a community level. This demand apparently received its impetus and sense of importance from the same blind respect and trust in psychological and psychiatric infallibility which prevailed at the time the Psychiatric Field Service was first organized.

Here again, the self-assured, tangible quality of a definite numerical rating and an apt classification system offered a firm handle which both the judge and the correctional administrator could grasp in his need for making a precise and logical decision with regard to an otherwise harassing disposition of difficult cases.

The "clean sweep" of a new administration suddenly wiped out what might have been the correctional acme of community based psychiatric services. Even today, this goal remains an unfulfilled dream of clinically oriented treatment personnel. The new governor, himself a successful business man, was motivated by his own hard-headed philosophy and a rigid budgetary need to put the state on a completely objective, businesslike basis.

Naturally, the governor brought into top administrative positions those people who, like himself, were successful business men. One of these, a self-made immigrant industrialist with a generous, but completely biased and untutored need to provide for the unfortunates in our criminal population, became director of the State Department of Public Welfare. It was his contention, as he blatantly informed me in his brusque, "old-world" accent on his first visit to the prison, that "all of these 'IOQs,' between you and me, don't amount to very much."

I, along with the Psychiatric Field Service director, was, however, most "tolerantly" recommended for retention as the lower half of an essential skeleton force. This recommendation, we knew, was meant to appease a sympathetic minority, and to tone down current editorial opposition to a complete eradication of clinical diagnostic facilities. Verbally, the psychiatric director was given to understand that, as a two-man staff, we were being retained purely on the basis of seniority. There was also an implicit agreement of the fact that minimal clinical personnel was deemed necessary for psychological evaluation and related psychiatric commitment purposes.

The deep disappointment and dark despair involved in a sudden about-face on issues which one has come to regard as of paramount importance, sometimes has a very stimulating effect in the direction of redoubled efforts and incentives toward perfecting a new approach. And, as it developed, the businessman's oversimplification of the human equation in a mixed population of criminal offenders settled its own fate in about the same length of time that it took to raise and wipe out the five-man psychiatric team.

In a little more than two years, which included the national disaster at Pearl Harbor and our nation's precipitation into World War II, a succession of fantastically impossible businessmen's crumbling promises came to a shattering conclusion. As chairman of the parole board, the welfare department director had functioned with omnipotent convictions and a grandiose misuse of power which soon provoked adverse publicity and accusations of politcal influence and favoritism in his pawn-like handling of prisoner's sensitive emotions.

At the heart of this egocentric, power-twisted administrative decay was the collapse of the director's inmate-management, labor relations dream of a prisoner's grievance committee which had degenerated into the viciously uncompromising nucleus of a prison riot. A full scale rebellion developed, with uncontrolled but predictable certainty, into a violent subjugation of hostages, and an unreasoning destruction of property followed equally unreasoning demands for an immediate redress of grievances.

The end result was the inevitable containment of mob rule through sheer force of the disciplined numbers of a hastily summoned National Guard unit.

All of this great fuss on a state government level, however, had finally boosted the stand of an inmate minority to headline proportions. It had the effect, thereby, of temporarily satiating their demands for recognition—granting them the emotional buildup of a "powerful" splattering of the kind of attention which they really craved.

The final scene in this highly emotional drama was that of the hoped-for administrative shakeup, along with the demonstrated peril of the prison guards' position which called for an increased wage scale to compensate for the now proven hazards of his essentially indispensable occupation. And well in the center, but behind the scenes and pretty much in the shadows of all of this publicity, the lone psychologist and his somewhat embittered and cynical director were prodded into a much more sensitive awareness, and a considerably more profound observation, of his institution clientele.

RORSCHACH RATIONALE

It was in January 1944, within weeks of the final screening and subsequent solitary commitment of about 40 of the most aggressive rioters, that the first Rorschach test was given in the Wisconsin State Prison. Since its use at this time evolved from a need to "put the finger" on personality conflicts which might expose the insidious beginnings of a prison riot, one cannot escape a "Big Brother" connotation in our increasingly involved Rorschach analyses[87] as applied to the offender's behavior and treatment needs.

It was a time, of course, when public focus was on corrective security measures, and when the results of seriously disruptive tendencies were in evidence all around us.

The first candidate, who might also be remembered quite literally as the first "victim" of the Rorschach test, was an emotionally disturbed sex pervert. He had been reported as having performed the most degrading acts of fellatio at the bidding of his more aggressive fellow inmates during the long night that the inmate rioters' rampant emotions took over the institution. He was picked as the first Rorschach subject because of the scandalous indications of degenerate behavior and warped thinking which might provide a key to associated vicious acts on the part of other inmates.

Instead of an average of 20 to 30 responses to the ten ink blot stimulus patterns represented in the Rorschach test, this first subject gave a total of 110 percepts. All of his responses were bleak, anxiety-ridden projections of his own inner tensions and guilt-saturated makeup.

He compulsively twisted each card with an uncertain spiraling and "edging" mannerism which was in itself highly suggestive of mental imbalance. He otherwise intently studied remote stimulus areas at arm's length, as well as in myopic detail, reevaluating irrelevant and insignificant form to the point of exhausting himself and the examiner with an endlessly unpredictable revelation of his intense inner turmoil.

He was, nonetheless, under tight security control which "necessitated" his escorted return to a solitary cell wherein his now fluid emotions, and the first indications of loose and disorganized thought processes, were to be rigidly capsulated. Under the circumstances, of course, he had no way of knowing the real purpose of the test to which he had just been subjected. He was, likewise, shakily unaware as to whether he would have to wait a week, two weeks, or a month or more, for the results.

A real threat was added to his unlimited range of imaginary ones, and the reality of the situation was that he was forced to await an indefinite week or two of scoring and formalizing a projective evaluation report prior to the psychiatric appraisal of the visiting psychiatrist. Then, too, it must be remembered that the latter, who was also the clinical administrator, worked primarily on the basis of personal requests which took precedence over much of the deep despair and terminal needs of one who had so disgracefully ostracized himself from "normal" institutional participation.

As we have long since concluded, the inmates most in need of psychological and psychiatric attention are often those who have neither the inner strength, nor the degree of trust, necessary for instituting a personal request for help. Those who do put in requests through a chain of command from the supervising officer to the deputy warden, and thence to the clinical division, do so with the knowledge that a week or ten days or more might elapse before they are called.

This form of neglect, no matter how unavoidable, necessitates that the problem in regard to which the request had been made has at least temporarily resolved itself before the inmate is called. The precipitating need, in other words, is no longer an urgent one, and the motivation, assuming it to be genuine at the time that the request was made, is no longer a potent force.

Actually, then, as so frequently happens, the bulk of requests are discovered to have been initiated by so-called psychopaths, the childish attention seekers, or institution-wise chronic offenders who use their clinical audiences with the ulterior objectives of some purely manipulative, personal gain.

The irrelevancy in this situation of turning a highly trained, professional ear in the direction of the chronic complainer is still prevalent today. The reason, from a security standpoint, is an obvious one, in that institution authorities, while clamoring for relief from the headaches of the agitating minority, are indifferent toward the "silent majority" whose bottled-up feelings cause them no particular institutional concern.

At the same time, we know that a purely objective, institutionalized discipline, while offering a sheltering arm for the more withdrawn and submissive conformist, tends to be morally devitalizing and in no respect geared toward the exercise of a much needed personal initiative. This inmate, although otherwise well behaved in terms of institution regulations, may be most fearful of "normal" interpersonal tensions, and totally unprepared for outside, competitive pressures at the time of his release.

My first Rorschach "patient" might have been somewhat vaguely classified as a "constitutional psychopath," but there was no question regarding his need for psychiatric attention. Nor was there any question, on the basis of his Rorschach response pattern, of the intensely conflicting, unbearable emotional pressures which he carried back with him to the equally intolerable enclosure of his solitary cell.

He had neither the emotional strength nor the incentive of hope in any personal request for help, but the need to escape the black phantoms of his own guilt was, nonetheless, an overwhelming one. At the first opportunity, while being ordered for leg-stretching purposes along the top tier corridor with other solitary isolates who now contemptuously ignored him, he dove to a gory, head-shattering death on the concrete floor 20 feet beneath him.

The newly appointed deputy warden, a Ph.D in education who had previously functioned as the prison school principal, was genuinely shocked at his own negligence and absence of understanding in this particular situation. But, true to the tradition of a veteran army officer and stern disciplinarian which he had carried over from World War I, he allowed himself to see only the overall picture of necessary security for the welfare of many.

Like the psychologist, who had blinded himself to the "victim's" need for an informal chat before a formalized determination could be made, he rationalized his position as one which called for a protection of the "good guys" from the "bad guys" as a primary and all-inclusive consideration. The psychologist's diagnostic interests and clinical concerns were not, however, as easily brushed aside. This was particularly true, since his was an individualized form of diagnostic evaluation, and a much more subjective interest in human behavioral difficulties.

The psychologist had not yet, of course, reached the stage of individual treatment which at that time, and for at least another decade, was regarded as the sole function of the psychiatrist. The psychiatrist, however, was so occupied with routine interviews and administrative diagnostic procedures that he, himself, had little time for treatment analyses, much less a traditional form of psychiatric follow-up.

The tragic circumstances of the above described incident, however, had the effect of spurring a much overworked, two-man clinical team into still greater efforts in the direction of projective evaluation and associated behavioral analysis. The psychologist was compulsively driven toward further experimentation with a wide variety of projective techniques, while the psychiatrist was provoked into a "shortcut" penetration of the inmate's "phony" exterior with the projective analysis results as his most potent weapon.

The psychiatric director had, in other words, learned that any direct confrontation of the inmate with the psychoanalytical interpretation of his own response pattern, had the effect of wearing down the inmate's resistance to the point of an inadvertent confession of his inner conflicts.

This new approach afforded an individualized opportunity for ventilating otherwise secretly withheld personal feelings, the trusting disclosure of which had an intangible, and therefore, highly controversial, benefit on the emotional well-being of the inmate offender. It was, nonetheless, the beginning of a psychoanalytical form of treatment which, in effect, told the inmate that he was fooling no one but himself, and that if he ever expected to make parole, he had better level with the psychiatrist.

It was also, unfortunately, geared toward a fulfillment of the psychiatrist's own biased needs, since the latter practiced a form of "one-up-manship" which placed the inmate in a mutually confidential, but completely submissive role in relation to the therapist. It was not, in other words, the kind of therapeutic relationship which promotes an inner sense of self-sufficiency and emotional well-being so much as it tends to fortify already deep-rooted emotional dependency needs.

In addition to this, the method tended to evoke a rebellious projection of early instilled sibling rivalries which could not be resolved in this particular context so long as the psychiatrist was, in fact, giving preference to those who had the psychopath's attention getting aptitudes for chronic complaint. And, of course, here again, those who were most manipulative of authority figures, and who were, consequently, most skilled in the art of instituting challenging personal requests for psychiatric assistance, were the ones most likely to be granted an interview.*

The underlying diagnostic proficiency of the clinical team was, nevertheless, greatly advanced, and with this advancement came a much greater awareness of the offender's basic needs, and the manner in which these needs might be most effectively corrected.

---

*This is not meant to imply any lack of sincerity or drive on the part of an otherwise dedicated Psychiatric Services director who, in addition to the administrative demands of an increasingly complicated clinical correctional program, had himself exhaustively screened and personally honored up to 20 requests for individual attention during the course of a single day. It does, however, suggest some rather glaring faults within a penal correctional "system" which provides no feasible check against the inadvertent projection of even the most conscientious clinical worker's personal needs and biases at the expense of any real consistency in our treatment of the criminal offender.

Chapter 4

THE SWING TO A MORE OBJECTIVE APTITUDE EVALUATION

An awareness of the offender's subjective needs, no matter how revealing, must be transmuted into tangible objectives with "foreseeable" results before efforts in the direction of resolving those needs might become authoritatively acceptable. Even an inmate's new awareness of the compulsive qualities of his unconscious drives toward a particular offense, does not necessarily imply that he accepts this premise on a feeling level. He may, in fact, lean on an intellectualized explanation of the unconscious nature of his difficulties as a justifiable reason for future irresponsibility and consequent asocial behavior.

Even when an intense emotional response gives a "felt" assurance that he accepts the psychiatrist's analysis of his difficulties, there is no way of knowing, subjectively, that this acceptance, in itself, would fortify him against the commission of further crimes. Nor could anyone, including the therapist, lay claim with any degree of certainty to any sudden insight or understanding as responsible for an offender's changed behavior when it does occur.

As indicated earlier, the tangible results of psychological testing, despite a highly questionable IQ designation, had been utilized over a prolonged period as a means of fulfilling a much needed index of mental capacity and associated behavioral responsibility (see pp. 21-23). This "solid" numerical rating eventually became confused with the intangibles of a shifting nosological classification with reference to personality defects and the adverse effects of emotional interference.

The psychiatrist was valued from an administrative standpoint primarily because of the authoritative, clinical backing which he was able to offer in regard to touchy security problems. His astute professional evaluations were never questioned so long as they supplied the need for an "institutionally perceptive," socially protective disposition of medically irresponsible offenders whose disturbing behavior might otherwise call for their transfer as mentally incompetent or criminally insane.

It seemed paradoxical in the immediate postwar years that, along with an increased awareness of the offender's individual needs, he should be subjected to a tightening hold on his capacity for individual expression. The riot of 1944 (see pp. 25-26), while elevating the personal status and overall training qualifications of custodial personnel in the direction of a more understanding approach, stressed an apt diagnosis of institution security risks as the most important function of the psychologist and psychiatric supervisor.

Of secondary importance, but also from the standpoint of institution rather than individual needs, was the increased emphasis on inmate training, both academically and vocationally, to conform with existing, inadequate facilities. There was, at this time, a decided swing away from a psychoanalytic, diagnostic approach in the direction of a more tangible, quantitative analysis. Consequently, and despite the perennial shortage of available funds, an increasing pressure was uniformly exerted for more staff to handle an increased load of both individual and group administered aptitude tests, as well as the more clinically oriented psychometric and projective evaluations.

From an administrative standpoint, the theoretical aspects of an apparently advanced rehabilitative program within the walls of the Wisconsin State Prison did not want for an enthusiastic champion. They were, in fact, authoritatively proclaimed with a great deal of practical punch and fervor as far back as 1940.[21]

At that time, a new warden, who subsequently offered his penological skills as an army major in the military correctional framework of World War II, focused on a program of prison administration which strongly denied the concept of punishment as a cure for crime. In recent years, we have been made brilliantly aware of a unified need for this stand as it was so ably presented in *The Crime of Punishment* by Dr. Karl Menninger, a firm and convincing exponent of the importance of individualized attention and integrity in our dealings with the criminal offender.[80]

The seeds for this program had, of course, been intermittently dropped on sterile administrative soil as far back as the early 1900's and the first indications of psychiatric services in a penal environment.[54]

There were the staunch, but plaintively unheeded admonitions of those eloquent proponents of prison reform: Professor John L. Gillin, Stanford Bates, and Austin H. MacCormick, to name a few. There was even the suggestion of a change in the "damning" pretentiousness of the prison as a correctional institution through a change in its name. At this early date, on the threshold of our most profound economic depression, an intensely sincere, and courageously hopeful psychiatric voice was echoing from the broad background of both a medical and a law degree, the insights of a coordinated need for an acceptance of psychology as "stronger than stone walls or iron bars," which "do not alone a prison make."[89]

In 1940, the new warden's correctional enthusiasm, as well as his foresight, was made apparent in a publicized account of the pressing need for inmate training comparable to that required in a free setting[21]. He emphasized increased educational opportunities, and the development of correlated habits of industry and vocational skills, while at the same time stressing moral and religious training, physical, mental, and emotional health, and an adequate utilization of leisure time activity.

The punch line, however, was that of an envisioned "prison of the future" as developing a system of "positive" training and rewards for persistent effort which would be coordinated in the findings of a representative classification committee. Herein, at the close of the "debilitating thirties," and just prior to the demoralizing shift of priorities called for by our precipitation into World War II, was a highly commendable, but idealistically premature, concept of prison reform.

It, nonetheless, provided a utopian glimpse of uplifted morals and renewed strength which would have moved the offender up the rungs on a ladder of personal attainment, thus allowing for a gradual reduction of his custody needs. Eventually, and in terms of a coordinated focus on the part of a "dedicated" staff, it would have provided for a gradual application of institutionally instilled, adaptive skills, thereby assuring a characterization of "the prisoner of today as the parolee of tomorrow."

Although these lofty objectives were invitingly presented with the contagious enthusiasm of a new and youthful prison warden, they have, more than three decades later, remained discouragingly unfulfilled. From the standpoint of coordinative goals, or, for that matter, from the viewpoint of an enlarged and increasingly enlightened administrative staff, they have, in fact, failed in the main purpose of promoting meaningful changes in the offender's *personal incentives* for change.

In those energetic postwar years, this failure did not in any way result from a lack of staff incentives or effort toward promoting a changed approach in the offender's proven inadequacy in a free environment. Nor did it result from a lack of official emphasis with respect to the earlier conceived, and so-called "positive" approach to the inmate's training needs. Within the prison, a classification committee composed of representative disciplines, including the director of education, social services supervisor, clinical psychologist, a medical assistant, director of prison industry, deputy warden, and the prison chaplain, was, in fact, formed as planned.

The clinical psychologist continued to merit a very important function at this time in that he dutifully constructed an appropriately coordinated rating system for purposes of an objective classification of inmate potential. Each individual offender was subsequently evaluated on a scale ranging from those who were most amenable and best motivated to the more passively indifferent and less tractable inmate, and on to the other end of a continuum representing those who tended to be most aggressively asocial or psychopathic in their reactions.

For classification purposes, the psychological findings were integrated in terms of mental capacity or learning potential as related to actual functioning level, and in the light of specially determined vocational interests and comparable skills. At the same time, an evaluation was made of the offender's personality composition, his custody allocation on a scale ranging from minimum to maximum, and the manner in which his psychotherapeutic needs might be reflected in his interpersonal adjustment, intrapersonal conflicts, and motivational goals.

The classification committee, in addition, regularly evaluated the offender in terms of his school progress as compared with his initially determined achievement scores, his demonstrated moral and religious incentives, his leisure time interests, hobby activities, social history, and the extent and quality of his familial contacts. Of more immediate interest were the work progress reports on his institution job assignments, his institution disciplinary record as related to the nature and extent of his criminal history, and overall interpersonal attitudes which might affect his custody needs.

From the standpoint of the institution, of course, security requirements were an ever present and primary consideration. As the weekly meetings continued, and the coordinative effort of the various committee members became routine procedure, the practical impact of their more refined determinations became increasingly less potent. Volumes of paper and hours of staff time, however, continued to be used on psychometric test results, personality evaluations, and a measured index of the offender's vocational interests and aptitudes in relation to a recommended job training assignment which, more often than not, was unavailable.

Despite overriding security problems and an absence of available opportunities, however, a vocational training program geared toward the "fulfillment" of individual needs continued to merit the spotlight of current rehabilitative effort.

As it appears now, from the safe distance and time-mellowed perspective of a 25-year-interval, there was an overwhelming concentration of effort on a paper program reflecting a flurry of "rehabilitative" activity which could not work out in practice. There was then, as there is now, an insidious ebb and flow of strong undercurrents in a power struggle which tended to build up with each bright, new focus on specific issues.

Like the confused convolutions of a tortured childhood, this subtle struggle continues to follow a pattern of ingrained hypocrisy wherein an administrative red light is flashed against any authoritative clinical "infringement," while at the same time showing the green light of official concern for the impoverished offender. The autonomy of each "parent figure" is threatened in the sense that, on the surface at least, custody restrictions appear to be incompatible with a genuinely positive expansion of inner needs.

The clinical psychologist, nonetheless, proceeded on the assumption that tangible results, scientifically determined, might eventually prove to be most acceptable, and, therefore, more conducive to a more profound assimilation of individual emotional needs. A liaison function was, in fact, introduced at this time which tended to promote a much needed verbal understanding between the shop foreman and the disciplinary staff on the one hand, and the clinical services on the other.

It was a time when the correctional psychologist merited more than usual recognition as one whose advice could be sought, and realistically considered, on questions of disciplinary infractions and job placement, as well as on those relating to emotional and mental strengths and consequent readiness for parole.

"DOWN SIDE UP" OF CRIMINAL "REHABILITATION"

As it developed, however, the "cart before the horse" analogy was amply demonstrated over a two-year-period of intensive aptitude analysis. The "cart" in this case was an extensive job analysis and vocational aptitude testing program which sought to gear the offender's training needs in accordance with those of the United States Employment Service.* The "horse," of course, was the driving power emanating from the inner resources of the offender—the motivation which he, himself, was able to muster in the direction of making this authoritative "thing" a practical reality.

Considerable research went into this venture between 1948 and 1951, and the administrative heads of three adult maximum security institutions were involved in the project. It was first advanced by the Corrections Division director in a state-wide attempt at providing a coordinated approach to a program which would, theoretically, place the inmate offender in a position of vocational merit comparable with that of anyone who applied to the U. S. Employment Services for an appropriate placement in a free society.

The prison psychologist, who now supervised inter-institutional

---

*The Division of Occupational Analysis, United States Employment Service of the U. S. Department of Labor, Bureau of Employment Security, had prepared a two volume, second edition (March, 1949) of the *Dictionary of Occupational Titles,* with Vol. I as *Definitions of Titles,* and Vol. II as *Occupational Classification.* A third edition, 16 years later (1965), defines as many as 23,000 different occupations in more than 230 different industries. This latest edition enjoys a widespread use which extends far beyond that of the Federal-State Employment Service and some 65 other governmental agencies. It has at times been called the "Bureaucratic Bible" because of its extensive use as a dependable counseling and reference source.

programs involving the work of four other correctional psychologists, was appointed as chairman of the vocational aptitude testing procedures. Several weeks of intensive training ensued under the tutelege of state representatives of the U. S. Employment Services who sought to introduce a General Aptitude Test Battery into the correctional program.*

It was an era of statistical analyses, fact-finding inventories, an intensive job market evaluation, and a search for dormant skills which closely paralleled the overall postwar effort to bring war casualties and other handicapped persons in line with our nation's readjustment needs.

The psychologist's rationale at this time centered in a recognition of intelligence tests, and associated personality evaluations, as mental candle power in a spotlight on special abilities and aptitudes. The merits of any single psychological test, no matter how valid or revealing of inner dynamics, were, for the most part, discounted in favor of a concisely administered battery of verbal and performance tests stressing a statistically determined vocational trend.

It was noted that even a superiorly endowed person might be quite unaware of the special skills and abilities which lie dormant in his makeup. Many of the personality conflicts and frustrations resulting in an individual's incarceration, it was postulated, were the direct result of misdirected energies in a vocational environment ill-adapted to his needs and talents. It was reasoned, furthermore, that the higher the intelligence of the person in question, the more glaring the discrepancy, and the more aggravated his sense of frustration.

There was a great deal of stress placed on the fact that abilities which make for success in a particular occupation are found in combinations of varying degrees. The following excerpt of an article, taken from the official Wisconsin Department of Public Welfare publication in the immediate postwar period, will reveal the psychological trend of correctional thinking at that time[111]:

> An adequate vocational aptitude testing program takes into consideration six major abilities—academic, mechanical, social, clerical,

---

*The General Aptitude Test Battery, prepared by the Occupational Analyses, (Standards and Methods) Division of the U. S. Department of Labor for use by the U. S. Employment Services (March, 1947), utilized 15 tests in the measurement and conversion of ten test scores, which were then interpreted in terms of 20 occupational aptitude patterns.

musical, and artistic. It would be highly unusual, if not actually detrimental to ambition and drive, for any one to possess all of these abilities in equal amounts. Nor could one conceive of a steadfastly successful person being gifted with a superabundance of any one ability to the exclusion of all the others. Abilities which make for success in a certain occupation are weighted and distributed according to a certain pattern for each job, trade, or profession.

A topnotch lawyer, broker, newspaper reporter, social worker, or writer, for example, requires an A academic rating, an A social ability, and a B clerical skill, but the fact that he rates D in mechanical, musical, and artistic talents does not interfere with his success in his chosen field.

A high grade technical engineer or inventive genius, on the other hand, requires an A mechanical skill in addition to an A academic rating, but a D rating in social sensitivity and only a C clerical ability have no particular bearing on his ultimate success. In fact, each job classification represents a pattern of interests and abilities actually demonstrated as necessary for success in those particular occupations.

The technical engineer with artistic ability might well become an architect, sculptor, or stage designer, whereas in the lawyer's pattern of abilities, an A rather than a D rating in artistic talent might quite possibly be a distracting influence responsible for throwing chances of success in that particular field off balance.

In the ensuing five years, between 1945 and 1950, aptitude designations were refined to include the U. S. Employment Services General Aptitude Test Battery which presumed to point up special skills relating to 20 aptitude patterns. The specific job categories relating to these 20 fields of work were defined and classified in the *Dictionary of Occupational Titles* (see pp. 36-37). We had, at this time, regarded ourselves as far removed from the rigid, narrow-minded conclusions of "the regimented years" in that we now perceived the prison population, insofar as innate abilities are concerned, as comprising a fairly close approximation of the average person in our society.

In the process of this realization, however, we became increasingly aware of one major difference, and one apparently insurmountable difficulty. In view of the fact that a considerable number of normally endowed institution charges are subject to personality defects or conflicts of feeling, their professed interests or preferences are understandably colored by their emotional needs. Any scaled analysis based on inventory evaluations, no matter how statistically correct it may appear to be, must first of all meet the highly unreliable test of "confined incentives" in an abnormally depressing prison environment.

Scientifically measured results, particularly those with inflexible scores, or arbitrary numerical designations which are presumed to be objectively correct, are subject to a great deal of egocentric manipulation. This may be true from the standpoint of an unmeasured apathy on the part of the examinee, or because of the personal ambitions of the examiner who more or less unconsciously seeks to establish a satisfying correlation.

Subjective analyses, on the other hand, are lacking in statistical validity, and although they offer a more profound clinical picture of the total personality, they are actually no better than the clinical insight and judgment of the psychologist who utilizes this form of measurement in his diagnostic evaluations.

In any event, it has become increasingly apparent that the reaction of a vast majority of our criminal offenders is subject to an intense need to cover up their "weaknesses," or to alibi their inadequacies, by maintaining a false front. They are, under these conditions, incapable of any direct response. Since they cannot be themselves, and because they are unable to face facts squarely, they are continually driven to reroute their energies in a wasteful expenditure of frustrated emotion. Every correctional worker, inside or outside of an institution, is aware of the job hopping propensities of the criminal offender who appears to have no settled goals, and whose reactions are indicative of an extremely short attention span for most of his professed vocational objectives.

A thorough program of vocational aptitude testing and counseling, in order that it may be effective, therefore involves an almost impossible sifting of innate abilities and special skills in terms of consistency of effort which is, quite obviously, tuned to the strength and direction of an emotional drive. In addition, a complete vocational evaluation necessarily involves a comparison of scientifically measured interests against demonstrated abilities and intellectual potential in each of the 20 major areas of work which the General Aptitude Test Battery presumed to point up.

Inevitably the conclusion is reached wherein it is apparent that the very frustrations which might be corrected through a diligent application of an adequate vocational program in themselves prevent its effective indoctrination. In the end, we are back to the original problem of an overall personality evaluation which assumes proportions overshadowing the more tangible mental functions.

We are, at the same time, faced with the futility of utilizing a so-called modern approach in an obsolete prison system which is geared primarily toward the containment of a "vicious and socially disruptive element." This undesirable element, which actually comprises no more than 20 percent of our total prison population[23,56], is otherwise described as saturated with "destructive qualities," the very nature of which negate any demonstrable "merit" for more advanced appropriations of the taxpayer's already "desecrated" funds. As it is, we are caught in a "rehabilitative cul-de-sac" which offers no realistic expectations of either the necessary incentives or the required skills for future adjustment in a competitive society.

For purposes of illustration, let us consider one offender of high average mental capacity and better than average incentives for future adjustment who ran the gamut of our most intensive vocational aptitude and reclassification analyses in this "enlightened" postwar period.

This was a 25-year-old man who had been "forced" into marriage in his late teenage period, and who, at the time of his commitment, was the father of three children. He was a first offender who had experienced only one prior arrest for disorderly conduct wherein he apparently saw himself as trapped into marriage by the exacting demands of a "benevolent" law enforcing authority.

His current armed robbery offense, for which he was sentenced to a prison term of three to five years, was the consequence of his involvement with three other young men who used his car in the actual offense. He, himself, disclaimed any personal complicity other than the fact that he knew about the robbery, and that he had shared in a division of the stolen money.

He was described psychiatrically as a situational offender who was outwardly well-mannered and cooperative, but who gave every indication of being emotionally constricted and preoccupied. He was seen as apprehensive and devoid of self-confidence, apparently laboring under marked emotional stress which he sought to conceal under a bland and noncommittal exterior. His offense was regarded as the outward manifestation of his need to escape an unbearable marital situation, the true circumstances of which he tended to gloss over as in no way responsible for his present predicament.

He was one of many emotionally traumatized offenders whom the psychiatric director had initially referred to the psychologist for projective evaluation. He was subsequently confronted with Rorschach findings, focusing on his heterosexual incompetence and associated fear of exposure before his peers, as one with insufficient masculine strengths. He appeared on his own request for regular psychiatric interviews about the same time that he was scheduled for reclassification, along with the committee recommendations for a thorough aptitude evaluation.

It was originally noted that this man's high average intelligence was characterized by a good fund of general information and a high level of arithmetical reasoning ability. Routine learning, however, was described as poor, and an inconsistent and erratic test response suggested that he was blocking on certain significant test items. Special skills were, nonetheless, apparent in his demonstrated capacity for concentrated effort in the more impersonal situations calling for quantitative thinking. His actual intellectual potential was, therefore, estimated to be that of an emotionally repressed, but superiorly endowed person.

The fact that he was underfunctioning because of emotional interference was again demonstrated in an 8.5 grade level on the school achievement test as compared to a 10th grade attainment in a free setting. Even so, it was apparent that a dropout at the tenth grade level in an individual of superior mental capacity had to be the result of indifferent application in one who had long been in need of professional help with his emotional problems.

While these emotional factors were finally getting the recognition which they deserved, an appropriate allocation of specific needs, and the time scale upon which they should have been systematically resolved, was not even discussed. The "pendulum," in other words, had again swung out of range of any global consideration of interlocking needs. The psychiatrist, however, continued his extremely "confidential" approach, while the psychologist was prodded for more tangible evidence of an aptitude evaluation which starred as the main play on the current rehabilitative stage.

INTER-PROFESSIONAL BIASES IMMOBILIZE
THE NEED FOR CHANGE

It was inevitable, therefore, that our underfunctioning inmate's emotional reserves should become involved in a psychiatric confrontation on psychic impotence and masculine identity problems at the same time that he was being asked to participate in an energetic vocational aptitude testing and training program. The clinical facts of his emotional blocking and consequent underachievement, together with his urgent need for peer recognition, were, of course, aired at the reclassification sessions dealing with his particular case. There was, however, no coordinated psychiatric follow-up on "highly personal material," the "untimely" revelation of which it was feared might undermine a jealously guarded, psychiatric rapport.

The gap between the psychiatric and administrative functions widened with an insidious emphasis on custodial versus clinical needs, and a neutralization of authoritative objectives was the inevitable result. A very realistic "treatment" conflict was superimposed over the one with which the offender was already struggling at the time that the offense was committed. His awareness of a conflict of interests, and consequent rejection of the authoritative "phoniness" which he saw in his prison surroundings, was exceeded only by an unbearable sense of frustration and a need to find relief through the most comfortable of the available channels.

These avenues of escape are, as we have seen over and over again, nothing more than postponements of the problem with which he had been confronted throughout a major portion of his lifetime. It was all the more difficult to face for the reason that it had been previously sidestepped by both the inmate and his "jailers" at the time when the going was rough.

The subject of our illustration, however, did not want for either professional attention or innate abilities upon which to rejuvenate his entire existence. When subjected to the General Aptitude Test Battery, he had, in fact, startled everyone by qualifying at a better than average level for 18 out of 20 fields of work.

The test results proved that he was particularly high in mechanical capability. Since his measured interests also focused on a high level of mechanical skill commensurate with the obviously superior quality of his visual-motor coordinative power, he was most enthusiastically recommended for assignment as a machine shop trainee.

Six months later his case was reviewed. Instead of the machine shop, he had been assigned to the main lobby as a radio operator. This was because the radio operator's job was vacant, while machine shop jobs were in limited supply. It was also a "tentative" assignment which fulfilled a need for the institution, and which was, furthermore, "justified" as a most desirable location for one who was interested in attending the institution school.

A much more important reason centered in the production demands on key men in the machine shop which tended to discourage time out for related courses of study. It was certainly true that shop foremen in a prison, conditioned over the years to the production needs of a tightly budgeted and otherwise efficiently operated institution, frowned on those who had introduced "a new form of goldbricking" by "escaping on pass" to both the psychiatrist's office and to the institution school.

As it developed, our most promising inmate protégé did not even feel inclined to take a course of study in the institution school. Nor did he ask for a University Extension course, or for any form of self-study to fulfill his recognized potential for a highly skilled level of vocational training and subsequent readjustment in accordance with his superior intelligence.

He did like the element of "trust," as well as the inmate status, which was extended to him in his otherwise key position as a radio operator in the lobby. He also liked the freedom of movement, and the readiness with which he was enabled to make the "most desirable contacts." He "conformed" and "exerted" himself to the extent that he eventually became a minimum security risk. He developed into a "natural" as the warden's special chauffeur after he had "proven" both his mechanical skills and his "good judgment" as a garage mechanic on the institution farm.

Whereas he had failed miserably on personal integrity and self-achievement, despite clear indications of a coordinated need for both psychiatric attention and vocational training, he readily succeeded as an apt candidate for the institutionalized mold of a trusty who had only to put in his time in the easiest and most ineffectual manner possible.

When an offender with these qualifications succeeds on parole and is not heard of again, he has managed to readjust himself to the competitive demands of a free world in spite of, rather than because of, the attention which he has received. The only benefit which he might have conceivably realized as a consequence of his prison commitment was one of self-awareness with respect to certain mental assets and emotional deficiencies which he may not have considered earlier.

Although unfulfilled in his vocational training incentives, and allowed to take the easiest way out, he may have recognized certain shortcomings, as well as personal skills, which would tend to develop a new perspective with respect to his own responsibilities. He would, under these circumstances, be less inclined to blame others for his past mistakes, and less apt to become criminally involved a second time.

Certainly, and despite the shock of a callous confrontation, he had achieved some emotional benefit from his brief, sex-oriented interviews with the psychiatrist. After all, he was diagnosed as a circumstantial offender whose main problem centered in the emotional frustrations of an inadequate marital relationship which time alone might help to resolve.

Realistically, however, he had been let down by an extensive program of rehabilitation which neglected to establish priorities for his most pressing needs. He was, first of all, denied a recognized need for training as a machine shop apprentice because there was no opening available to him at the time. Secondly, he was a minimum risk whose need for status, and whose natural craving for a trusty location, worked against the prolonged application and consistency of effort which would be required of him in a more disciplined approach. A complacent neglect was, therefore, allowed to fortify his earlier indicated tendencies toward a less profound and more immediate emotional gratification. It also fulfilled an "urgent" institution need which, in effect, tended to cement already inherent dependency needs in the offender.

In the end, the vocational aptitude testing program was perceived as failing the expected beneficiaries of this intensive endeavor on six very important issues:

1. It failed to recognize the more amenable screening needs and priority levels in regard to which the accidental, or situational

offender, might derive an immediate benefit from a vocational aptitude training program.

2. It overlooked the emotional conflicts which first needed to be resolved before a consistency of effort and outlook might be expected on long range training objectives.

3. It failed to recognize the overwhelming influence of peers in a prison environment; that of chronic offenders whose main objectives are those of undermining incentives which may be in any way fulfilling of the authoritarian approach.

4. It promoted a school related program which was incompatible with the obsolete physical facilities and budgetary requirements calling for an "institutionalized" level of production on the part of prison industry.

5. It failed to provide either work habits or job training comparable with that found in a free setting.

6. It made no allowance for the fact that those who are best motivated are also the best security risks. They are, thereby, subject to minimum security designations which permit their "escape" into more comfortable locations far removed from the more consistent and arduous demands of their training objectives.

SECURITY HIDES BEHIND ITS OWN EMOTIONAL BLOCK

One other influence of grave importance which might be considered in this era of advanced liaison activity on the part of the clinical psychologist is that of the offender's relationship with the guards, or correctional officers as they are now called. After all, the guard's daily surveillance brings him in close contact with his prisoner over much of his eight-hour, five-day workweek, whereas comparable contacts with clinical personnel are seldom of more than two hours duration for the entire week.

On the basis of the extent of interpersonal relationships with authoritarian figures, and whatever influences these contacts may imply, the personality of the guard is deemed to be of considerable importance in the potential reshaping of constructive incentives in the rehabilitative plan.

With this thought in mind, therefore, the prison psychologist in the vocational aptitude evaluation era was pressured with just one more demand on his already overburdened temporal resources. While the vocational aptitude testing program was in full swing, and while he was being flooded with referrals from the psychiatrist for individual Rorschach analyses, he was asked to evaluate the personality of probationary guards with the same subjectively significant projective approach.

The clinical psychologist, by this time, had completed hundreds of Rorschach interpretations, all of which were highly prized by the psychiatric director as an opening wedge in his psychiatric "breakthrough" to the inner layers of previously undisclosed emotional material. The psychiatrist was, in effect, sold on the unconscious potency of this projective instrument as a means of crashing the offender's otherwise impervious barrier of defensive denial to the inner core of his private life.

It was felt that the same might be accomplished, with highly beneficial results, in a projective screening of the most desirable qualities in probationary guards. With the aid of an assistant clinical psychologist, who took over the load of other institutional referrals and routine classification procedures, the chief psychologist became intensively involved with the prison deputy warden in an analysis of potential officers whom the deputy had indicated his intention of hiring.

This part of the program, of course, was highly experimental, but it was given a thorough trial over a period of more than a year. The psychologist conscientiously evaluated each guard candidate, most of whom were fairly young World War II veterans of high school graduate standing, in an interview which involved an analysis of the family, marital, and social backgrounds of each in the light of the Rorschach and other indicated projective test findings.

The basic instability of nearly half of the applicants at this time showed up on the Rorschach analysis in the form of marked emotional constriction and unhealthy withdrawal tendencies. There was, in fact, qualitative evidence in the projective evaluations of some guard candidates of an incapacity for warmth or empathy in human relationships, an essential ingredient to any understanding interpersonal approach. The examiner was even startled at times with strong indications of sadistic thought processes which necessitated the writing of a negative report, including recommendations against hiring this type of individual.

The hard-earned rapport which had been established between the clinical psychologist and the custodial staff subsequently became rather distant and strained. Despite both oral and written interpretations of the test results, questions were raised regarding the validity, and even the authenticity, of the reports which had been so earnestly solicited. Here, again, a great deal of conscientious effort and valuable staff time was lost in the dead bulk of clinical files bulging with administratively neglected, and otherwise unacceptable, results.

As it finally developed, the very individuals who were labelled on the basis of the Rorschach findings as being emotionally calloused, authoritatively rigid, or sadistically inclined, were often the ones who were hired. Those whose projective analyses showed considerably more flexibility, sensitivity, and empathy in their human relationships were as often discarded on the surface indications of an "undesirable" humility, or impassioned "vulnerability," despite their inherently positive Rorschach protocols.

These discrepancies were most apparent under conditions which encouraged critical reporting of inmate behavior without regard for the more intangible prison pressures involving the uniquely helpless personality characteristics of the man himself. The insidious personality clashes behind the impulsively unpredictable acts of violence on the part of one inmate against another, for example, were seldom considered in the subsequent disciplinary action. The unwavering, authoritative stand held that "it takes two to make a fight, and both must, in all fairness, be punished, since the feelings on the part of each involved inmate are much too high, too contagiously unreasonable, to allow for any separation of blame."

Fighting between inmates, no matter what the provocation, was regarded as a most serious offense meriting solitary confinement for all active participants. It was authoritatively perceived as a moral breakdown of discipline which, except for the tardily arranged, ring-placating "grudge fights," could not under any circumstances be tolerated. Neither could the true, underlying causes of a prison "blow up," for "reasons of security," be aired publicly without a heavy amount of security conscious editing, if not absolute silence.

The clinical psychologist, for similar reasons, was never informed of the fact that his analysis regarding the suitability of a particular "officer candidate" was, or was not, acceptable. Passive resistance, in this instance, matched that of the most engaging psychopath, and the issue was eventually allowed to end in a quietly unresponsive and unheralded demise.

It did, however, become quite obvious that the subjective analyses by trained psychological personnel had lost favor because the findings did not conform with the preconceived ideas of the deputy administrator as to what personal qualifications constituted a good correctional officer. It had, in fact, become apparent that the alertly watchful characteristic of a man who was capable of being both coolly efficient and authoritatively conforming in the exercise of his duties, whether or not he was sadistically inclined, took precedence over all other personality attributes as the most essential quality in an "effective" prison guard.

We are, therefore, obliged to add one more point to our list of failures during this stage of a "coordinated" effort in the direction of a more realistic approach to the overall training program:

7. This point, and perhaps the most important one, indicates a dearth of any real communication between the clinical and custodial staffs with respect to the emotional needs, and long range objectives, of criminal offenders. Then, as today, our own egocentric needs continue to promote a controversial, or more often, "stand-offish," approach to this problem despite the fact that we must eventually assimilate the offender with all of his pent-up hatreds and interwoven tensions into the feeling warp of our rejecting society.

Chapter 5

THE DIP FROM DIAGNOSIS INTO TREATMENT

Early in 1952, the psychiatric services staff had almost completely withdrawn from vocational aptitude analysis in favor of a more refined diagnostic endeavor. For a brief space, a newly appointed supervising psychologist concentrated on research projects designed to lend weight to more effective testing procedures. It was at this time, also, that the first of a series of articles was published which gave promise to some rather pointed comparisons of inmate Rorschach protocols in relation to those of probationary guards.[27, 28, 112]

These projects, however, did not even scratch the surface of our prison communication problems, and the clinical services, in effect, continued to function in a relatively isolated state. There was, nonetheless, a more profound expansion of diagnostic effort during this period which tended to make psychological services a total and all-absorbing consideration. These services were now fully devoted to intensive projective analyses on an increasingly greater number of inmate referrals. Any consistent research endeavor was, as a consequence, crowded onto the sidelines of voluntary, extraprofessional activity.

The emphasis was once again on psychiatric diagnosis, together with a much more erudite and all-inclusive report structure, for the most part meaningful only to clinical services personnel. The psychiatric staff, at this time, had been increased to two resident psychiatrists in addition to the psychiatric director, and the demands for psychological testing from a purely clinical point of view had naturally increased. While contact was still maintained with the reclassification committee and with the parole function, the psychologist's physical presence was replaced by an "appropriate" report form with indicated recommendations which were often ignored.

From the standpoint of the institution administrative function, custody needs continued to merit a primary consideration. The psychiatrist's lengthy, and sometimes involved report, was seldom heeded except insofar as he was able to offer a definite opinion with respect to an offender's mental competence, or medical responsibility, in a prison setting. Then the issue became one calling for the alternatives of hospitalization, transfer, or "responsible" disciplinary action under conditions which took the heat of any public reproach away from an otherwise uncertain administrative decision.

It was at this time, also, that the psychiatric scene began to shift so as to embrace a more specialized concept in line with the public clamor for an appropriate diagnosis and treatment of the sex crimes offender. The Wisconsin Sex Crimes Law became effective in December of 1951, and the Wisconsin State Prison was designated as the main facility for both diagnosis and treatment of those who were thereby committed. At this stage in time, and for a period of five to ten years thereafter, the prison psychologist refined his diagnostic tools for an apt determination of the extent and quality of a convicted offender's sexual deviations.

The mechanics of the law entailed a 60-day-observational period, during which time the presence or absence of sexual deviation was psychiatrically decided on the basis of clinical observation and psychological test results. The question of "dangerousness" and treatability within the environment of the prison was also determined at this time. It was, in fact, the psychologist's diagnostic task to formulate a practical psychological basis for these decisions prior to the ultimate staff hearing with the psychiatrist.

The psychologist's area of influence had thus been expanded to include a determination of the offender's potential for treatment, as well as offering evidence regarding the level of his emotional growth and the integrity of his thought processes. He was expected to provide psychological determinants with respect to the sex criminal's inner resources, while highlighting the disintegrating influences of underlying psychosexual fixations, obsessive thinking, or compulsiveness in his behavior.

Even more important, from the standpoint of society and the protective concerns of "public policy" under the criminal code, was a psychological analysis of the offender's capacity for exercising inhibitory controls against an otherwise unpredictably violent discharge of impulses.

This, then, became the climax of an intensive diagnostic effort which laid the groundwork for an individualized treatment program centered almost entirely on the mandatory requirements for treating sex crimes commitments. The psychologist, although indispensable on the basis of the exhaustive mental and emotional spadework which he was obliged to do, was, at the same time, rigidly excluded from the actual treatment process. Treatment, as defined by the psychiatric director of that period, necessitated a medical degree in addition to the other essentials of acceptable psychiatric experience, all of which narrowed the treatment function to a disturbingly limited and chosen few.

The ultimately unexpected precipitation of the psychologist directly into the treatment parlor of this sacred psychiatric citadel will be discussed at length in a succeeding chapter. In the meantime, and until the increased demands on the psychologist's diagnostic skills had necessitated a comparable expansion of the ranks and training qualifications of the clinical psychologist, he had little time for anything beyond repeated staff conferences and the intricate fulfillment of advanced testing procedures.

In addition to a supervising psychologist with administrative duties embracing other state correctional institutions, we now had four staff psychologists at the prison who were involved in various diagnostic phases of the Psychiatric Services sex crimes program. Previously, and up until the readjustment period following World War II, the allocation needs of an overflowing prison population, ranging from chicken thieves to bank robbers and embezzling bank presidents, called for routine screening procedures on the part of one male psychologist.*

But throughout the 1950's, and until the original Psychiatric Field Service label had been contracted into a shorter, but more expansive

---

*It should be noted that the Psychiatric Field Service had also employed a female psychologist whose extensive psychometric duties at both juvenile and female correctional institutions in the emotionally impoverished atmosphere of the depression years required a spiritual commitment and dedication of effort which today is a rather rare quality. Nor should one forget the medical students and correctional career people who offered transient, but nonetheless, enthusiastic psychometric assistance over many years of our congested institution's greatest need.

Clinical Services designation, there was a heavy hand on a frustrating mass of arbitrarily conceived concepts and questionable statistical data. The accepted informality of approach during this period, however, had erased much of the earlier conforming rigidity, making room for a "man to man" confrontation which, in the psychologist's office as well as in that of the psychiatrist, welcomed an uncensored release of freely verbalized feeling.

By this time, both the psychologist and the psychiatrist had been blessed with appropriately furnished offices in a new hospital building which provided ample room, as well as a treatment atmosphere, for a more advanced form of mental evaluation. There was also the proximity with the institution medical staff, and from the standpoint of both physical surroundings and personal care there was a much more relaxed approach to the individual problems which the inmate presented.

Along with all of the pressure for a more involved personality evaluation in the immediate postwar period came a much more understanding approach to the inmate's problems in terms of tolerance for his emotional difficulties. He was, consequently, allowed more time for an expression of his verbalized needs, and mental note was made of his behavioral reactions as an aid to projective analysis.

Little or no factual information was at this stage recorded on a verbatim basis; instead the examiner assumed an unhurried, and for the most part, acceptant attitude with the specific intent of promoting some degree of emotional honesty in the response of his client. At the same time, the psychologist was busily occupied with an alert observation of the inmate's mannerisms focusing on hidden feelings of much more significant import which lay behind or between the literal interpretation of his habitual utterances.

Usually, the Wechsler Adult Intelligence Test Scale[119] was the first measuring device to be presented, although the test order was frequently varied in accordance with the subject's reaction and the needs of his particular situation. If, for example, it was established that he was illiterate, or perhaps educationally defective, a performance scale involving manual mediums of intellectual expression was the first in a series of tests to be presented.

This initial testing evaluation might be followed by a test of visual motor coordination in the form of the Bender Visual Motor Gestalt

Test, and more often than not it was supplemented with a short projective evaluation utilizing the inmate's version of a Human Figure Drawing.* A vocabulary, word association, or sentence completion test was supplemented only in those instances wherein a minimum of verbal facility had been demonstrated in the initial interview.

As staff was added to take care of the increased diagnostic and more profound psychoanalytical needs—greater emphasis was placed on the psychologist's clinical judgment and flexibility of approach. It was up to the psychologist, for example, to select the most appropriate tests, the order in which they were given, and the extent to which pertinent response patterns were utilized in the psychological report.

This new latitude in the psychological workup, while purposefully far removed from the abortive rigidity of earlier testing procedures, sacrificed one very essential quality. It gave up a uniformity of approach and concensus of diagnostic effort, the lack of which threatened to undermine faith in the decision-making scaffolding from which the offender's emotional rehabilitation was being erected.

As it developed, with each new addition of professional clinical staff on a hierarchy of advanced degrees and academic proficiency, came a new set of testing procedures, a new set of diagnostic evaluations, and a new set of recommendations. For the inmate offender, as well as for the custodial staff, it ushered in a confused set of values, and ultimately, a lessened respect for the integrity and effectiveness of clinical services personnel.

Progress, of course, thrives on new ideas, and flexibility of approach is the inevitable heritage of an alert and competent psychologist. A willingness to change, despite repercussions in institutional security which threaten further confusion for both "doctor and patient," is a sometimes painful, but necessary spur, to self-directed change in the inmate offender.

INADVERTENT REINFORCEMENT OF A PSYCHOPATH'S MANIPULATIVE GOALS

It might be helpful, under these conflicting conditions, to survey

*The tests referred to are those of Bender, L.: In L. Lowrey (Ed.): *A Visual Motor Gestalt Test And Its Clinical Use*, Research Monographs, no. 3, New York, The American Orthopsychiatric Association, 1938; and Machover, K.: *Personality Projection in the Drawing Of The Human Figure*. Springfield, Thomas, 1947.

the diagnostic sequence of a particularly difficult case from the time of the initial interview to the date of the offender's ultimate release. In the course of a complicated, clinical-custodial interaction over a period of many years, we might then be able to note the good in relation to the bad, and thereby separate the strengths from the weaknesses in a particular diagnostic approach.

The inmate we are about to observe, and to whom we shall refer as Mark Stout, was one of many hundreds of seriously involved criminal offenders who ran the gamut of our postwar diagnostic efforts. He first appeared on the prison scene with a six-year-term for assault and robbery, unarmed; this being the criminal code label for a largely unrecognized, and much more profound, emotional problem. As it developed, he, himself, did not recognize the true nature of an underlying motivation which had none of the premeditated qualities implied in the robbery offense with which he was charged.

Unlike the broken home situation of so many criminal offenders, Mark came from a socially acceptable, and otherwise comfortable, middle class home in which the parents appeared to have shown every concern for the welfare of their only son. He was, however, the second of two children, the oldest being his academically brilliant sister, four years his senior.

Physically Mark appeared to be in good health, but he was regarded as overweight and subject to a glandular disturbance in early childhood. Parental overanxiety about this condition had unquestionably precipitated serious emotional problems. There was, for example, an associated enuresis which extended into his twelfth year, and there were also indications of an unacceptable visual defect calling for corrective glasses which he greatly resented and refused to wear in his elementary school age period.

The negative impact of this early emotional trauma is indicated in the fact that, far from following the lead of his conscientious sister, he showed a dearth of interest in his school work. His neglect worsened to the extent that he avoided all competitive situations, including those in the area of sports activity which might have made him more acceptable to his peers. He became increasingly sensitive to a pervading incapacity for self-assertion, which he perceived as falling far short of the potential implied in his stocky build and apparently strong physique.

Since he feared the turbulence of his own emotions, he hid behind a wall of indifference, and a hostilely aggressive reaction became his most dependable weapon against exposure of vulnerable feelings which, to him, meant complete loss of control. He found himself caught up in a vicious circle of impotence, the very preoccupation with which seemed to incapacitate him more. Throughout his growing years he had made the painful discovery that the more sensitive he became, the more emotionally drained and incapacitated he found himself to be in his struggle for acceptance by others.

He had no dates because he was fearful of his capacity for adequate performance, and, thereby, threatened by the belittling consequences of almost certain rejection by the female. His only escape was through alcoholic indulgence, and it was under this condition of lowered inhibitions that his criminal career had its beginning.

Over the years, until age 25 when he first came to the prison, Mark had a history of truancy, speeding violations, auto larceny offenses, and aggressive sexual behavior toward a female. He came to the prison on a six-year-term for snatching a woman's purse and forcibly removing her wrist watch. He was apprehended in his car while attempting to leave the scene of the offense, and after he had impulsively broken his key in the ignition lock.

At the time of his prison commitment, Mark was subject to a detainer on an attempted rape offense in another state, and he had a prior record of desertion following two military enlistments over a nine-year-period. He was married for less than a year prior to his prison sentence, and it is significant of an underlying emotional dependence that he picked a self-sufficient girl, three years older than himself, whom he described as physically plain and unattractive while lauding her good housekeeping characteristics.

In the initial interview, Mark freely admitted the offense for which he was charged, but he was, true to the pattern established by many other offenders, unable to offer any logical reason for his act. His main premise was that he was under the influence of liquor at the time, and that he was, consequently, not himself, and inclined to do things over which he had no control.

This stand, which tended to shift responsibility away from himself and onto causes of unknown import, made it easier for him to admit other irresponsible acts of truancy, AWOL, and auto theft.

He was even able to confess the "possibility" of earlier suspected, but legally unsubstantiated, rape offenses.

The first impression was that of a man who was outwardly co-operative, but inwardly resistive and self-centered in his makeup. He tended to be impulsive and generally superficial in his response to the test situation. He, nonetheless, classified as superior in his mental capacity, scaling on a superior level verbally, compared to a high average rating in manual performance.

He showed evidence of a good fund of general information, together with social comprehension of high average calibre. But, whereas superior visual motor organization was shown, routine learning was revealed as relatively poor, and the overall indications of his approach to the testing situation were those of a person who was inclined to apply himself in a flighty and irresponsible manner.

His work experience was that of a grossly under-functioning individual who had been only spasmodically employed as a salesman and laborer. He verbalized vocational inclinations in the direction of small business management, with a view toward starting a restaurant or baking business upon release. At the same time, he professed a high cultural interest, and it was obvious that his intellectual incentives were far beyond his emotional capacity to fulfill.

Under pressure of the personality evaluation he reluctantly admitted that his acts under the influence of liquor were illogical and unnatural, and that he was in need of treatment. At the same time, he was careful not to reveal anything, in either his family or marital history, which might suggest any adverse emotional conditions or circumstances.

He denied any traumatizing experiences in his youth, and he was quick to reject any suggestion of favoritism on the part of either parent toward his talented older sister. He, in fact, lauded his parents as exemplary in every respect, and he was obviously offering the clinical manifestation of a sociopathic personality, or alibi artist, whose "phony" exterior served the purpose of adroit manipulations for personal advantage under pressure of authoritarian controls.

He described his heterosexual experience, unconvincingly, as extensive and entirely satisfactory during almost a decade of military duty. His contention was, of course, at variance with the behavior disorder displayed and contrary to the projective findings in his case.

The clinical indications were those of one who was nourishing a great deal of repressed hostility toward the female, and whose emotionally immature and dependent makeup was characterized by an aggressive camouflage of his otherwise inferior self-concept and confused sexual identification.

The initial psychiatric recommendations took note of an underlying phobic reaction, related to unresolved sex conflicts, which indicated a need for psychotherapy. Although cognizant of his need for psychiatric assistance, he appeared to be totally nonacceptant of his basic difficulty. He was only, at this point, evidencing a self-conscious awareness of guilt-anxiety tensions, the true nature of which he was very reluctant to disclose.

Individual psychiatric interviews were begun on the projective evidence of emotionally dependent, but strongly repressed, hostile feelings toward the female. There were also indications of underlying panic reactions, associated with the policing tactics of an exacting father, which had precipitated his mistrust of all authoritarian figures. His father, for example, had insisted on a daily report of his son's grades and behavioral reactions in school, thereby cultivating an attitude of mistrust based on the father's own misguided suspicions.

It was further noted that Mark was subject to immature phantasy ruminations, emanating from longstanding authority conflicts, which he was inclined to act out in an impulsive and unpredictable manner. At the same time it was revealed, also as a consequence of projective analysis, that he did possess the necessary intellectual and emotional resources for achieving a deeper insight into his needs.

His main handicaps, insofar as psychotherapeutic intervention was concerned, centered in a lack of feeling tone in his interpersonal relationships. For example, instead of allowing himself any real warmth or concern for the feelings of others, he bent every effort toward maintaining rigid intellectual defenses which served to deny any emotional awareness as to the true nature of his deviated acts.

Within two months of his commitment, Mark was approached by the psychiatric director in individual sessions which, first of all, bluntly informed him of the projective findings, including his "phony" exterior. He was, in effect, offered the ultimatum of total rejection in the form of a negative report, or professional help in the direction of an earlier release. The latter, he was informed, hinged on his capacity for periodic "confessions" of the emotional tensions and specific sexual conflicts to which he was subject.

The message which was implicitly conveyed to him, at this point, was that of his need to level on a "tell all," "father-son" basis, before any of the psychiatrist's powerful influence could be utilized in his behalf.

It should be remembered that it was during this period, extending over approximately ten years following the conclusion of World War II, that the treatment function was the sole prerogative of the psychiatrist. His was the ultimate authority, and inmate offenders at this stage of criminal growth were quick to recognize that his favor not only advanced their chances for parole, but also their possibilities of attaining desirable hospital and trusty locations. They were very much aware, also, of his influence on the deputy warden in regard to farm or camp assignments which were perceived as only a step removed from parole.

It was a time when the psychiatric director still wrote his overly confident, direct to the point, "nail-on-the-head," reports which were either good or bad in terms of an inmate's behavioral difficulties, institutional adjustment problems, and ultimate chances for release. All the inmate offender had to do was to "confess," admit his guilt, concede his "phony" makeup, and attempt to make amends. This he did through a remorseful, and, for the most part, subservient admission of highly personalized material, the details of which no one but the psychiatrist and himself would be aware.

Mark was, of course, no exception to this form of approach. He had all of the basically insecure, but outwardly "tough" qualities of a sexually conflicted person who was exercising a rigid intellectual defense against exposure of his vulnerable inner self. Breaking a man like this, from the emotionally constipated and egocentric individual that he was into a carthartic release of pent-up emotion, was quite a challenge.

But, whereas a direct confrontation in terms of emotional response did evoke attitudes suggestive of varying degrees of success, it somehow served to solidify the already tight defenses of Mark all the more. It was, perhaps, a carry-over of his father's earlier attempts at "breaking" him during his adolescent and early school age period. In any event, it didn't work, particularly when the psychiatrist had bluntly, and somewhat tactlessly, spilled out a Rorschach test comment to the effect that he had been found to have homosexual tendencies.

In the light of subsequent events, Mark was obviously not ready for this form of disclosure. It came within six weeks of the initial psychiatric interview, and after the patient had "generously" conceded difficulties with his parents, a sense of inferiority in relation to his sister, and a certain inadequacy in his sexual relationships.

It was more than he could take, and he characteristically reverted to an earlier pattern of behavior. His defense in this case was one of angry withdrawal. He responded in an impulsive and primitive manner by banging his fist on the desk, kicking over a chair, and slamming the heavy office door in a hasty exit.

Many months elapsed before he again put in a request to see another psychiatrist. He signified his willingness to continue treatment only after provoking his righteously indignant father into complaining to the family attorney about a lack of the kind of psychiatric attention to which the father felt that his son was entitled under the law.

Mark was again seen on an individual basis for a period of one hour each week. After several months of regularly spaced, psychoanalytically oriented sessions, it became obvious that he was giving only a token expression of feelings which were essentially unchanged from those evidenced at the time of the first interview.

It was apparent, however, that he did cooperate to the extent of "seeing" a psychiatrist, and his overly solicitous father continued to exercise a "helpful" influence through persistent contacts with a competent attorney. On the outward indications of a compliant attitude, Mark received an early parole to the custody of his parents. Once this was accomplished, he was remanded to the supervision of his physically unattractive spouse. As a result of this authoritative manipulation of unresolved dependency needs, the basic conflicts inherent in an emotionally castrating mother figure were again given the unbridled opportunity of an insidious fruition.

When one takes into consideration the nature of preexistent pressures, indirectly fostered by the mock gestures of helpfulness which characterized his first parole release, the second rape offense would appear to be quite inevitable. The emotionally ambivalent marital situation to which he returned was certainly not a test so much as it was a precipitating cause for the revival of early instilled adjustment difficulties over which he had learned no adequate controls.

Mark was out less than ten months when he was apprehended on a rape offense, and the actual intent, in this instance, was beyond question. He, however, showed evidence of relief, rather than remorse, for his assaultive attack on the 18-year-old girl whom he had forced into his car. He freely admitted to slapping her across the mouth and tying her hands behind her back, while alternately engaging and threatening her with a number of indecent acts. Nor did he deny that he had naively requested a snapshot of her, and he appeared to derive a certain perverted pleasure from his frank admission of having gotten her to agree to a subsequent date.

A SOCIOPATH HONES HIS RATIONALISTIC TOOLS ON EGOCENTRIC PLOYS

He was apprehended at the time of his reappearance on what he contended was good faith in trusting the girl to maintain her end of the promised agreement. Now that she had "tricked" him, he felt justified in an increased sense of hostility, rather than a feeling of remorse, as a consequence of his assaultive behavior toward her.

At the time of his second commitment, Mark appeared to be glossing over the most significant details of his deviated acts, and a comparison of his verbalizations with other sources of information showed that he was still withholding pertinent material with regard to his marital and heterosexual experience. Far from a sense of guilt, his feelings centered in his conviction that the girl was "a good actor." He saw her as devoting all of her energies into deceiving him into thinking that she was greatly impressed by his behavior, pretending to welcome his attentions to the point of leading him into a police trap.

At this point, and despite his earlier extensive exposure to an individualized form of psychiatric therapy, it was apparent that the intensity of his basic conflicts remained unabated. The only significant admission which he would presently make, focused on his strong attraction for young, physically attractive females who were in no respect comparable with the plain, bespectacled woman whom he had married.

He conceded, with a head-shaking negation of his own dependent feelings that he was actually ashamed to be seen with his wife in public places. At the same time he was quick to maintain that they had never had an argument, this in itself being evidence of a deeply repressed hostility which he feared might come to the surface, and thereby sever his dependent relationship.

During the course of succeeding interviews, he appeared to be keenly aware of the fact that he and his wife had been making arrangements to move into a house trailer only weeks before his arrest. These homemaking qualities, he admitted, were also on the verge of realization just prior to his original offense. In the latter instance, he conceded that he had been preoccupied with the fact that his wife had informed him of her pregnancy, and that he was unaccountably shocked by the prospect of being the father of her child.

Mark, obviously, felt dominated by the marital situation in the sense that he was, by his own admission, never out of his wife's sight for more than an hour or two during his free periods while out on parole. Here, again, it was quite apparent that he looked upon his wife as a mother figure—a maternal balm for early psychosexual fixations and unsatisfied emotional dependency needs. Since these needs conflicted with those implied in a deeply rooted sense of masculine insufficiency, his feelings toward his wife were strongly ambivalent.

He had, in other words, found himself unable to reconcile the preadolescent cravings of an affectionally deprived boy with the "cool" of a physically strong and self-sufficient male. He, therefore, kept battling an emotionally depleting, and otherwise intellectually abortive war within himself.

At the end of a long, twisted line of confused feelings, he found himself far short of the exacting demands of his perfectionist father. At the same time, he was as much as ever removed from the love of his hypochondriacal mother whose neuroticism his father had managed to control with studied guile, and with his own self-sufficient brand of hypocritical deceit.

Mark wanted his measure of control also, but instead, he found himself helpless in the grip of an inner turmoil which had precipitated the forcible release of an unreasoning hostility against what he perceived as the seductively fickle female.

Actually, the only current evidence of change in Mark's attitude was that he had expressed a need to be free of his wife's dominating influence. This was, of course, without any apparent realization of the dependency fulfillment which he would be giving up, and against the loss of which he would be staking his as yet unattainable masculine competence.

At this stage in time we had moved into the late fifties, and the 1951 Wisconsin Sex Crimes Law under which Mark was now committed had been tested to the statistical satisfaction of clinical personnel over a period of approximately nine years[26, 51]. That is to say that the treatment focus on sex crimes offenders appeared to result in a recidivistic rate of not more than ten percent, as compared with three to four times that figure among those of the general prison population who were committed under the criminal code.

Mark was one of those inwardly resistive, and apparently intractable, sex crimes commitments who clearly demonstrated his incapacity for lifting himself out of the ten percent minority of repeated failures. He had, in accordance with an increased pace of changing conditions, been exposed at appropriate intervals to a wide variety of both group and individual test situations. He had also been subjected to every form and angle of treatment which our more advanced clinical services team could devise.

Psychological measurements on this particular individual, over the years, embraced the most widely acceptable standardized tests, as well as the less tangible projective and experimental techniques. All of the test situations emphasized the underlying character disorder, and variously defined sociopathic characteristics which this man so typically presented. It was also consistently noted that he was endowed with a superior mental capacity which was directed primarily toward the furtherance of his self-centered interests.

Despite the lack of any real evidence of change in either his basic emotional conflicts or his general outlook, he was again released in late 1960, four years after his second commitment. No one could ever say that he was not involved in a most progressive sex crimes treatment program. It would, nonetheless, appear that he won his second release on parole purely on the basis of his manipulative abilities, his attention-getting aptitudes, and his otherwise superficial involvement in whatever the institution had to offer.

It is highly significant of the inherent weakness in treatment consensus and coordinated rehabilitative fulfillment at this time that

Mark was again paroled to the emotionally castigating influences of his unattractive spouse. The attraction, from his point of view, most obviously centered in the fact that he was still inclined to dump the burden of his institution-fostered dependency needs into her solicitous lap.

Outwardly, Mark gave every indication of conscientious cooperation and willingness to abide by the rules of his parole. Never, at any time during the course of regular reports to his parole officer, did he give any indication of the marital tensions which were so obviously present in a repressed and insidiously accumulative state.

Within eight months of his release, Mark was again in serious trouble on a charge of vicious assault and the attempted rape of a young divorcee with three children. His swollen hand attested to the force which he used in beating up his victim, and although he did not deny the charges he contended that details of the offense were hazy as a consequence of his steady consumption of large quantities of alcohol.

It was only then, and for the first time since his release on parole, that he admitted to the fact that his wife did not satisfy him sexually. Again, as previously, he showed no remorse for his victim, but blamed his therapist and the parole system for his failings. His new admission of marital incompatibility involved little or no emotional insight, and he was still able to indicate only a childish self-pity over the fact that he must once again return to the prison for "treatment" under the sex crimes law.

Back in prison, many months again elapsed before Mark was able to discard his need for a projection of blame against the "system," and more specifically, against his victim. He, however, continued to see her as a frustrated female who had been on a flirtatious binge, tempting and leading him on at a time when she was as desperate for male companionship as he was for a truly affectionate female.

When the promised affection was not forthcoming, and at a time when his inhibitions were grossly reduced by alcoholic overindulgence, he rationalized his behavior as an "irresistible impulse" which no man under similar circumstances could normally be expected to control. He did not, of course, offer any logical explanation as to why he did not discuss his true feelings earlier, or why he did not insist on a separate existence in accordance with his earlier realization of his need to be free of his wife's dominating influence.

The first psychatric report, within a month of Mark's readmission to the prison sex deviate facility, indicated "a pattern of behavior wherein the offender's sexual impulses sought immediate gratification without regard for the feelings of others." The report further suggested that it was impossible for him to view his abnormal behavior objectively, that he was reacting to an overwhelming need for narcissistic gratification, and that the consequences of his act were subordinate to his needs of the moment.

He was described as amazingly comfortable in situations to which most people would react with anguish and despair. Since he had allowed himself to feel neither shame nor guilt, whatever self-criticism he was able to verbalize served the purpose of creating a favorable social impression at the expense of any real concern for his own shortcomings.

Mark was, at this point, regarded as psychotherapeutically inaccessible because of a rigid unbending need to be constantly liked and gratified to a degree which took precedence over everything else in his life.

A second psychiatric report by another psychiatrist approximately 18 months later, concurred with the earlier diagnosis in saying that the offender was highly manipulative, and that he would tend to make a mockery out of most types of therapy which might be available to him. It was, however, recommended at this time that he be "exposed to an intensive type of individual or group psychotherapy which would generate anxiety, and thereby uncover characterological defenses upon which he would discover that he could no longer rely."

It was suggested that he be "confronted in a group situation before his peers with the realities of his strong passive-dependent needs, and the manner in which these needs had been satisfied through a perverse, ego-syntonic form of incarceration." His therapist was, in other words, advised to provoke whatever hostile feelings he could in this man's interpersonal reactions, and thereby shock him out of the complacency and absence of any positive movement which was apparent in a too comfortable state of institutional adjustment.

The therapist was, furthermore, warned against the seductive nature of a man whose superior intellectual capacity gave him every advantage in the use of defensive mechanisms and ploys. In retrospect, it was pointed out how his disarming manner and appealing facade had, on countless occasions, won over administrative and professional personnel alike, to the satisfaction of his egocentric needs.

Except for the most objectively oriented research analyst, the practical application of these recommendations posed an almost impossible task. It called for a certain emotional distance, or callousness of approach, which was incompatible with the psychotherapist's inherent sensitivity to emotional needs.

The deliberate promotion of hostile feelings in a group situation was, in other words, anxiety provoking for the therapist as well as for the patient. It conflicted with his own inner need for recognition as a helpfully tolerant and understanding person. It was, indeed, threatening even from the standpoint of institution security controls, the repressive nature of which tended to make the therapist's task an extremely frustrating and essentially intolerable one.

Instead of a tolerant sensitivity with which the therapist normally responded to an interacting group of criminal offenders, he was being asked to confront his patient in a blunt and uncompromising manner with the cold evidence of his defensive manipulations. The therapeutic aim in this instance was one of triggering otherwise repressed hostile feelings, the destructive aspects of which might hopefully be aired and thereby be publicly dissipated in the emotionally charged reactions of his peers.

The question in this form of approach, however, is one which anticipates what would appear to be an almost superhuman combination of empathic concern, along with its antithesis of apparent indifference and rejection of the inmate's basic needs. In practice, it involves the astute timing of various blends of understanding manipulation geared toward reversing the sociopathic maneuverings of a select group of criminal offenders with deeply ingrained patterns of antisocial behavior.

Here is where an appropriate screening of inmate clientele, and an apt selection of therapeutic personnel in a sequential and coordinated approach, would be most desirable. It is where diagnosis with regard to mental capacity and personality composition should be followed by a staff consensus as to the basic treatment needs of each offender in relation to his demonstrated potential. Then the question of individual or group treatment, separately or in combination, and particularly the inmate's unique capabilities on a time scale best suited to the needs of each as an individual, should be aired and documented for future reference.

Experience has shown that in any effective psychotherapeutic approach an empathic bond between the therapist and his client is an essential ingredient. In the event that gross resistances are encountered and a personality clash becomes increasingly evident, the therapist's personal pride or ego involvement should under no circumstances interfere with his willingness to exchange his patient for one who had been assigned to another therapist with similar problems.

Equally important in the eventual resolution of both intrapersonal and interpersonal conflicts is the proper assignment of individuals who show a natural trend in the direction of reliving a particular role in the group interaction. It is imperative that the resultant verbal clashes occur between persons whose makeups and biases would serve to dissipate, rather than tend to fortify, emotional problems which are known to be basic to criminal behavior in each case.

Following the psychiatrist's latest recommendation, Mark Stout became number five in a special group of rape offenders who were regarded as dangerously assaultive. All had committed earlier offenses of a similar nature, and each had demonstrated an impervious reaction to previous forms of treatment. Like Mark at the time of his assignment to this particular group, and because of repeated failures and the absence of any demonstrative change in their asocial patterns of behavior, each had been psychiatrically appraised as therapeutically inaccessible.

Chapter 6

THE SHIFT FROM INDIVIDUAL TO GROUP PSYCHOTHERAPY

L IKE the first Rorschach at the Wisconsin State Prison, group psychotherapy had its beginning in the midst of correctional transition and turmoil. It was introduced under pressure of "treatment needs" within an overburdened psychiatric staff rather than because of any sudden insight into the benefits which might accrue to the individual offender. The fact that it did eventually work out in favor of both was an accident of clinical adaptability to the medico-legal requirements and pressures for treatment under the sex crimes law.

The sex crimes program had ushered in a new challenge for specialized treatment with a Freudian appeal which stimulated a profound interest in the abnormal aspects of this apparently regressive and uncontrolled biological urge. The psychiatric director centered on a psychoanalytical approach which had certain didactic advantages for his colleagues, since the public was awed by the underlying motivations of the sex crimes offender whose apparently bizarre behavior was shrouded in so much mystery and misunderstanding.

The psychiatric treatment function was, at that time, an exclusively individual handling of a highly confidential, doctor-patient relationship. It was a time when a concise "prescription" was offered, including definite recommendations on the part of the psychiatrist to the Special Review Board with respect to the offender's readiness for parole.*

*The Special Review Board, apart from the regular parole board which passed on criminal code commitments, was especially created to decide the parole releases of those who were sentenced under the more indeterminate provisions of the Sex Crimes Law. This board consisted of three professional members representing their respective disciplines in psychiatry, law, and social work. Two were university professors, while the third, also a member of the regular parole board, held an administrative position with the Wisconsin Department of Public Welfare.

During most of this mid-century decade, the program had a confidential and psychiatrically authoritative ring which was substantiated beyond expectations in a recidivistic rate (with respect to any new sex offenses) of less than 10 percent.[26, 51, 82] Motivation for treatment was high, and the status of the psychiatrist was boosted in the eyes of both correctional and legally constituted personnel.

Under the law, it was mandatory for the courts to commit all offenders who had been found guilty of rape, attempted rape, or indecent liberties with a child to the prison sex crimes facility for diagnosis and whatever treatment might thereby be indicated. In addition, the courts also had the option of committing others whose offense and behavior might, in their opinion, suggest sexually deviated trends. When, with the passage of time, a statistical analysis of the recidivistic rate showed what appeared to be a highly successful treatment program, the number of commitments under the law was greatly increased.

At this stage in the mid-fifties, the psychiatric services director, and his two highly trained colleagues, found it necessary to reduce the number and extent of their treatment interviews. The treatment, in some cases, was limited to ten or 15 minutes of interview time, and the balance of the patient's hour was given over to assigned reading from a select list of books. The idea was that of providing a controlled learning experience which would then be discussed and psychoanalytically assimilated.

Actually, the reading-discussion method of treatment helped to conserve the psychiatrist's valuable time without lowering the time interval of his focus on a particular patient. Nevertheless, as the number of treatment cases increased, less and less time was available for the better motivated and more promising offenders whose increased interest in emotional self-betterment begged for more and more of the psychiatrist's individual attention.

The psychiatrist, consequently, became more "positively" selective in both the quantity and the quality of the case load which he felt that he would be able to handle effectively. As a result, the hard-core offender was ultimately neglected in favor of the more tractable and less serious deviate. A growing number of sex offenders, many of whom eventually complained about being denied their right under the law for more intensive treatment, had actually become psychiatric rejects.

This was the stage wherein thought was given to a group approach as a means of fulfilling the minimum requirements of treatment. The best psychiatric opinion of that period, however, offered little hope of any positive change through a method which would, in effect, detract from the personal prestige and authority of the psychiatrist.

The group approach was, in fact, implicitly regarded as a clinically acceptable "dumping ground" for those offenders whom the psychiatrist viewed as a waste of his time. Far from any psychotherapeutic benefit, he foresaw in the group only a possible socializing advantage which, at best, might help the offender to adjust to the problems involved in his immediate prison surroundings. The psychiatrist was, however, keenly aware of the manner in which the group method could relieve him, the therapist, of some overriding pressures, while at the same time affording a reasonable "alibi" for whatever complaints might arise on the issue of treatment.

Group psychotherapy under a dubious, but otherwise tolerant psychiatric direction, first penetrated the comfortable defenses of custodial rigidity as an experimental aid to disciplinary control. This "revolutionary" approach achieved tentative acceptance in 1951 as a medium for testing out refreshingly hopeful research incentives under a new, supervising psychologist. A clinically inspired staff of four psychologists worked patiently and energetically toward turning this new flexibility of effort into a practical reality.

But, whereas the group approach did have a gratifying effect in reducing the incidence of disciplinary infractions, it opened up a new avenue of attention-grabbing manipulation on the part of a psychopathic minority. The group method, and particularly the psychodramatic approach, appeared to give license to an "acting out," or carry-over of feeling, which threatened the staid security of medieval concepts still lingering in the physical restraints of our prison "fortress."

DISCIPLINARY "NONENTITIES" MAN THE
FIRST PRISON THERAPY GROUP

It should be noted that, on this initial venture into group psychotherapy, the prison administration, and specifically the deputy warden, passed on all recommended "patients" for the group therapy experiment. The dozen or so who were first screened at the custody level, consequently, were somewhat biased in favor of the more passively resistant, or nonaggressively intractable, of the institution administration's disciplinary "headaches." The real troublemakers were, of course, very definitely isolated in solitary cells, or otherwise restricted under a form of punishment which denied participating privileges of this nature.

The new method, nonetheless, focused on a manner of airing repressed feelings which, despite the subtly nonacceptant attitude of the custodial staff, tended to advance communication objectives on clinical issues relating to institution disciplinary needs.

Once group psychotherapy had begun, its benefits to the individual became gradually, but increasingly, apparent. It was, furthermore, given the weight of a unified purpose by the initial inclusion of four therapists in one experimental group of criminal code offenders.

The first group consisted of eight "volunteers," none of whom were sex crimes commitments, although all had been clinically appraised as problem cases with deeply ingrained authority conflicts. While the psychodramatically oriented supervising psychologist was recognized by virtue of his training as the group leader, the psychiatric director gave his official sanction and clinical stamp to the experiment by delegating a staff psychiatrist as an observing participant.

As a consequence of verbal agreements to the effect that the custodial and psychotherapeutic aims within the institution need not be regarded as incompatible, attempts were made to bridge the most obvious differences before the group therapy experiment was begun.

From the standpoint of the psychiatric services, group psychotherapy was, first of all, accepted as a unique professional function calling for medical direction, and, thereby, not to be confused with the more routine institution disciplines relating to custody allocation, job assignment, or leisure time activities. It was also understood that the psychiatric services personnel were in the best possible position to decide who was most in need of treatment, and the manner in which therapy within the group itself should proceed.

The institution administrator, on the other hand, exacted assurances to the effect that each new candidate for group psychotherapy was to be screened by the deputy warden, and that his was to be the ultimate authority as to whom among the proposed candidates would be eligible. This would, of course, be determined primarily on the basis of custody restrictions. The warden, in addition, reserved the right to discontinue the group treatment process if it were, in his judgment, at any time to have negative implications, or tend to detract from the morale of the institution as a whole.

Other important but less significant areas of agreement dealt with the behavior of the group members outside the group, including the need for maintaining confidentiality of personally expressed material. It was agreed that, while no group participant was to be pressured for information which he had given out in the group discussions, neither were any of the therapists to allow threats of riot, harmful assault, or escape plots to go unresolved. Nor were any of the therapists to allow any of the inmates to play one group against another, and thereby create seeds of dissention within the institution.

The four group leaders, between themselves, agreed on a form of procedure which, for a period of at least six months, would be a learning experience for everyone concerned. It was decided that we would be working with an "open-ended" group of no more than ten, and no less than eight members. We would have regular 90 minute sessions at regular weekly intervals, and each therapist, in a team of three psychologists and one psychiatrist, would be the group leader in alternating sessions over a 12-week-period. This would mean that each therapist would be in charge of the group for three out of 12 sessions.

After each therapist had become thus acclimated, and the apparent strengths and weaknesses of his particular approach had been aired in frankly honest discussions with the other therapists, each was given a "graduation" test extending over four consecutive sessions under his special leadership. The unique qualities of his total psychotherapeutic effort were then noted and evaluated in turn by each therapist. At this point, he also ran the gauntlet of each inmate-participant's personal opinion as to the benefits which he, himself, had realized from a particular approach.

Even at this stage, it was decided that no one approach might be singled out as most effective, or as more desirable, than the others. Rather, it was felt that the degree of spontaneous enthusiasm which was generated in the process had a great deal to do with the resultant emotional catharsis and the individual progress which was being made.

GROUP INTERPRETATION PROVIDES AN OPENING WEDGE

Before each therapist finally took over his own group, the following approaches were given a thoroughly intensive trial by each of the four "neophytes" in group psychotherapeutic techniques:

The first meeting, characterized as a general session, dealt principally with the aims and purposes of a group therapy program within a penal institution. It provoked a great deal of lively interest among the eight inmate participants. A large measure of enthusiastic support was, in fact, generated as a consequence of the therapists' indicated respect for whatever questions, opinions, or dissentions they might have to offer.

The questions revolved about the advantages of group therapy in relation to individual therapy, how far each participant might be expected to go in disclosing his innermost thoughts, and the extent to which each might be trusted to keep the confidence of another. These questions were clarified so as to invite a freedom of emotional expression, the unique qualities of which were tempered only by a group member's fears and inhibitions in the exercise of personal responsibility. The understanding of a need for inner incentives toward a common objective on the part of each was, thereby, greatly enhanced.

They were, of course, also very much interested in the manner in which each, as a "charter member" of a new psychotherapeutic method, had been selected. When informed that each had, in fact, been clinically appraised as having the potential as well as the need for treatment, and that none had been condemned as a threat to the institution, the beginnings of self-respect and hope for the future readjustment possibilities of each had already been advanced.

The air was also cleared as to what, or how much, would be required in the form of verbal expressiveness from each participant in the group interaction. Although no measure of verbal fluency was offered as in any way more favored than sincere attitudes on the part of "interested listeners," individual opinions based on the previous experiences of each were eagerly solicited. Among other things, it was noted that educational and vocational training, except insofar as emotional strength and feelings of self-sufficiency were generated in a new sense of personal worth, had little in common with group psychotherapy.

The tendency to confuse the acquiring of new information, or intellectual understanding, with emotional self-betterment was explained as the antithesis of group psychotherapy in the sense that rigidly acquired learning patterns might, thereby, be defended rather than alleviated. In a penal setting, it has frequently been demonstrated that increased knowledge without emotional insight can enable one to become more rationalistic, and consequently, more defensive of his otherwise inadequate position.

In response to the question as to how one might be made aware of the fact that he was being therapeutically benefitted, a personal realization of increasing tension and anxiety, followed eventually by an inner freedom of feeling and a new continuity of thought, was offered as a likely result. Each inmate participant was also assured of a certain relaxation, along with a new lease on his capacity for concentrated effort, once he found himself able to release feelings associated with certain "bad" experiences which he had heretofore been unable to disclose to anyone. The true facts of his situation, however, must somehow be faced and accepted by him before this "miracle" of self-realization might first be sighted and positioned to occur.

The first session, involving one therapist as the group leader, followed the relatively unstructured pattern of a nondirective procedure. To begin with, one of the eight participants was asked to introduce his particular problem to the group. This he proceeded to do with the "spontaneous" enthusiasm of one whose dependency needs had been encouraged in the direction of "free verbalizations" during the course of previous interviews. He had learned how to anticipate a favorable nod from his therapist in the earlier individual sessions which had carried over to the present situation.

There was, however, no question about group motivation, and this particular session stimulated a new interest and a new life in the intensity and perspicacity of the questions which followed. The spuriously confident exterior of the inmate-participant under observation was, consequently, shaken by the insinuations of "phoniness" in his manner of presentation. Although a certain pat analysis together with a great deal of unexpressed feeling was obvious to all, the session was allowed to terminate on an unresolved note of tension, and without any attempt at summarizing or highlighting significant material.

In the following session, both the inmates and the therapists were somewhat critical of an uncomfortable lack of closure which they had experienced as a consequence of this first nondirective approach. The one psychiatrist, thereupon, utilized his much more directive skills in an interview method focusing on an inmate participant with whom he was acquainted as a result of previous individual sessions.

This interview was psychoanalytically spiked to point up unconscious motivation, and it was, likewise, structured to include a round robin of opinion polls and comments from each group participant during the last 30 minutes. The therapist then summarized the underlying consensus of thought and associated feelings, together with some added conclusions of his own, all of which revealed a profoundly logical and authoritatively correct, psychiatric analysis.

The next session, conducted by the third therapist, attempted to provide an artificial stimulus for the projection of feelings and identity problems by calling for inmate volunteers as interacting citizens in a typical community. The actual setting consisted of a miniature village, utilizing scale model homes of different types and locations, into which the representative group members were to project themselves.

In addition to a miniature church, a garage, and a tavern near the center of town were a colonial home, a couple of Cape Cod and ranch style houses, an apartment building, and an exclusive country residence set aside from the rest of the community. At least three of the participants, rather significantly, chose the latter as a place to live, and only one cared to live next to the church.

The discussion revolved about a hypothetical situation in which each of the "residents" assumed significant roles in the community reaction to a murder offense which had been reduced to a manslaughter charge on the accused man's plea of guilty. The "victim" was the garageman's teenage daughter who was found to be pregnant after she had been killed in a car "accident" under suspicious circumstances. The accused driver was the only son of a big real estate promoter who lived in the country estate. Each participant, including those who assumed the roles of the married offender, the respective parents, the clergyman, and the judge, reflected their special biases in the manner in which each sought to justify or discredit the offender's actions before and after the offense.

A later discussion resulted in a rejection of this method of group psychotherapy as emotionally too distant, and too academic, in its connotation. It was regarded as generally ineffective in the sense that it tended to take the spotlight away from the participants as individuals. It was, however, a lead toward an otherwise insightful projection of conflicting feelings which gave the supervising psychologist his cue for a trial run of the psychodramatic approach.

The fourth session, then, attempted to surface the actual feeling behind a deeply traumatic emotional experience in the life of one of the participants. The inmate, first of all, related the circumstances of a bind in which he had been placed by the deceptive manipulations of his overly solicitous but affectionally rejecting parents. The main participants in this potentially violent situation were then instructed in their particular roles out of hearing of the others. Each was, in fact, secretly goaded toward increased emotion in the dramatization of his particular part.

At the height of the interaction, which the therapist in each of the staged scenes subtly prodded with painful intensity, a reversal of roles was suddenly demanded with a startling clap of his hands. It was at this point that each participant was expected to recapture, with his own intense feelings, a part of the mood and antagonism which was felt by the other.

This approach, as evidenced by later repercussions, expected too much, much too soon. The interaction, in order that it might be effective, called for the very emotional adaptability and flexibility of effort which we were trying to instill through psychotherapeutic techniques. One who is emotionally conflicted, and consequently under tension, is naturally far from relaxed. Least of all is he capable of adjusting himself to a situation which makes immediate demands on his constricted emotions, or which taxes his very limited capacity for empathy with the opposing moods of another.

The psychodramatic method in this restricted penal setting, in fact, had the effect of promoting more unresolved tension with which this particular individual was forced to cope. Actually, since he was unable to internalize his feelings, he had no alternative between sessions but to act out against the increased pressures inherent in his physical restraints. The approach might have worked out had its proponent been more patient and less demonstrative. Instead, it ended in solitary confinement for one otherwise hopefully motivated participant, and postponed the incentives of others in the direction of any equally dramatic psychotherapeutic attempts for many years to come.

The easing of tension among the participants of group psychotherapy was, nonetheless, apparent in many other, less dramatic, ways. Variations of many experimental forms, utilizing the more emotionally productive methods of the earlier approaches, were being continually tried and evaluated.

A projective approach, employing the tangible comparisons of an inmate's self-concept through individually produced human figure drawings, was introduced as a stimulus to a lagging group discussion. Written autobiographical sketches were also submitted by the more verbally fluent group members as a leverage for opening up a discussion on personal material. A milder variation of the psychodramatic approach was cautiously attempted in a hypothetical disciplinary court scene involving an accused inmate offender, as opposed to group-selected authoritarian figures with whom he could more realistically identify.

We were all in agreement that spontaneity was the very essence of group psychotherapy; that no one session could, or should be, structured to conform with any rigidly, organized plan. It was felt that no therapeutic deadlines could be realistically contemplated during the initial stages of treatment, nor should the attainment of any specific objective rule the content of any one particular session.

As we moved from one session into the next, we became increasingly aware of recurrent ups and downs in the spirit of the group interaction. We encountered unexplainably sullen and depressed moods which encompassed the entire group. There were, at the same time, hostile undercurrents interspersed just as suddenly and unpredictably by a spirited and emotionally uplifting session which was a joy to all.

It was, however, gradually recognized by inmate participants and therapists alike that real progress was necessarily painful, and that emotional insight, unlike intellectual understanding, did not always make one feel good. It sometimes appeared to take a step backwards before gathering momentum for the one and a half, or two steps ahead. This stage of indecisiveness, self-doubt, and emotional strain was as trying on the therapist, in terms of effort and feelings of discouragement, as it was for the inmate offender.

Out of it all, however, came the realization that we might best reach the offender through a tolerance for the rough edges of his feelings. We gradually became aware of the adverse effects of our own emotional impatience, realizing that the forcing of an insight before the inmate was ready for it might also force a defensive jamming of the "emotional door" to his inner self beyond our ability to repair. Through repeated contacts and conferences came a more profound understanding of needs which only constant effort and prolonged experience can promote. The following developments and refinements in the group treatment approach to the criminal offender were, consequently, the product of almost 20 years of group psychotherapy in a penal environment.

GROUP PSYCHOTHERAPY GETS A FRAGILE "FOOT IN THE TREATMENT DOOR"

Throughout the sixties, and until spiraling costs and a new administration had caused an unfortunate shift of the Sex Crimes Law responsibility in late 1970, a peak of group psychotherapeutic endeavor in a penal atmosphere had been reached.* There were as many as twenty interacting groups in the Clinical Services prison unit alone, and innumerable others were picked up in the institution Social Services category during the course of later years.

It should be noted that group psychotherapy with sex crimes commitments was energetically pursued for the first time in 1956, and the relatively neglected criminal code population was, thereafter, taken over by the institution Social Services department.

From a clinical standpoint, and except for the so-called "orientation" or "didactic" groups, eight to ten members per group was deemed to be most conducive of the interacting process. Many groups relating to a particular type of offense, like, for example, homosexuality, were tried with somewhat discouraging results in the sense that defensive rationalization of a particular criminal pattern

*Instead of the long awaited and thoroughly planned reception and treatment center proposed by the Bureau of Clinical Services in the Corrections Division, the sex crimes program was summarily shifted to well established, but differently oriented, treatment facilities in the State Hospital for Criminal Insane under a new authority in the Mental Hygiene Division.

was, thereby, promoted. As the behavioristic psychologist might justifiably contend, the negative aspects of their personalities tended to be undesirably reinforced.[7]

Experience has shown, therefore, that heterogeneous, or mixed offender groups, are better motivated toward group interaction and a resolution of their emotional difficulties than the more homogeneous groups which attempt to bring offenders of a particular classification together.

There may, of course, be definite exceptions to this, as indicated in the Synanon movement.[124] It was necessary, also, from a purely practical point of view, to separate groups of criminal code offenders from those who were committed under the Sex Crimes Law. This was because of legal differences which tended to complicate efforts in the direction of working out personal problems which might be overshadowed by a need to manipulate for some technical or legal advantage. Then, too, it was sometimes advisable to segregate into separate groups those who consistently denied having committed the offense for which they were confined.

An intellectual level which would provide an average to superior capacity for comprehension was found to be most desirable in terms of an effective group interaction. The exceptions, again, were in the didactic groups which were especially geared to the needs of the mentally retarded or educationally defective individuals.

The didactic approach might also apply to certain paranoid personalities, "fixed" character disorders, or culturally deprived and irresponsibly naive offenders who have shown themselves to be unamenable to the usual psychotherapeutic techniques. In these instances, a structural analysis at their own level of mental or emotional growth might prove to be most effective.

It has, in fact, been demonstrated that "even the most seclusive or vehemently projective individual, may suddenly become interested in the relative abnormalities of his own preoccupations while elusive didactic impressions are being reviewed or reinterpreted. The sharing of ideas, particularly sexual ideas in a group situation, even at this level, appears to provide some impulse neutralization and communication skill that may lead to a more socialized life adjustment."[106]

By far the most important characteristic in any positive group interaction is found in a combination of both the potential and the

motivation for change. In this connection, and for purposes of a
group experience, it is sometimes desirable to invite, by way
ample and a provocative verbal instigation, the distorted manipulations of the institutionalized and self-defeating psychopath. It may
be a help, rather than a hindrance, to have at least one, and sometimes two, verbally aggressive, asocially defensive, or sociopathically
demonstrative individuals in the same group with six or seven of the
more passive, but otherwise socially amenable individuals. A morally
rigid, or inhibited person, opposite an anxiously confused or less re-
strained morally loose inmate, also provides the psychic atmosphere
for an emotionally productive session.

It is, likewise, a benefit rather than a detriment in terms of an insightful group interaction, to have a group of individuals within a
fairly wide age range so that both peer and interfamilial relationships
may be tapped in the process. Even more desirable, although somewhat impractical within the tight restrictions of a maximum security
institution, would be occasional sessions with selected female delinquents, female social workers, and just prior to an anticipated release, with interested members of the inmate's family.

As indicated earlier, group psychotherapy in a penal environment
allowed for many variations in the manner of resolving an offender's
emotional difficulties. The approach differed primarily in accordance
with the personal interests and biases of the group leader or therapist. Regardless of the method, however, a sincerely helpful attitude,
together with an understanding flexibility in the face of changing
circumstances, were essential qualities in every group psychotherapist.

The sincerity of the therapist is a measure of the depth of his appreciation for the intense effort which the inmate offender must put
forth in order to keep his confused feelings under control. It is the
extent of genuine care which he is able to show for every positive
gesture—even a small attempt on the part of the inmate to lift himself out of his emotionally helpless state. It is most of all, his perceptive awareness of the need to inspire within the offender a willingness
to suffer the pain of exposing long-hidden feelings without causing
greater deterioration to his self-respect, and thereby throwing an already shaky integrity off balance.

The therapist varies his approach within the limits of his personality and overall capacity for keeping this effort alive. This means that

he may evoke his best response from the nondirective approach, or it may mean that the opposite extreme of a highly structured involvement may at times become necessary. Perhaps he has reached the stage wherein the more drastic prodding of the so-called "hot-seat" approach might prove to be most helpful.[114] These are decisions to which the therapist must adapt himself with all of the insight and empathy at his command.

Because of the fact that the criminal offender has been repeatedly subjected to the hard arm of authoritative restraint, the nondirective approach has often proven to be most beneficially productive for the inmate of a penal environment. This is because the therapist encourages a ventilation of feeling without being rejecting or in any way defensive of his position in the role of group leader.[93, 94] He remains flexible in the sense that he is always ready and willing to explore the thoughts of a man who has a need to speak out at a particular moment. For this reason, a spontaneous, or open-minded approach to a given session can be much more helpful, in terms of emotional insight and understanding, than the more elaborately organized group sessions.

The nondirective approach may, however, be interspersed with varying degrees of structure, depending on the mood of the group and the particular situation in which the therapist finds himself at a given moment. There is, for example, the "Behind-Your-Back Technique" wherein group pressure forces a man to turn his back and remain silent, while all other participants to whom he has just related his life history, discuss the pros and cons of his situation.* Final comments would then be invited from the other group members with respect to the effectiveness or inadequacy of his presentation before the group.

The silent treatment has, in fact, often provoked the most anxious person to speak out on a feeling level at a time when superficial pleasantries, insincere manipulations, or chronic complaints against an irrevocable social system begin to dominate the group discussions. Obviously, we cannot tear down the walls of a maximum security institution, or tolerate a group fortification of complaints against outside pressures which it is beyond our power to control.

---

*This approach was first introduced by Corsini, R. J. in The behind-your-back technique in group psychotherapy. *Group Psychotherapy*, 4:55-58, 1953.

But we can provide the emotional atmosphere for a look within the person himself by an unexpected shift of focus which serves to provoke an anxious bid for recognition within the sphere of the group's own influence.

Anxiety about oneself is often the first step to emotional insight, and this is especially true in a group situation which forces some form of rationale, however inappropriate, for the feeling which is thus displayed. It stimulates an inner drive for a realistic escape from a commonly shared tension, much of which is absorbed in the genuine concern of the interacting group members.

The fact that the group leader may, himself, be subject to anxious moments in the group interaction, does not detract from either the learning process or the emotional insight which might, thereby, be realized by all participating members. The therapist who finds it necessary to become suppressingly defensive, or overly reactive to an expression of hostile feelings which challenge his value as an authoritarian figure or group leader, also finds that he has closed the door on the kind of relationship which will help an inmate to get the self-understanding he needs.

The therapist must have the combined qualities of an enthusiastically interested, sensitively concerned, spontaneously flexible, and socially creative person who can adapt himself to the best features of a constantly changing interaction. He must be able to apply himself to the positive aspects of the dual therapeutic, or "devil's advocate" approach, as readily as he can to the "looking glass" perspective of tape recordings on a closed circuit TV.

In the former approach, one therapist may assume a permissive, or more or less maternal role while the other presents himself as the opposite side of the coin with rigidly authoritarian ideas. The group members then evaluate the proceedings in terms of their feelings and reactions to the absence or overemphasis of authoritarian direction in their lives.

Very often, as a consequence of this approach, they are able to discern an analogous situation in their relationship with their parents. The associated emotional conflicts, thereby, become more rapidly apparent because of the opportunity for reliving one or two emotionally traumatic situations in this manner.

On the TV tape, by comparison, the offender is offered a new perspective, looking over his shoulder so to speak, by hearing and seeing himself in action. In this way, certain verbal inflections, hesitations, and blocking of speech, together with mannerisms of which he, himself, may be unaware, become part of his self-concept. He begins to see them, not so much as handicaps, as the "hallmarks" of an individual which are now available for integration into the total personality.

The ultimate in therapist adaptability might be that of an intentionally provocative, or adverse psychotherapeutic approach. The therapist unexpectedly assumes the role of one who appears to be apathetic, disinterestedly uninvolved, or actually rejecting of his group. He may seem depressed, moodily impatient with his clients' reactions, or plaintively "out of sorts." Hopefully, thereby, he may provoke an opposite reaction among those who have been most obstinate, as well as in the response of those who are searching for some form of rationale, some real meaning behind their confused behavior.

This method must not, of course, be handled deceptively, but only as a spur to the much more honest release of feeling which the therapist then strives to resolve before the close of a particular session.

The psychodramatic approach, which appears not to have worked out effectively in a penal setting, also calls for considerable flexibility on the part of both the therapist and the interacting participants. It does require a great deal of directive action on the part of the group leader, and it has its value principally in the degree to which the inmate participants are enabled to apply themselves to specifically assigned roles within the family constellation.

In this connection, the psychodramatic method can be made to conform to an emotional experience which the offender attempts to act out at emotionally significant levels in his psychosexual development. A reversal of roles at crucial points in the emotional build-up, together with the assimilation of an "inner voice" in the so-called alter-egos, calls for a brand of physical dynamics and internal flexibility which is notably absent in a penal environment. It should be reserved for later, and more relaxed, socially interacting situations, preferably in a post-institutional setting.

Group therapy, at a much less profound, but nonetheless stimulating level of verbal exchange, may lead to more meaningful insights as a consequence of the initially more structured focus on a common topic. In order to insure a more than casual interest in the group discussions, a subject should be chosen which is most strongly related to the personal feelings of each group member. We might list several of these topics which have been utilized as the beginnings of a group psychotherapeutic relationship involving the therapist and a new group of sexually deviated offenders:

1. What is normal, and what is abnormal about sex? The therapist might pose, by way of illustration, a more specific question as to the therapeutic readiness of one who is an admitted homosexual. Due to no fault of his own, this "offender" may have never experienced sexual stimulation from the opposite sex. Consequently, while being otherwise conforming and amenable to supervisory controls, he may have no desire to change in this respect.

This particular topic might compare the relatively more accepting homosexual with the much more confused rape offender who is pretty much "on the fence" as to the direction of his sex drives. Because the latter is less able to tolerate the self doubts and frustrations of conflicting sex interests, might one, therefore, be justified in saying that he is more dangerous than the other?

2. What effect does fear or anger have on the sex drive? A fear of impotence is often the most threatening, and at the same time, the least discussed of the emotional problems with which the offender is faced. This question, then, seeks to make room for the initial contemplation and the hope of a later confrontation, with the psychic effects of these emotions on the sex drive.

Does he find himself impotent and inclined to temper tantrums when frustrated or ridiculed because of his apparently poor performance in the sex act? And to what extent may a violently aggressive act on his part stimulate his lagging sexual potency? These are questions with wide emotional ramifications which are much too frequently overlooked for the reason that they are so distastefully avoided in the psychotherapeutic process.

3. Is it right for the female to be aggressive in the sex act, or should she be completely passive and altogether submissive to her partner's demands? In what manner does aggressiveness or passivity on the part of the female affect the offender's affectional, or psychic capacity, for adequate performance in the sex act? It is surprising how pitifully naive an apparently sophisticated, and otherwise world-

ly appearing criminal offender, may be in regard to these questions.

4. Is he a chronic complainer, and inclined to ventilate his gripes indirectly, or is he able to seek out and face the right person when looking for an answer to a particular problem? Most criminal offenders are notoriously incapable of making decisions which focus on the immediate source of their difficulties. They avoid any acceptance of personal responsibility, particularly that which calls for a direct confrontation on issues with which they are most sensitively involved.

5. Who is best motivated toward changing his behavior, and to what extent must he become emotionally involved in order to make this change? This question invites a form of introspective analysis which focuses on the importance of personal effort. It directs attention to pertinent examples in the group interaction wherein the persistence and tenacity of certain sincere individuals become the signposts of success in overcoming their emotional difficulties.

It also raises a somewhat more complicated question as to the apparently premature release of certain relatively innocuous offenders, despite evidence of little or no effort on their part in the treatment program. From an opposite point of view, the treatment milieu must be cleared with respect to the more serious offenders whose effort is unquestioned, but who present a continuing danger to the public because of the deeply ingrained nature of their criminal patterns.

6. The most emotionally provocative, as well as the most evaded questions, center in a discussion of conflicts within the realm of family relationships. It is here that we find an accentuated projection of sibling rivalries which have become interwoven with deceptive parental attitudes of rejection or favoritism, the tangled emotional consequences of which were never resolved.

In this most sensitive area, pertinent questions explore the comparative status of the oldest or youngest son in relation to each other, in relation to a middle son, or to an older or younger sister. Might one be better off if he were an only child? Would he prefer an older or a younger sister, and whom might his parents most likely favor? A discussion with respect to the comparative role of the mother and father in the home naturally follows, together with the extent to which the offender is inclined to identify with one or the other. Does he sense a favoritism toward him on the part of the mother, and how does this tie in with a probably belittling attitude on the part of his father?

Eventually, the question comes up as to the extent to which his father's negative attitudes, for example, those implied in an abusive or chronic alcoholic pattern, have been inadvertently copied by him. As has so frequently developed, an offender's intensified need to prove his real worth may be negatively expressed in a need for punishment in order to ease the tension created by a deep sense of failure.

Assuming that his psychotherapeutic needs are fulfilled, this failure may finally be recognized as a direct result of his anticipated inability to match up to the expectation of authoritarian figures, beginning with his father. After a sometimes prolonged, and frequently painful bout with many shades and gradations of his mixed feelings, he ultimately perceives his continued incapacity for sustained effort as a result of his own perpetuation of these interfering preoccupations.

CONCLUSIONS OF A GROUP PSYCHOTHERAPIST

Almost two decades of experience with group psychotherapy in a penal environment provide a delicately exposed relief of salient features on a treatment globe of deceptively quiescent, but potentially volcanic feelings.

It seems pertinent that both the therapist and the inmate-participants in a group interaction should have a common goal in the direction of elevating the offender's self-concept, or self-respect, in association with his peers. The sights for this goal are, first of all, lined up from the special viewpoint, and on the comparative discovery of each group member that he is not as abnormal, nor as obnoxious to the others, as he at first thought himself to be.

He gradually becomes aware of certain blind spots in his makeup through a recognition of another man's blind spots, and the depth of his understanding is increased accordingly. As his capacity for self-realization through this interpersonal form of self-alignment progresses, he tends to see himself in another man's inferiority feelings and sensitivity to ridicule. He, for the first time, views the contrasting harshness and devitalizing effects of his own silhouetted tendency to block up emotionally. Thereafter, he becomes increasingly conscious of a detouring waste of vital energy in his defensive need to lie or to evade a painful expression of his true feelings.

He begins to recognize himself as a confused bundle of affectional impoverishment, mixed with indiscernible elements of fear, anxiety, and anger which tend to overflow in some areas of his life, and which interfere with his capacity for love and understanding. Eventually, he comes face to face with the self-defeating effects of an overwhelming sense of rejection, and the manner in which he, himself, had invited this rejection because he had grown to expect it. He perceives himself as one who was rejecting the very affection he so desperately needed because his "undeserving self" would not allow him to assimilate it.

Eventually, and at a more specific functional level, each man comes to recognize the sex drive as a measure of his vitality and zest for living. He begins to see the intensity of this sex interest as a normal, healthy development which is not wrong in itself, but only in the manner in which it was expressed.

In the area of sex alone, for example, the criminal offender enters the treatment program with many erroneous concepts, the distortive severity of which is only gradually recognizable. Any frank and open revelation of these most sensitive areas must necessarily await the first indications of trust in the therapist and other group members before they might bypass whatever defensive inhibitions are inherently ingrained in the personality.

In this connection, we are frequently confronted with the early instilled conviction that masturbation tends to undermine, or to destroy, one's manhood. Even the best of the medically approved, authoritative assurances, for example, often fail to convince a sexually deviated offender that his penis is not too small, or that his sexual potency has been harmed only in the psychic aggravation stemming from his debilitating misconceptions.

Then there is the conviction that they are "oversexed" because of the fact that their preoccupations with sex provoke a need to make as many female conquests as possible. This drive is, of course, more realistically defined as the result of a basically inadequate or prohibitive sex life. It is the result of a need which had become most intense because of the persistent frustrations involved in an inability to perform in a satisfying manner. In this context, the sex drive, as such, might be regarded as weakened in the sense of any relaxed biological fulfillment, while being strengthened in the intensity of his need to prove his masculine competence.

There is, also, the very persistent rationalizations of alcohol as a cause, or excuse, for deviated behavior. Repeated analyses and reassurances in the other direction often fail to convince the offender that alcohol merely permitted the expression of psychosexually immature or regressive drives which were already there.

Most of these misconceptions are tied in with the need to project blame for their misbehavior onto external causes, such as an unfortunate marriage, an early, traumatic sex experience, neglect of their physical and affectional needs, or a generally abused childhood. This projective need emanates from an inherent emotional dependence on external controls which it is extremely difficult to overcome. It is only after a prolonged struggle that the awareness of the need for change within themselves is recognized as being, first of all, dependent upon the ability to accept some measure of responsibility for their own actions.

Because of the need to evade or to bypass unpleasant issues, the therapist has to be continually on the alert for evidence of feeling, as opposed to the intellectual rationalizations which most inmates have developed as a smoke screen for their sensitive feelings.

The purpose of the group interaction is, of course, always one of provoking real feeling about what is going on in relation to another member's attitudes, comments, or reactions. This involves getting into highly sensitive areas which sometimes provoke a great deal of hostility toward the therapist because of the jealously guarded fears and inadequacies he seeks to uncover. Until new peer reactions have been tested, a hostile rejection of feeling is the inmate offender's only learned way of defending himself against a vulnerable exposure of his inner world.

Most of those with whom we work nourish a deeply repressed, and otherwise uncontrollable, resentment against family members, parental figures, siblings, or peers who appear to challenge the inmate offender's intense need for acceptance as a virile male. Deep seated fears of violence, as associated with a gnawing apprehension of ridicule or humiliation against which repression, withdrawal, or denial of feeling appears to be their only defense, are common to many of the inmates with whom we interact in group psychotherapy.

There appears to be an unconscious, but consistent transference of infantile emotional needs to a marriage wherein the inmate offender unconsciously seeks a wife who will baby him. He, at the same time, greatly resents the dependent emotional bind in which this unsatisfied oral craving places him. Intertwined with this need is the impossible ideal of a long-suffering, self-sacrificing mother which he is unable to find in the woman he marries. This frustrating situation understandably results in a psychic incompatibility, and an aggravated emotional tension, frequently culminating in the offense for which he is confined.

Although they are reluctant to admit it, most all of our most productive group participants eventually achieve insight into the perverse nature of the attention which has been extended to them by their most intimate family members. They gradually become aware of the fact that they appear to merit more in the direction of a solicitous concern from their parents and wives *after* they have gotten themselves into serious difficulty with the law.

This increased attentiveness has the effect of substituting, and to a large degree promoting, a dependent psychic relationship in place of the more responsible contacts which are now denied to them. It also leaves room for considerable apprehension and doubt on the part of the offender as to whether or not the more personally fulfilling physical contacts can ever be satisfactorily consumated in a free setting.

These conflicting tendencies should, of course, be given every opportunity for a verbal airing and eventual resolution through properly coordinated, pre-release family therapy sessions. This should precede, rather than follow, any of the more intimately controlled, and impatiently sponsored, conjugal visits.

Practically all of our inmate clients have an acute sensitivity, along with a pronounced aversion to "phoniness" in other inmates, as well as in authoritarian figures. They associate this concept of phoniness with attitudes and overtures of praise which they tend to see as geared to make a man work harder, or as a ruse for taking advantage of him in some underhanded way.

They perceive praise as a deceptive device—a "nice," authoritative, manipulative tool—which is "really intended to whip more and more out of the inmate" in the form of self-centered, institutionalized credits. They cannot, or will not, allow themselves to view these "condescending attitudes" as being prompted by any genuine concern for their own personal achievement. Even though an inmate's personal accomplishment were the primary aim, the offender's otherwise ingrained fear of falling short on expectations might thereby be accentuated, thus adding to the severity of the emotional problems and tensions of which he already has too much.

An intense fear of failure, as associated with anticipated rejection, is a common hindrance to the kind of motivation and stimulation of self-confidence which we strive to produce in our inmate clients. For this reason, it is good to bear in mind the fact that the therapist must be in a position to offer the offender something in the form of increased self-respect, or actual advancement in his capacity for self-control, before he can take something away. One cannot expect him to give up deeply entrenched, long-standing defensive needs, no matter how ineffective or self-destructive these defensive reactions may be, if in so doing he feels more empty, more insecure, or more anxiously threatened than he did before.

An inmate who has a need to slug a tenaciously persistent, but otherwise nonviolent homosexual, for example, cannot be expected to admit that he is defending a state of panic with regard to his own homosexual inclinations. He must first be guided into the most effective ways of saying "no" to these apparently unwelcome attentions, thereby convincing himself of his capacity for less destructive, but equally masculine methods of control. Only then might he have sufficient emotional fortification to concede his unconsciously hateful reaction to his true feelings.

Our most common mistake, and perhaps our greatest weakness as an effective therapeutic source, lies in the fact that we still tend to be inconsistent in our demands for punishment at the expense of promoting a greater sense of personal responsibility and self-control. Apart from the more obvious physical and affectional restraints, punishment may be perpetrated, most insidiously, in the form of a psychic rejection, or inadvertent denial of normal identity needs (see pp. 26-28).

We otherwise compound the error of emphasizing a particular psychotherapeutic fad, an almost obsessive concern for the success of a new approach to emotional problems, without arranging, or allowing for, a coordinated follow-up of efforts in terms of continuing needs or priorities in the treatment process. Above all, we consistently fail to take into consideration a common goal of necessary psychic fulfillment for the inmate offender before the inner incentives toward more concrete objectives may be anticipated (see pp. 44-45).

The psychological conditions favoring the emergence of an emotionally integrated, and potentially adjustable, inmate offender, will be discussed in a final chapter. At the moment, and as indicated in the previous chapter recounting the psychotherapeutic experiences of Mark Stout just prior to his assignment to a special group of rape offenders, we will follow the uncertain progress of this "therapeutically inaccessible" group.

We will take each interacting offender through the emotional turmoil of his grossly inadequate and recidivistic reactions into the final testing ground of a free world. After all, we cannot escape the fact that we must eventually assimilate, in one way or another, the motivations of even the most viciously assaultive and "intractable" offender.

Chapter 7

TRANSACTIONAL ENCOUNTER IN A GROUP OF SEXUALLY DEVIATED OFFENDERS

As INDICATED at the close of the previous chapter, five rape offenders regarded as dangerously assaultive were brought together in an attempt at resolving their emotional problems through the group approach.* They were, at the time, between 29 and 34 years of age, since each had been previously exposed to many hours of individual psychotherapy extending over a period of five to ten years. An average to superior intellectual endowment, which contrasted markedly with an otherwise inferior functioning level, had been demonstrated by each.

All five were serving indeterminate sentences with a mandatory provision for treatment of their sexual aberrations under the Wisconsin Sex Crimes Law. Four of the five had been released on two successive occasions as sufficiently advanced in the treatment process to try out their emotional legs in a free setting. All four were returned under the indeterminate commitment for a new sex crime following a pattern similar in nature to that noted in the original offense.

Only one of the five in this special group had not been released because of the legal complications of an attempted murder warrant, charging him with a crime under the criminal code, as well as under the sex crimes law. Three of the others had earlier records of prior conviction for auto theft and harmful assault. None of these earlier

---

*This does not, of course, conform to the ideal of a heterogeneous group situation, as outlined in the previous chapter (see p. 78). But, because there are some who refuse to accept any personal responsibility for their behavior, and who consistently hide behind the defensive shield implied in what Dr. Thomas A. Harris describes as the "I'M OK—YOU'RE NOT OK" position,[60] they might be made to realize an interacting futility at their own level of egocentric awareness in this much more selective approach.

offenses, surface-wise at least, gave any hint of sexual implications. Two of the five were single, and three had been married and eventually divorced following their commitment as sexually deviated.

Four of the five were, of course, regarded as exceptional cases, since less than ten percent of those released on parole under the sex crimes law over a nine year period were returned with a new sex offense.[51, 82] All five, from a psychiatric viewpoint, had been variously described as sociopathic or schizophrenic in makeup, revealing obsessive-compulsive drives along with sadistically toned oral interests in the sexual areas of their existence. In spite of these deeply entrenched behavioral traits, all five became indirectly, but nonetheless actively motivated toward an eventual resolution of their sexually deviated urges.

Each offender frankly admitted an obsessive phantasy life along with a compulsive urge in the commission of his crime, over which he had no conscious, rational control. One even revealed a compelling need, almost immediately following his last release, to visit and attack his uncle's wife who lived in a community some distance from his own. Like the others, there were some humiliating aspects to his phantasy life which he admitted to having held back. This was because he feared the displeasure of his therapist over a tardy disclosure which would expose his deceptive nature and militate against his need for acceptance at this late date.

One group member conceded that, whereas he could express himself readily on paper or in a tape recording, this was markedly different from talking out his feelings to members of the group, or before the Special Review Board. As he had indicated many times, hearing himself on the tape recorder or listening with other members of the group to his autobiographical sketches in written form served the purpose of detaching his feelings to the extent wherein it was the tape or the paper which took up the emotional impact of any first hand observation. It was an entirely different matter when the words conveying the feeling had to pass inspection directly through his own lips.

It is highly significant that, whatever the medium of expression, frankness in disclosing morbid or bizarre detail was not one of their shortcomings. For this reason, a false impression of insight and adjustment potential was generated. These men assumed a conforming exterior, backed by an intellectual understanding of their morbid confessions which completely obscured any real emotional involvement.

Since each had retraced vital areas of his past experience in minute and shocking detail, the emphasis in these group sessions was on current interpersonal relationships. It was felt that too much time had been devoted to establishing a rationale for sexual dynamics, while overlooking the need for expressing the more primitive feelings in the offender's concept of love and dependency fulfillment as opposed to the hate of an accumulative sense of rejection. Hopefully, they would become more realistically aware of the manner in which their defensive denial of underlying inferiority feelings had precipitated aggressive impulses which were incompatible with a realization of their affectional needs.

Each of the five offenders was asked to think of other group members, including the therapist, as people with feelings rather than as objects to be manipulated for the purpose of demonstrating their superior insight. They had come to realize, through many ups and downs in the treatment process, that one might reveal a keen intellectual insight while, at the same time, solidifying his defenses against any genuine emotional release.

Through increased self-awareness and understanding of each other's emotional difficulties, they were able to concede a deep, underlying fear of exposing a vulnerable core in their makeups. They were, consequently, asked to view each person in the group as an individual with hostile feelings covering anxieties and fears very much like their own. Operating on the assumption that everyone tries to cover up feelings which accentuate a sense of inferiority in his makeup, the focus of attention was shifted from one group member to another, eventually involving the therapist as one who might have difficulty in expressing his own feelings.

As it developed, the emotional involvement of the therapist became a crucial factor in the ultimate release of feeling on the part of other group members. Each had expressed his dissatisfaction at various times with the extent and quality of the treatment he was getting. Each had had the agitating experience of several erudite rejections from the awesome three-member Special Review Board. All five had experienced the ultimate authoritarian impact of penetrating eyes sharpened in the critical disciplines of law, psychiatry, and social work.

The more genuine words and feelings, which each had promised himself to voice before this august body, refused to come out. Each parole conscious group member found himself reverting to a superficially verbal, desperately nonchalant, and otherwise rigidly defensive stance, while the calm, impersonal comments of their inquisitors focused on their repetitive or unchanged patterns of behavior and consequent need for further treatment.

The expected hostile reaction was often sidetracked in the direction of some apparently unrelated issue, or for the most part, repressed under a bland and conforming exterior. But then came the unexpected cancellation of a group meeting almost immediately following one of these frustratingly noncommittal, but obviously rejecting, Special Review Board hearings.

The group reaction was one of an accumulative hostility, the expression of which had, up to this moment, been withheld. Within a week, angry feelings emanating from the reinforced authoritative rejection sensed by each group member had built up to unreasoning proportions. There were none who were adult enough to accept logic in the fact that the earlier group meeting had been postponed in order that individual attention might be tentatively given to a recalcitrant member who had suddenly asked for a new therapist.

This one cancellation of an anticipated session loomed ominously in the shadows of succeeding meetings as a grave injustice which had been deliberately perpetrated against them. It was subsequently interpreted as rejection of the group by the therapist because someone had had the courage to speak out his feelings. The therapist was tacitly accused of a deceptive combination of indifference and favoritism which sparked hostile attitudes associated with early sibling rivalries and childish deprivation.

The member meriting special attention had written a letter already branding the therapist as emotionally distant and insincere, while at the same time berating the other group members as "phonies." This letter significantly preceded his pending Special Review Board appearance wherein he was reenacting a lifelong need to justify an anticipated failure. The letter, as read before the group, had the effect of putting the therapist and one manipulatively supporting

"Parent" on one side, and the four other members who expressed their doubts, and who challenged their leader's integrity, on the other.

In the heated exchange which followed, one member lapsed into a fearful silence, while the author of the derogatory letter visibly gloated over the commotion he had caused. The raised voices and twitching features of the participants attested to the genuine quality of feelings which threatened to get out of control.

It was at this point that one of the protagonists rasped his disapproval of the distant "fatherly" attitude of the therapist, while another blurted out a disjointed comment to the effect that he saw a certain resemblance to his smug, older brother.

It was the emotional pressure of this interaction that stimulated a reawakened interest in the treatment potential of the group. One of the members, who had remained deceivingly cool in his denunciation of the therapist, now impulsively suggested that each be given the ultimatum of facing whatever emotional pressures the others had to offer for as long as it might take to break down his defenses.*

Previously, the pressure had been applied most intensely to the particular member who was next scheduled to appear before the Special Review Board. Or, it was at times inadvertently provoked by one whose "phony" attitude aroused the ire of the others. Too often, however, the pressures were alleviated by the supporting tactics of another whose own anxieties drove him into sidetracking the issue by diverting attention upon himself.

Now that all of the members were aware of this tendency, and agreed on the need for a concentrated test of their capacity to withstand an attack on their sensitivity to shame and ridicule, the group moved into a new plane of emotional understanding. At the moment, they moved in unison against the dark-haired, meek-appearing inmate with an otherwise deceiving manner and a contagiously dis-

---

*We might recognize this as the "Parent" of the "Child" in a transactional exchange originated by Dr. Eric Berne,[15] and so realistically presented as "A Practical Guide To Transactional Analysis" in group treatment by Dr. Thomas A. Harris.[60] Although the group interaction, as presently described, took place in the early 1960's and without benefit of the teaching experience implied in transactional analysis, the otherwise distinct personality components of "Parent, Adult, and Child" are evidenced in many of the highly manipulative and emotionally conflicting interactions in which this group indulged. The "Adult" personality, as portrayed in the "I'M OK—YOU'RE OK" position,[60] is generally submerged in these ingrained character disorders under an overwhelming surge of feeling from the rejected "Child."

arming smile who had dared to suggest that each should be tried to the breaking point.

Group Member One: During earlier individual sessions, Delbert Newfondel* had disclosed in naive and voluminous detail a homosexual relationship with a much older man, beginning when he was nine years of age and ending with the event of his first marriage at the age of eighteen. At that time, the man affectionately known as "Uncle Jake," committed suicide. During this entire nine-year-period, the boy's parents were completely unaware of what was going on. Although this evidence of emotional distance between Delbert and his parents was pointed out to him, he defensively avoided any admission of tensions in the home which might reflect against his parents.

During the period of his first commitment under the criminal code on a charge of assault with intent to murder his father-in-law, he became aware of a situation in his relationship with his wife's father which was analogous in nature to that earlier experienced with "Uncle Jake." He was, however, released on parole without having worked through any of the more potent feelings inherent in his early family relationships.

He was returned under the sex crimes law on a charge of breaking into a dwelling with the intent of raping a sixteen-year-old babysitter. He denied the intent of rape, claiming that he mistook the girl for his paramour, the divorcee for whom the girl was babysitting. He did, however, admit a strong urge to kill, and he described several incidents wherein he had actually beaten certain women acquaintances into a state of unconsciousness.

He was committed for a 30-day observational period to the State Hospital for Criminal Insane, but subsequently returned to court as a sociopathic individual without any evidence of a psychosis. His admissions of seriously assaultive behavior were found to be gross exaggerations since the brand of insanity was much more tolerable to him than the abnormally obsessive interests which he must now face.

At this point, he had no recourse but to disclose strong voyeuristic interests and orally obsessive drives, wherein it was more impor-

*Although the case histories are real, all names herein indicated are fictional. Any reference to real persons, actual or implied, is, therefore, purely situational, and for purposes of illustration only.

tant for him to get down and make a close visual inspection of the female sex organ than it was to perform in the normal sex act. This was the basis of his literal denial of an intent to rape the involved girl, since he had "only tried to stifle her screams" long enough for him "to get a good look." It was also the reason for his assaultive reaction whenever his victims offered strenuous resistance, or otherwise tended to reject and belittle the need for his advances.

He now began to open up on his early incestuous interest in a younger sister, and the severe reprimanding which he received when caught peeking at her through a keyhole in the bathroom door. It wasn't until much later, however, while undergoing intensive analytic therapy with a consulting psychiatrist, that he uncovered the beginnings of a deep-seated castration complex. A morally strict, matronly woman who acted as a mother substitute in his early years caught him masturbating, and told him that she had a dog which could sense what he had been doing and would bite it off if he continued.

He phantasied this as having already happened to his sister, and since she had replaced him as the baby of the family who was most deserving of his parents' attention he sought an identity with her passive-dependent attributes, while at the same time striving to maintain his masculine standing as a competent male.

He was paroled as one who had made remarkable gains in self-understanding, and whose effort, despite evidence of a violent and unpredictable behavior pattern, appeared to be constructively oriented.

He was out just 12 days when he assaulted a woman who had picked him up in her car, and when she turned him over to the police, likewise assaulted the arresting officer. During the year following his return to the treatment facility, he showed evidence of a mentally confused and rather severely agitated state. During this period, he hinted at traumatic incidents as yet not revealed, and admitted that he had slapped the girl with whom he was last involved because of her belittling remarks when he attempted sexual intercourse with her.

At the time of his admission into the group with four other assaultive rape offenders, he had conceded that it was not possible for him to achieve an erection while he was being visually stimulated, and that slapping the girl helped him to maintain a necessary advantage in the performance of the sex act.

His revelation of psychic impotence, associated with cunnilingus obsessions, struck a sympathetic chord in the other group members. All five had reached four general areas of agreement in the course of about 25 weekly sessions:

1. As has already been indicated, they voiced the opinion, either implicitly during the course of the group interaction or more directly in private interviews with the therapist, that they had never actually become emotionally involved with their problems, despite a frank disclosure of morbidly obsessive sex interests.

2. All five related a history of an emotionally distant, punitive, or rejecting father-son relationship, while experiencing a morally condemning, almost smothering control over their capacity for emotional expression on the part of the mother or mother substitute.

3. Each had come to recognize a need to degrade, and at the same time emulate, the feminine qualities of a sister or sister substitute who appeared to be a favorite of the father.

4. A growing awareness of a homosexual problem, together with a nonacceptance of the passive-feminine characteristics which come under the homosexual label, was verbalized by each.

The emotional insight into this ambivalent situation, through a group provoked transference reaction, was the aim of the current focus on sensitive areas which, heretofore, had been successfully parried.

The stage had been set for Delbert, whom the other group members noted to be characteristically side-stepping, time and time again, any real expression of feeling about his parents and siblings. He impatiently stated that he had been through all of this before; that the narcosynthesis which he had sweated out in the research endeavor of a consulting psychiatrist a year previous had the effect of thoroughly airing his feelings in this area. The group, however, persisted with relentless determination to ferret out his feelings, reminding him of the fact that it was he who had suggested this harassing approach.

He suddenly turned on the therapist as the heartless conniver of the treatment which he was now receiving. He elaborated on what he called the therapist's unconscious, defensive block against any new understanding on his part. He based this on the disappointment which he felt that he had caused the therapist and consulting psychiatrist by a rapid reversion to his original pattern upon release. He indicated that this was especially true, since neither the therapist nor the psychiatrist wanted to admit a mistake after having committed themselves in highly optimistic and glowing terms regarding the depth of his understanding.

It was highly significant that the cause of the therapist, who remained uncomfortably silent during this tirade, was actively supported by the other group members. This support could not have been elicited had the therapist's anxieties about being put on the spot provoked him into the expected authoritative defense of his position.

The therapist was, however, fortified by the recognition of a healthy surfacing of hostility which, for the moment, was being projected against him. This recognition accepts all of the discomforts of a necessary and inevitably tense situation. Far from the nodding acquiescence of an intellectually stimulated journey into sexual dynamics, it is the tremulous, dry-mouthed utterances and moist-skinned friction of these submerged feelings which signals the therapist that his group is on the move.

One wonders, because of the unavoidable unpleasantness which this experience entails, how much has been lost in therapeutic effort at the moment when the offender's challenge of the therapist's status indicates that the goal is within reach. It is a moment when the group participant is both defensively hostile, and childishly demanding, of authoritative relief from the pain of his most excruciating emotional conflicts.

With the group forcing him into the narrow confines of his own evasions and contradictions, Delbert found himself in an emotional dilemma which called for the revival of feeling involving a dreaded homosexual experience. It was a feeling which tore at the life line of his affectional need for a man whom he had wanted to trust and respect as his own father.

Since it was not possible for him at this point to trust an open expression of his fears, he wrote out his thoughts in the form of a letter as he had done many times before. Only this time his feelings were much more turbulent. He began by explaining that he felt he was being "cut off" each time he tried to bring it up, but perhaps this was just another example of his own confused outlook.

He went on to say that, if there *was* a form of therapy of the nature which he was about to describe, he was at a loss to know why the therapist picked him, knowing how he felt about a man laying his hands on him. "Suppose," he continued, "that it were a woman whom the doctor had put to sleep, and then seduced? That would be a form of rape punishable under the law. With me," he wrote, "it is called therapy!"

His letter deviated in emotionally vivid and troubled detail to the point of branding the psychiatrist as one who had deliberately caused him to relive his experience with "Uncle Jake." He described this reliving, with childlike innocence, in terms of actual physical contact. He saw himself, under the influence of sodium amytal and hypnotic suggestion, as the "helpless victim" of one who had, once again, forced him to "submit in a homosexual act."

He now shored up his tortured feelings by stating that he had been fully awake, and acutely aware of what was going on. He described a posthypnotic suggestion which, in his mind, was intended to serve the psychiatrist's own "deceptive" purposes in causing him to forget everything that happened except for the traumatic beginning of his castration fears. Because of his otherwise "passive submission to a superior will," he felt very strongly that a trusted and highly responsible medical authority had reduced him to the same level of shameful secrecy which he had experienced over so many years with "Uncle Jake."

A second letter, written two days after the first, pointed up a recurrent need to counteract the projected threats of his own incapacitating attempts at severing the umbilical cord to his dependency strivings:

> Why do I try and twist things around so that I appear to be the poor little boy who is always offended? Am I really seeking understanding, or am I trying to cover up something about myself. And why, all of a sudden, has it become such a big issue? The fact that I've got it on my mind, I think, bothers me more than the thing itself. I realize now, as I write this, that I was trying to cover up by getting myself to believe that I was being used, mistreated, or taken advantage of, and that I had to submit if I wanted a parole.
>
> But what I see as most fearful about the whole ordeal is that I couldn't gain what the doctor was working so hard at offering. The one thing that I am able to accept is that, had I really been asleep, I wouldn't have been back, nor would I have needed any further treatment. There is something about being awake when I was sup-

posed to be sleeping that makes me feel so guilty and ashamed. Like I allowed myself to be used almost because I wanted it that way.

I tried to make myself used in my last letter, also, in order to cover up and give myself a reason for not having learned anything at the time. I wanted to convince you of why I failed last time, and I figured that you would say: "Well, Delbert, now I see why you didn't stay out, and I can see now why you were so confused. You felt so dirty rotten and fearful of the future for having let a man use you again that you just couldn't discuss it."

Unlike the group member who had taken the therapist to task as one in whom he could generate little confidence, Delbert was not called for an individual session previewing his "shocking" disclosures. He was, in fact, asked to read his first letter aloud before the group, and with the full understanding that this was no family secret.

He appeared startled and reluctant to proceed, hesitating over the first page of his letter for one long moment before he began. As it developed, however, he managed to retain his emotional control up to the point of voicing what he had written regarding the psychiatrist's instructions for him to disrobe for a test of his reflexes.

At this point, he suddenly dropped his head onto his arms, and as the other group members sat motionless in their chairs, the convulsive trembling of his sagging shoulders could be felt along the edges of the pencil-gouged, cigarette-scarred table. Several long moments of silence followed this unexpected display of feeling in one whom the others had gotten to know only as a bland, self-satisfied person with soft-spoken mannerisms and an innocent twist to his mask-like smile.

"I don't know what hit me," he finally sputtered, while blowing his nose and shaking back a stubborn forelock of ruffled, black hair. Then, gulping apologetically, he let go of the real feeling behind his last offense. "I guess I must have cried like that when the girl drove me to the police station. Then there was the time when I got married and 'Uncle Jake' committed suicide. Sure, I'm a homo all right. I just never admitted it before."

"I know now, too, why the doctor here reminds me of my older brother. I had a feeling all the time that my brother knew about me and 'Uncle Jake,' and I wondered just how much he had told my parents. Just as I wondered how much the doctor had told the Special Review Board."

"For a whole year, I kept thinking, what is wrong? If he knows, why doesn't he want to discuss it? I kept thinking and dreaming that the psychiatrist was 'Uncle Jake' come to life again. I wanted to tell how I felt about what he had done to me, but thought that since you knew and didn't say anything, I'd better not. Just like my older brother about 'Uncle Jake.' "

"I couldn't sleep; even woke up in my cell one night holding my shorts out toward the door and yelling: Sign it, damn it! I guess I was on the fringe, and having trouble deciding what was real and what wasn't. Now I know that the whole bit with the psychiatrist was all my imagination, and that I was really asleep when I thought I was awake. It's got me sweating plenty, look!" He raised his arms to expose the obviously damp, irregular patches of perspiration encircling his armpits.

The mask-like smile had been pushed aside, and the stumbling intonation of his voice, with words slapping, one into the other, was like a dammed-up stream gurgling through a new outlet. The intent faces of the other group members reflected their awareness of his changed attitude. Exposed as they were to a gush of feeling in one who had long been defensively complacent, the others not only showed more respect for him as a person, but became more genuinely motivated themselves.

Group Member Two: There was Pete Pamperson, for example, who repeatedly swallowed his hostility, even nodding in agreement when one of the more verbally aggressive members spoke of his patronizing manner and "wishy-washy ways."

"It's not so much what you say as the way in which you say it," he was told. Pete, who was also serving a six-year-term under the criminal code for attempted murder in addition to his commitment under the sex deviate statute, straightened his narrow shoulders and jutted his lower jaw forward.

"Guess, I'm next," he said simply. But his smoldering eyes, searching the faces of the others in petulant defiance of his own apparent submission to the coming ordeal, blinked a nervous rejection of what he knew would be a relentless prying into his private life.

During his five years under the treatment program, Pete had worked out a thoroughly logical analysis of his early traumatic experiences, culminating in his present sexually deviated state. He had, from the first, freely admitted an overpowering need to steal women's undergarments. His vicious attack on a middle-aged, neighbor woman followed his unexpected discovery of her presence in the home after forcing entry for the purpose of pursuing his morbid sex interest.

He had listed, in systematic and painstaking detail, all of his early sex experiences, including an older girl's seduction of him at age four or five. He even admitted his intense fear of being forever disowned by his mother after she had caught him in a homosexual act with another boy.

He attributed both his fetish for women's clothing and his repressed hatred for his mother to her deceptive handling of a childish infatuation which he had had for his uncle's niece. Although he was barely six when she was 20 years of age, he recalled in vivid detail the manner in which he had been deceived into thinking that she would "hold up her birthdays" and marry him when he grew up.

He elaborated on the sensual stimulation which he received from stroking her nylon-covered legs, as he had witnessed her boyfriend doing without reproach in her aunt's presence. Pete's description indicated that incestuous desires were provoked up to the point of obvious excitation on his part, at which time his fingers were slapped, and his frustrated emotions held up to ridicule by the more "responsible" family members. He also recalled how his mother, catching him in an act of masturbation, had stood over him like a mythical harpy, saying, "If you ever, ever do that again, we will have to send you to a doctor and have it cut off!"

Then, before he reached the age of seven, as he recalls it, he suffered a most agonizing emotional upheaval. He was rudely informed that his maternal ideal, in the form of his uncle's niece, had gone away to be married. He screamed and stamped his feet, receiving a severe beating from his father along with the threat of total rejection from his mother after all efforts at pacifying him had failed.

His next recollection was one of searching the niece's abandoned room in order to assure himself that she had really packed and left. He remembered picking up a pair of nylon hose that she had left behind, brushing their silky softness against his skin, and experiencing the same exhilarating sensation he had known while being jostled on her knee. Only now he was able to enjoy this pleasure without the dreaded risk of rejection and ridicule.

Pete had come to realize all of this during the first three years of his confinement under the treatment program. But he was still his "wishy-washy" self, full of fears and hates which he could not express openly.

To be sure, he had passively "confessed" his homosexual tendencies, and he did not deny that he probably wanted to make himself over into a woman by adorning his body with the nylon stockings and undergarments he had stolen. Hadn't he overheard his father say that he should have been a girl, and wasn't his father always playing up to his mother's sister's daughter and ignoring him?

Then, when he grew up and married his wife on the rebound after being jilted by another girl, hadn't his father practically adopted his daughter-in-law as his own "pet" daughter? The only time, in his recollection, when his father had shown any affectional concern for his son was when Pete's infant daughter had died shortly after a premature birth.

Even this concern, as he concluded later, came only because he was unable to present his father with the gift of a baby girl that the father had always wanted. Maybe that was why he stiffened and froze when his father put a consoling arm about his shoulder. Maybe it was the reason why he stiffened up when anyone tried to warm up to him.

These thoughts turned endless gyrations in his mind, while he pessimistically struggled toward a happier solution to his difficulties. It was not until this moment, however, five years after he had first begun treatment, that he was able to admit to having lied about the true nature of his thoughts at the time the offense was committed. He had previously led everyone to believe that he had beaten his victim while in a dazed, panic-stricken state, after she had surprised him prowling about in her home.

He now admitted that he had phantasied the most degrading perversions with the involved woman, and that his vicious assault had taken form in his mind from the moment that he discovered her presence in the home.

Once he had struck her and failed to make her unconscious, he admitted that he was obsessed with a compelling need, quite apart from any sexual desire, to strike and strike her again. He continued to hit her, even though she begged him to stop and promised to do anything he asked. He admitted that there was no telling how far he would have gone had not a neighbor appeared to investigate the commotion. Then, inexplicably, and like one in a daze, he meekly withdrew and turned himself in to the police.

At this point, Delbert asked him if he didn't think he was a homosexual. When Pete tartily replied that he had already admitted that he had homosexual tendencies, Delbert accused him of splitting hairs on something that he had never really been able to accept. He asked Pete, quite seriously, if his real intention wasn't one of wanting to kill off his mother, or someone who reminded him of his mother, so that he could feel free to play the female with his father.

Pete lapsed into a smoldering silence, the muscles at the corners of his jaw contracting spasmodically with the pressure of his churning emotions. When he finally found his voice, the words snapped out between his compressed lips like barbs from a blowgun.

"You know," he burped insolently, "you got the same dirty ways, the same silly smirk—all the damn, feminine filth and meanness about you that—" he stopped with a choking cough and cleared his throat with considerable effort.

"Of course, you wouldn't realize it," he continued hoarsely, and in a much more subdued tone, "but you're a helluva lot like my mother!"

The session closed in a rather futile attempt at smoothing the more obvious wrinkles in a jumbled harassment of mixed feeling. The group meeting was finally dispersed on a note of mounting frustration over surfaced hostility which, like the frayed end of thread in the eye of a needle, could not be quite grasped.

It wasn't until a week later, when the group reconvened, that the circumstances which precipitated Pete's outbursts were recalled in a more relaxed atmosphere. It then became clear to him that, while he had no sex urge toward women in the usual sense, he did, as Delbert expressed it, *want the wanting* of a woman very badly.

Since everything she did, beginning with his mother, belittled and worked against his achieving this want, his big urge was toward degrading and destroying her condemning femininity. He then admitted for the first time, and with obvious emotional distress, that he had beaten his wife when she threatened to leave him and that he would then defend her against his own villiany by trying to comfort and console her as she lay whimpering on the bed.

Group Member Three: Pete's voice began to break, and Elric Jungfeld, with obvious agitation, cut in to say that he thought we had been "badgering this man" long enough. It had become increasingly apparent during the six consecutive sessions that the spotlight was focused on Pete, that Elric had been counteracting the pressuring tactics of the others with disturbing regularity. This was particularly noticeable since it was he who had authored the derogatory letter labeling the group members as "phonies," and deriding Pete as a patronizing weakling with "wishy-washy ways."

When the inconsistency of his defensive shielding of Pete was pointed out to him, Elric smiled in his characteristically aloof and emotionally detached manner. The group members, however, noticed an intense quality about him which was not apparent in his usual shocking disclosures. There was both fear and anger in his high-pitched voice when he finally admitted that Pete's hostile feelings were a double for his own.

This was Elric's third commitment on forcible rape offenses extending over a period of more than ten years since he was originally admitted for treatment under the sex deviate law. He had, over the years, written out at least 100 pages of autobiographical material. But, even more revealing were his extensive tape recordings covering an extremely bizarre phantasy life. They were monumental examples of obsessive sex ideation in one whose sharp intellectual defenses called for a morbidly detached front.

He had, from the beginning, freely admitted the bizarre quality of his sexual phantasies, confessing a morbid interest in preadolescent females, and verbalizing dissatisfaction with anything but the idea of conquest in the sex act. At the time of his last appearance before the Special Review Board, he had flatly declared that he must be a homosexual, and likewise admitted in a blandly defensive manner that he had a fear of killing someone. He later conceded that he was motivated, in these admissions, more by a need to produce a shocking effect than he was toward expressing himself in a favorable manner.

The other group members bluntly suggested that he was asking for an unfavorable report in order to ease his conscience about his own mean impulses. Elric evaded comment on this point, while freely admitting his last offense as a need to degrade a young, teenage girl by forcing her into perverted sexual relations with him. This, he confessed, was after he had witnessed her sexual performance with a teen-age boyfriend earlier in the evening. He explained how sexual stimu-lation for him was synonomous with his capacity to force the girl into obeying his will; how important it was for him to reject before he, himself, could be rejected.

When asked if it would have been just as important had he not observed the performance of his friend, Elric suddenly "clammed up." It wasn't until close to the end of the session that he conceded a strange, new realization of the fact that he had actually been seek-ing acceptance for his "masculine aggressiveness" from his teenage male companions. Now, perhaps, he was seeking acceptance from the other group members with the same callous, emotionally detached reaction. Despite the fact that he had called himself a homosexual before, this was his first real insight into the unacceptable nature of his homosexual urges.

He now recognized both his tendency to repress, and the manner in which he had attempted to justify, unacceptable hostile feelings by inviting rejection upon himself. He saw this as a lifelong pattern which had remained unchanged up to the present time.

He recalled his early resentment toward a younger brother for being a "lovable invalid" who merited more than his share of atten-tion from his parents. He recalled his father's wordless condemna-tion of him after he had "accidentally" chopped off his brother's toe with a hatchet. He turned for affection to his coy, younger sister whose frightened refusal of his incestuous advances made an indelible impression upon him, and set the tone for his aggressive acts toward immature females.

But, most of all, he resented his own frightened reaction to his father's unpredictable outbursts. These followed the pattern of vio-lent rages over trivial matters which had the effect of aligning his mother beside her abused son in an emotionally seductive and con-spiring role against his enraged father. This was quite different from the peaceful calm which followed his father's sober concern and his mother's hurt reproach whenever he did anything seriously wrong like raping and degrading a female.

In view of these circumstances, Elric's "transference reaction," or transactional brush with the three ego states to which Dr. Eric Berne refers as the "Parent, Adult, and Child,"[15] was particularly revealing. He was not nearly so concerned about the morbid effects of his shocking disclosures as he was about the temporary withdrawal of anticipated attention.

Shifting him from individual sessions, where he had had the therapist all to himself, to a group situation involving a dreaded interaction with attention-grabbing "siblings" was bad enough. But when the therapist exposed his tendency toward annoying little contradictions for which the others demanded a reasonable explanation, the situation became intolerable.

He suddenly experienced a revival of the tensions he had known with his father. This, then, was his father getting him all stirred up again. So he branded the therapist as emotionally distant and insincere. He threatened to withdraw by asking for a new therapist, thereby slipping into his "helpless Child's game," geared toward earning additional support for his attention getting needs.

His "Child" gratifying rejection of his therapist had, however, occurred several weeks earlier and before Delbert's true feelings were brought into focus. Elric was now seriously engrossed in the self-defeating aspects of his own transference problems, and engaging Clyde Manley, the most seriously aloof and withdrawn member of the group, in the process.

Group Member Four: It was not surprising to find in Clyde a variation of the same basic problem that was discovered in the others. His father also gave vent to a vicious and unpredictable temper against his son without any explanation as to the cause. Nor did Clyde ever have the courage to ask. That is, not until he was challenged by Elric, who said that it was about time someone was digging into his "phony" front. The stubbornly regressive and belligerent exchange which followed left no doubt as to the surfacing of long repressed sibling tensions.

At the close of the session, Clyde announced that he was through with the group, that all of the abuse he was taking had gotten him nowhere, and that his only problem was one of achieving a better understanding with his parents. On the grounds that he owed the group an explanation of his feelings—one which would be demanded of him anyway by the Special Review Board—he was persuaded to return for one more session.

Then it came out that Elric's attitude in the previous session had reminded Clyde of his younger sister's manipulative influence over his father. It was also brought out that Clyde was reacting to feelings of rejection in the group in the same manner that he had reacted to accumulative tensions within his own home. It soon became clear to him that he had been behaving toward the therapist in very much the same manner as he had behaved toward his father.

At this point, it was fairly easy for him to admit his resentment toward those who doubted the veracity of his statements, thereby reflecting on his capabilities as a responsible person. Having opened up to this extent, he went into greater detail to explain the strong resentment which he felt against his mother because of the attitudes and covert insinuations of his father and favored younger sister that he was a "Mamma's boy" who couldn't do anything on his own power.

He was now bursting with a need to straighten out his confused feelings. He suddenly revealed what he had not been able to bring out during seven years of confinement under the sex crimes law. He admitted his obsession with the rounded abdomen of the 70-year-old woman whom he had assaulted and attempted to rape. It was the same obsessive urge which drove him into attacking his uncle's wife almost immediately following his last parole release. It turned out to be the source of a morbid concern which he had developed toward his mother whom he had imagined to be pregnant.

This concern built up to mountainous proportions in his mind as a consequence of his mother's solicitous condemnation of his masculine traits, whereas his father played up the "superior" capabilities of a younger sister. His mother's morally binding reaction to his developing emotional needs instilled within him an intense fear of any affectional involvement with a young girl because of the "terrible sin" which he would commit were he to get her pregnant. He couldn't touch his mother, but the idea of pregnancy in an older woman became an obsession with him that was displaced in the form of his behavior disorder.

In the silence which followed his last revelation, Clyde lowered his flushed face and ground a burned-out butt between trembling fingers. But he found himself lifted into an emotional state of wanting to remain in a group which he now saw from the point of view of one who had been rejecting, rather than as one who was rejected by the others. Elric remarked on his changed attitude, saying that it looked as though Clyde "didn't have to get quite so sore anymore."

It was quite apparent to the other group members, however, that Elric had also changed. While trying to defend himself in the unwanted role of Clyde's favored sister, Elric had become emotionally very much alive, treating the group to a facet of his makeup which rarely got beyond his rigid intellectual defenses.

At this level of self-acceptance and understanding, the group members displayed a new appreciation of several areas of emotional involvement which each had in common with the other:

1. They became strongly aware of repressed hostile feelings which each had nourished deep within himself under cover of a bland, outwardly conforming exterior. These feelings, they discovered, had their origin in a deep-seated fear of ridicule, calling for the protective armor of an emotionally detached front. They were reactivated through a group interaction which provoked a clash of feeling similar in nature to that earlier existent between a distant, rejecting father and an emotionally incapacitating mother.

2. All five confessed their need to degrade a woman sexually—mastery over her at the moment being more important than the fear of detection and punishment. This need was greatly accentuated by her belittling reaction which had the effect of robbing them of the desire for sex with a woman so necessary to the aura of manliness among their peers. It was a good feeling, therefore, to see the woman's shocked expression, and to know that she was fighting and kicking up a justification of their need to demonstrate mastery over her.

3. Each had finally come to recognize a deep-seated fear of physical injury, otherwise interpreted as a castration anxiety, which they had converted into a fear of expressing their own hostile impulses in an open and direct manner, particularly toward members of their own sex.

4. The admission of passive-feminine attributes underlying a basic homosexual problem was made possible by the activation of heretofore unexpressed hostile feelings in the group transference reaction. The incentives toward a more "Adult" resolution of this most painful emotional revival came with the realization of a need to invite rejection upon themselves before they could be sufficiently charged against their own fears to warrant an open expression of their true feelings.

Group Member Five: The final and most clinching evidence of an underlying need to invite rejection upon themselves was demonstrated in the attitude and reaction of Mark Stout. During most of an otherwise lively exchange, this new member, whose asocial background and individualized treatment over a prolonged period was recorded in Chapter 5, remained an emotionally distant and essentially uncommunicative person. He was, of course, the last to be admitted to this particular group which, in accordance with the psychiatrist's recommendation, appeared to be most conducive to the desired, anxiety-provoking impetus to change in his rigidly defensive pattern of behavior.

Although Mark appeared to be very intent on what the others were saying, the sparse quality of his verbalizations gave no indication as to the depth of his perceptions or the extent of his self-acceptance. There was growing evidence, however, that he had, during the course of heated discussions between the other group members, become increasingly aware of his own rejecting attitudes. It seemed likely, then, that he would also become aware of the manner in which this tendency had invited the Special Review Board's rejection of him.

It is significant that the one emotionally charged session wherein the group's relentless, uncovering process was inadvertently sidetracked against him followed the fourth consecutive denial of Mark's annual appearance before the Special Review Board. As before, the comments of all three board members were consistently negative, focusing on the conclusive indications of a viciously assaultive nature which showed no evidence of change.

He came into the group meeting on this particular day with only the noon hour intervening between this session and his earlier overwhelming rejection by the three highest authoritative disciplines ever to exercise control over his freedom. His broad frame exuded a sullen belligerence, and he was obviously morbid and depressed.

The group meeting quickly degenerated into a monosyllabic lethargy which was interspersed with glowering silences, and punctuated by apathetic yawning, insolent belching, or unrestrained coughing and rapping of ash trays. The attitudes of four out of five, in this particular session, reflected a pervading mood of defensive resistance against any form of understanding communication.

As in every psychotherapeutic session, however, smoldering silences present an anxiety provoking situation for at least one group member. In this instance, it was Delbert Newfondel who was driven to combat an intolerable sense of isolation through soft spoken introjections of parentally induced, "nice-guy" tactics in support of the therapist's attempted explanation of the Special Review Board's current decision.

Under pressure of this apparent hypocrisy in one of his own breed, Mark unleashed his otherwise unspoken thoughts regarding the "deceptive machinations" of the Special Review Board. He perceived these authoritarian "kingpins" as intent on satisfying their own "perverted" need to present themselves as the stoic, front-line protectors of an indifferent society.

He offered his own impression of authoritative contradictions in that while he was expected to change, he was not allowed to express his true feelings to the Special Review Board. To do so, he said, would, "in plain language, get my ass kicked out of the room."

Still, he contended, it was the aim of the psychiatrist and his therapist to push him to the point of a true expression of his feelings. "Isn't that right, 'Doc?'" This he added with a trembling lip, and in smug defiance of an acceptable explanation.

But, apart from this conflict in self-expression, he saw himself as being held up entirely on the basis of his past record. He sullenly proclaimed that his recidivistic pattern had, in itself, given him the label of one who was incapable of change. Any educated person, he said, knew that the highest court in the land would uphold the legal arguments for a mistrial in the event that adverse publicity would appear to have a prejudiced effect on the otherwise impartial findings of a judge or jury. Still, it was his contention that he was being judged and condemned in this very manner.

Everything he said or did he perceived as misconstrued or misinterpreted so as to lend weight to the authoritative conviction that he was no good.

At this point Delbert Newfondel, as the most experienced group member, took his "cue" to inform Mark that "you've got it all backwards." He told Mark that it was he, not the Special Review Board or his psychiatrist, who was misconstruing and misinterpreting his adjustment difficulties. This blunt reversal of the problem was, in turn, Mark's "cue" to enter into a heated emotional exchange in which Delbert was roundly criticized for his own "two-faced" brand of "institutionalized phoniness."

The 90-minute-session eventually worked its way through with Mark first coldly indifferent and verbally uncommunicative; then emotionally hot and obviously very angry against the "supercilious" authority which was so "unjustly" restricting his freedom. Finally, his tense, hostile manner softened into that of a subdued, quietly conversant person who was ready to admit his own compulsive need for recognition as a potent force. In the end, he cautiously admitted a tangential glimpse of the tendency on his part to turn his father, and other authoritative figures, into negatively fostered instruments of hate geared to justify his own need for chronic complaint against the social order.

At first characterized as a "dead session," this last meeting became the opening wedge in an intensely negative, nerve-flaying experience which was later recognized as a valuable exercise in an otherwise dreaded emotional catharsis. Others, including Dr. Carl Rogers, have noted negative feelings in "the process of the encounter group," as the first expression of "genuinely significant" emotion in the "here and now."[94] When tolerated as the first stage in a pending release of incapacitating feeling, these negative attitudes serve the very positive purpose of breaking down the artificial barriers to understanding communication.

But, it was the passively conforming, feministic label, and all of its implied dependency at a preadolescent level of emotional growth, which proved most difficult of acceptance. That was because it conflicted mightily with the masculine concept of an aggressive independence, and the adult need for self-assertion in its most potently acceptable form. As it developed, the recognition and admission of a passive-feminine orientation in a mutually experienced group interaction was one thing, whereas the resolution of these needs through actual confrontation in a free setting was quite another.

Chapter 8

THE BANE OF A RELEASED OFFENDER'S "FREEDOM OF CHOICE"

ONE of the great weaknesses in any effective follow-up of the criminal offender is in the absence of a truly coordinative appreciation of his basic needs. The therapist, like the parole agent, is subject to time limitations and jurisdictional restrictions which mitigate against anything but a superficial understanding of the other's problems in relation to those of his client.

Once an institutionalized offender is paroled, his therapist terminates an otherwise close relationship under the impersonal designation of "inactive" or "dead file" material. The inmate, at this point, sees himself as one who has "done his time," and "paid his debt to society," in many indescribable hours of enforced servitude, interpersonal tensions, loneliness, and solitary suffering. Many months of rigidly conforming, spiritlessly compressed mental anguish, in the offender's mind, emphasize a strong but seldom voiced conviction that he is most definitely entitled to "freedom from despair" in his current release from control.

The parole agent who takes over at this stage just as decidedly attempts to move his charge into the more objective light of environmental pressures and circumstances. This drastic change, however, calls for a mighty shifting of emotional gears to conform with the varied demands of a free society.

The agent will, of course, consult with Clinical Services personnel in the event that a new mental problem appears to be developing. But, for the most part, he is driven by his own specialized training, supervisory needs, and personal biases to regard his function as relatively autonomous. Apart from what his experience dictates as adequate supervisory controls, he is not motivated by any therapeutic concerns for the offender's more subjective needs which had been, theoretically, resolved prior to his release.

Attempts have been made, however, through a carry-over of family counseling and environmentally oriented group discussions under the direction of the parole agent, to bridge the obviously wide psychological gap between the offender and his capacity for adequate adjustment in a free setting. Even the clinical psychologist and the consulting psychiatrist are, nonetheless, inclined to emphasize institutionally conditioned strong points, while overlooking or disregarding a paucity in the offender's extra-institutional adjustment powers.

Clinical personnel, for example, seldom think of the released offender's choices in terms of the indecisiveness which springs from suddenly moving a simple mode of prison attire to a whole wardrobe of choices in which he has had no opportunity to become acclimated. And now, just as suddenly, he has equally unlimited vocational, recreational, and social choices that he must make in his attempts at asserting a vital independence against which his institution life had so insidiously conditioned him.

An acceptance of personal responsibility calls for a certain independence of movement. The strength and direction of this movement is, in turn, dependent upon an inner sense of self-sufficiency so necessary in warding off the creeping paralysis of a despairing and rebellious nonentity in a free, but indifferent society.

It has become apparent, time and time again, that the emotional obstacles implied in the long conditioning against any flexibility of choice in the assumption of personal responsibility have proved to be insurmountable for many offenders. This is, of course, particularly true of the chronic offender whose deeply ingrained emotional problems are inseparably linked with a repetitive pattern of criminal behavior.

We know, of course, that at least 20 percent of our adult offenders, particularly those who have experienced only one commitment, are situational offenders whose principal needs are met through proper screening, understanding supervision, and placement in accordance with their vocational needs and identity requirements in a helpful family circle.

The same is not true, however, of the recidivists who have committed 80 percent of all felonies. They are the unaltered majority of chronic offenders whom Ramsey Clark describes as responsible for four-fifths of our major crimes in America.[23] They are the ones who tend to repeat, either deliberately because of a deeply ingrained asocial pattern, or because the unaccustomed freedom and tensions of a free world present an unlearned, and consequently, intolerable situation.

The situational offender's amenability to changed environmental circumstances is certainly not true of that stubborn minority of criminal offenders who had, over a prolonged stretch of their most productive years, resisted all efforts toward change in their basically antisocial patterns of behavior.

It is this latter group, whose emotional and interpersonal tensions we have appraised in the group interaction of the previous chapter, whom we shall now attempt to follow in terms of their adjustment difficulties in a free setting at the time of their last known release from institutional controls. This 10 percent category is of paramount importance in terms of the immeasurable costs, quite apart from the incalculatable drain on the taxpayer's pocketbook, which they have perpetrated in an overlapping and interwoven warp of human misery.

The experience of these five group members, all of whom had been through many years of psychotherapy involving both the individual and the group approach, warrant a special assessment with respect to their adjustment capabilities in a free setting. This adjustment, insofar as the psychotherapeutic treatment program is concerned, is based on a movement from intellectual to emotional insight which, in turn, called for a genuine expression of feeling in certain highly traumatic and sensitive areas of their existence.

It is assumed that a revival of early repressed feelings, resulting in the intense emotional awareness and dissipation of tension noted in the foregoing group interaction, would allow for sufficient impulse control to guard against any future reversion to sexually deviated behavior. It would theoretically, for that matter, alleviate the compulsive thrill and thereby ease the need for any form of criminally motivated behavior.

The introspective highlights of the most electrifying psychotherapeutic exchange, however, may be snuffed out in the emotional vacuum of a more comfortable retreat from personal responsibility. The very intensity of the offender's glimpse into the dark recesses of his self-defeating behavior may produce a rebound in the direction of earlier learned avoidance techniques.

His characteristic withdrawal may be fortified by the fact that other group members have experienced an uncomfortable anxiety caused by the unwelcome surfacing of their own covertly expressed hostility. At these times, a pervading sense of futility reigns in the wake of his smoldering rejection and silent defiance of their persistent probing.

There comes a time when an emotional plateau is reached upon which the group participants languish until some unguarded moment when the protagonist's veracity is again challenged in the cross fire of a suddenly intensified outburst against the "phony" manipulations of another. Then, as in a symphonic crash of cymbals, the emotional crescendo spills over and as quickly subsides into a familiar pattern of indirect denunciation and projection of blame, while he attempts to reconstitute himself as a man. Finally, prompted by his own impatience and sense of boredom to feel his way again into the terrifying maw of his tangled feelings, he finds himself somewhat less frightened, just a trifle more confident, and a wee bit bolder about revealing his true feelings than he was before.

In view of this complicated interplay between longstanding characterological defenses and a chameleon of conflicting emotion, one can do little more than prognosticate a lessening of the dangerous propensities of this particular offender's tenuous adjustment in a free setting. It follows, then, that a man may be released after a suitable time differential involving community tolerance and "maximum" evidence of change, all of which tends to alleviate the serious implications of his particular offense.

Despite a long, intermittant exposure to the treatment program which tirelessly explored every turn and corner of his recidivistic background, his actual emotional awareness and acceptance of underlying destructive impulses may be transitory at best. But, both the offender and his therapist are in accord with the idea that he needs an opportunity to apply his new found insights. How else, the prison inmate justly proclaims, can he prove his capacity to take his rightful place as a responsible citizen in a free society?

His argument is especially pertinent because of the more tangible, although less profound, evidence of exemplary work progress reports, freedom from institution disciplinary infractions, and dutiful family concerns from the "safe" distance of his rule girdled prison. He might also be aided at this point by the genuine revival or final dissolution of a questionable marriage, the tempering effects of a reasonable time interval since the date of his last commitment, and what appears to be a favorable academic or vocational opportunity in accordance with his basic skills.

In the light of the foregoing interpersonal clashes and ambiguities, let us observe what happened when our five "dangerously assaultive" rape offenders were given their final release to a somewhat dubious, but otherwise receptive society.

Group Member Two: The first of the four to be paroled was Pete Pamperson who, concurrent with his indeterminate commitment under the sex crimes statute, had served five and one-half years of a six-year-term for the attempted murder of his middle-aged female victim (see pp. 102-105). Pete was released as one who had made real gains in understanding the "passive-aggressive" aspects of his personality disorder, as well as having achieved valuable insights into the underlying dynamics of his sexually deviated behavior.

Although an "intellectualized" awareness of his emotional difficulties provided no guarantee of impulse control in a basically immature and dependent person, it was noted that the ultimate test could only be made through a return to the competitive pressures of a free society. At the time of his parole, however, it was quite apparent that Mr. Pamperson had become considerably less anxious, and consequently much more spontaneous in his reaction that he was before.

On the whole, it was obvious from a more relaxed attitude and a lowering of his guard in his general interpersonal relationships, that he had experienced a positive change in his self-concept which had made some of his more primitive defenses an unnecessary accouterment at this stage of his emotional growth.

In view of his longstanding dependency needs, Pete had the advantage of several external factors operating in his favor at the time of his release. He was, first of all, paroled to a "halfway house" situation which provided moral support and counseling services during the first three months of his release. The pressures of an undesirable marital relationship with a woman whom he was psychically unable to satisfy had been previously resolved through divorce. The conflicting circumstances of an untenable home situation had also been eliminated because of his parents' decision to take up residence in another state. The economic timing was also right, since a job in accordance with his needs was readily available.

Another circumstance which strongly supported, and in no small measure replaced, these changed situational pressures came from a newly instituted follow-up of his group therapy experience. It was a field-promoted clinical approach which, at the moment, had all of the enthusiastic impetus of an experimental attempt at succeeding in that which is new and different.

Probably the most clinching factor in Pete's eventually commendable adjustment and discharge from control was the manner in which he handled his basic homosexual orientation and very limited heterosexual interests. His honesty in admitting his heterosexual incompetence had, first of all, cleared the air for a more realistic approach to this problem. When he frankly informed his parole supervisor of his marital intentions toward a widow 22 years his senior, however, there was considerable apprehension about the wisdom of a move which called up memories of his assaultive offense toward a woman of similar age.

Pete's affectional concerns later became more understandable through a clinical review of his underlying maternal needs as opposed to the distressing conflicts imposed by a younger and more demanding female partner. It is now quite apparent, after two years of marriage to what he readily accepts as a mother ideal, that his choice was a most realistic and mutually acceptable one. After more than five years in a free setting, he has shown no further indications of sexually deviated trends, nor has there been any evidence of behavioral difficulties of any kind.

Group Member Four: The same could not be said for Clyde Manley. He was the second of the five to be released, five years after his last commitment for the second of two compulsively vicious attacks on elderly women. Because of his admittedly morbid fixation on his mother, and despite an intensified awareness of the underlying dynamics of this situation, he was paroled with the understanding that he would not return to the source of his early emotional conflicts in his home community (see pp. 108-110).

He was, consequently, released under the sponsorship of two elderly bachelor farmers in a more distant locale. It wasn't long, however, before he found their obsolete methods and old world ideas even more restrictive and depriving of his emotional freedom than the prison community which he had just left. At least, there was a certain security in the communality of feeling and sense of belonging to which he had grown accustomed over a nine-year-period of enforced confinement.

He now saw himself in the eyes of the two brothers as one who was only capable of carrying out their menial chores, and he projected his smoldering hostility against what he perceived as old and decrepit buildings perpetuating a futile and inglorious past which was incapable of change. His mounting anxiety in this contrasting setting prompted his return, primarily on the insistence of his parents, to the more modern comforts of his own home pending a more appropriate placement.

Through the influence of his father, Clyde was offered tentative employment on the farm of a former schoolmate who was only a few years older than himself. This young farm owner readily agreed to Clyde's specific request for a greater show of confidence in his capabilities as a tractor driver, while at the same time indicating that he, the owner, was under a certain obligation to Clyde's father to keep him busy. He explained that, should he be forced through a lack of work to let Clyde go, the parolee's father would become angry and refuse carpentry skills upon which his young employer depended during the coming season.

Clyde was, thereby, placed in a bind which tended to recognize his capacity for independent performance on a man-sized job, while at the same time suggesting that he be held on this job only because of his association with a temporarily protective father. It was a *minor* incident which served to trigger a lifelong conflict of unattainable expectations. The main, underlying issue here, however, was one of acute emotional tension because the father's actions were being subsidized by those of a solicitous maternal image which was always looming in the background.

Early unconscious conflicts thus laid bare to the same emotional pressures which precipitated a regressive phantasy existence and a need to act out against the nurturing female again took possession of his reasoning. He retaliated on this occasion to the point of an angry, and apparently unexplained, destruction of household furnishings which was subsequently attributed to a mentally beserk or emotionally disturbed state.

Although he had some difficulty in explaining his feelings, Clyde was well aware of having rebelled inwardly with an intense burst of feeling, mostly because of the fact that both his mother and the family minister treated him "so nicely," and with so much solicitous attention to his welfare. They held his hand and patted his back, saying that this was something that could happen to anyone; that after all, he couldn't help himself, or, in his mind, "what else could one expect of a boy who had never grown up enough to pull himself free of his mother's apron strings?"

It is, however, highly significant in this episode of uncontrolled retaliation for being treated as an irresponsible boy (like his much more competent sister had treated him during his adolescent years) that he did not again revert to his considerably more serious assaultive behavior pattern. Since the same emotional build up had been noted in the group interaction which expressed both sibling and parental doubts about his adult capabilities, he appeared to have gained some measure of control, along with the awareness of just what had been making him so angry.

The knowledge of having demonstrated this degree of control was, in itself, therapeutic, and what might appear to have been a loss through parole revocation emanating from his emotionally upset state was actually a gain in terms of a specific focus of feeling at the true source of his difficulties. For he was now, more than ever, aware of the manner in which his repressed hostility had come to be displaced, and obsessively ventilated, in a need to act out against the reproductive function of the maternal image.

For more than a year since his last return to the sex crimes treatment facility, following his third, consecutive failure to adjust in a free setting, Clyde has resigned himself to the relative serenity of his prison farm assignment. He expressed a strong interest in the life of a herdsman, and he had an exemplary work record in the care of livestock and farm animals which had, in effect, removed him from the tensions of a competitive existence.

He remained a passively compliant and agreeable person whose outwardly acceptant and conforming manner belied the fragile personality structure underneath. The last psychiatric evaluation described him as one who "continued to be dependent upon his parents in a very infantile way, while at the same time nourishing a great deal of underlying hostility against his mother."

Earlier psychiatric appraisals over a ten-year-period focused on the same chronically malignant relationship between the offender and his parents. It is highly significant that psychiatric opinion preceding each release strongly advised against any parole plan which would place him close to home, and in a position where the pressures of this conflict-ridden situation might be reactivated.

The fact that he had, on each occasion, gravitated in the direction of this untenable home situation is a reflection of the inherent weakness, both within himself and in the application of supervisory authority which failed to recognize his needs.

This dilemma, calling for a more refined alignment of the paths of both the offender and the authoritarian controls to which he is responsible, is an issue of grave importance at both ends of the treatment continuum. It is logical to assume that until the total situation is remedied through a more consistent adherence to the offender's basic needs, he will not only become more confused and fearful of the world at large, but a mountain of constructive effort is in danger of being lost along with a proportionately staggering amount of the taxpayer's money.

On the basis of his otherwise stable work record and willing response to minimum security controls in an institutional setting, Clyde would, of course, again be given favorable consideration for parole. This time, hopefully, his increased awareness of the danger signals in his emotional life would coincide with a more personalized approach to his supervisory needs in a free world.

The main boundaries of these needs should allow for a full acceptance of himself as a person with something worthwhile to contribute in an area removed from the double-binded pressures of his home environment. As his experience has conclusively demonstrated, it is only under these conditions that he might have a chance to handle his dependency needs in a manner which would not fire the embers of his repressed hostile feelings against the female. Because of a lessened need to conceal a diminutive self-concept, he might then find the inner strength to curb the assaultive impulse which springs from a frustratingly inadequate show of his masculine potency.

Group Member One: Delbert Newfondel, the first of the five group members to test the merits of his own suggestion of the "hot seat" approach, was the third to be paroled, four years after his commitment on a new sex offense (see pp. 96-102). He spent his final year of confinement on the prison farm, since a staff consensus had determined that his primary need at this point was one of relaxed restrictions and environmental support of a parole plan tailored to his emotionally dependent needs.

He, too, had many external factors favoring his adjustment in a free setting, including a 90-day initial exposure to the services of the same "halfway house" rehabilitation center, and the same group therapy follow-up by a clinical services unit, to which Pete Pamperson had been previously exposed.

By far the greatest advantage he had, however, was that of a spray painting skill in which he had demonstrated so much talent that he was shortly earning over $200 weekly in the employ of a poster displays company. Since he had, unlike most of the others, never been deprived of his driving privileges, he had both the freedom of movement and the financial wherewithal for considerable choice in the exercise of recreational interests and personal responsibility.

Most of his free time was spent with his ex-wife in another city, and a large share of his earnings, likewise, was voluntarily turned over to her, supposedly for the support of their five children. The two younger children were the illegitimate progeny of another man, and a third child, which subsequently died, was fathered by a fellow inmate who had been committed for adultery during the period of Delbert's previous confinement.

It is significant of Delbert's continued emotional fixation that, far from blaming his ex-wife for her promiscuous activities, he saw only the magnitude of her deprivation of his presence as a desirable bed partner. He was, thereby, driven by a compulsive need to rectify this situation.

After several weekends of lavish expenditure and renewed sexual fervor, the unacceptable truth finally penetrated this narcissistic blind spot in his makeup. Arriving so as to surprise his wife and children with several expensive gifts, he caught her with another man.

She, in her exasperation at his unexpected appearance, told him what he had always feared but failed to believe earlier. She bitingly informed him that she had only been interested in finding out how much she could get out of him. Then, when he impulsively slapped her, she confessed that she quickly lost interest in him, or in any man for that matter, as soon as she knew that she had him hooked.

The stage had been set for the same kind of frustration, and the same kind of assaultive reaction, which Delbert had experienced earlier. And true to a delicately linked chain of underlying needs, the reactive qualities of which were again being triggered, he reverted to drinking and to a new association with a promiscuous female.

There was, however, one very notable exception to his previous encounters of this nature. The old voyeuristic compulsiveness was gone, and he discovered that he was no longer impotent; that he did not have to slap a woman around in order to maintain his sexual advantage. But the ardor of his sexual performance frightened the girl into thinking that she might be pregnant. In defense of her position with her regular boyfriend, she reported to the authorities what might, at the most, have resulted in a charge of fornication or adultery.

As it was, Delbert's confused feelings about this incident, and the still unresolved conflicts over his wife's rejection of "all that I had to offer her," prompted him to abscond from parole on an aimless journey to the west coast. He simply said that he had to get away, that he had to think things out in a manner which would leave no doubt in his mind about his sexual tendencies, or the extent to which he might still be emotionally bound to his wife.

Once he had settled in his own mind that he was not overtly homosexual, and that he was no longer bound by guilt feelings or a sense of obligation to fulfill his wife's needs, he made no attempt to conceal his whereabouts. He was, subsequently, returned to the prison treatment facility as a parole violator who was administratively tolerated as a "three-time loser," and otherwise accepted as a likeable and serviceable prison conformist.

It was quite obvious in this man's case, as it was in the case of those with whom he had over a prolonged period participated in a lively and psychotherapeutically productive interaction, that an emotional plateau had been reached. This level of emotional growth, from the standpoint of social mores, made him a less dangerous person than he had been in the past. A staff consensus at this time, however, suggested that he still presented "a facade of defensiveness oriented toward concealing underlying angry feelings, along with a basic unwillingness to recognize persistently strong emotional dependency strivings."

This latter deduction was based on the fact that he had placed frequent long distance calls to his parents, as well as to his ex-wife, since absconding from parole. Despite his contention that his ex-wife's actions had definitely eliminated long-standing guilt feelings and a sense of obligation toward her, current psychiatric opinion indicated that he had yet to extricate himself from the web of his unresolved conflicts.

The current appraisal characterized him as one who "still shows an inability to overtly express anger which, in the past, had necessitated an indirect release of feeling through antisocial acts and erratically unpredictable behavior." A specific focus on this area of his interpersonal relationships was presently encouraged. It took the form of continued active participation on the part of a small group of the more sophisticated parole violators who, like himself, had been particularly resistive to anything but a gradual reduction of deeply entrenched characterological defenses.

Group Member Three: Elric Jungfeld, one of the first to be exposed to the sex crimes treatment program 14 years previous, was also one of the last of the five group members to be paroled, six and one-half years after his last commitment. He had, like Delbert Newfondel and Clyde Manley before him, twice violated parole with rape offenses of a seriously assaultive nature (see pp. 106-108).

On this occasion, however, his lean, muscular build and ruddy complexion exuded an aura of physical well-being which was not apparent on previous encounters with the Special Review Board. He had just completed a year on the farm of a medium security institution to which he had been transferred for the socializing incentives which this more relaxed "halfway house" situation had to offer him. He had not, however, taken advantage of the academic opportunities which were so readily available to one of his superior mental capacity. Instead, he had contented himself with the more solitary and juvenile pursuit of model airplane construction during his leisure moments.

At the time of his Special Review Board appearance, he maintained his characteristic emotional aloofness, while aligning his intellectual defenses in an appropriately calm and dignified manner. His general attitude reflected years of practice in "correct" institutional procedure, and he had certainly had a most thorough exposure to the entire gamut of clinical services treatment facilities. Under the circumstances, there were none who could say that he had not received a "maximum" benefit from all of the available treatment "modalities" in an institutional setting.

A recognized mother fixation complex, however, still lurked in the background of his early adverse conditioning. The well documented, but pervading shadow of a controlling maternal image, like that of Clyde Manley, suggested the probability of a more responsible parole experience in an area many miles distant from his home community. Spring work opportunities in accordance with his mechanical, outdoor interests were readily available, and he was quickly engaged as a field man for a local canning company.

The hours were long and arduous, and as the summer days lengthened into the sultry temperatures conducive to the rapid growth of a large pea crop, the demands for an increasing work load became proportionately more intense. These excessive demands, as in previous situations calling for more than ordinary effort and disciplinary control, became the parolee's emotional justification for seeking temporary relief from fatigue through the use of alcohol and amphetamine.

A killing work schedule, provoking a gnawing, inner voice into crying for some form of maternal sympathy, also became the reason why he made the acquaintance of a 45-year-old married woman with seven children. She was separated at the time, and in the process of seeking a divorce from her husband who had chosen a military career over the needs and personal responsibilities of a large family brood.

This emotional situation provided a fertile climate for the reciprocal attentions of a frustrated "mother-seeker," and an affectionally starved "father-loser," both of whom were ripe for whatever affectional fulfillment each might find in the other. With Elric, however, the first intimacy conveyed a vague threat, associated with long-standing fears of rejection, which years of intensive analysis could not erase. The more intimate his involvement, the more fearful he became, and the more doubtful he was of his ability to fulfill his role as a husband and father.

It was at this point that his alcoholic excesses, paralleling his mounting anxiety tensions, precipitated an apparent memory lapse and near reversion to his earlier pattern of assaultive rape. In this case, however, the charges were not pressed because of the promiscuous reputation of the involved girl. It appears that she, in much the same manner as Delbert Newfondel's "pickup" during the course of his last release, reported the incident to counteract repercussions which she feared at home because of her own unsavory behavior.

There was, in any event, no evidence of the forceful rape or violence which characterized his earlier offenses of an almost deliberately assaultive nature. He did, however, abscond in great fear of an anticipated arrest, and during the next several weeks of tentative employment in a remote rural community he reverted to an earlier form of conduct disorder resulting in his apprehension for furnishing alcoholic stimulants for a teenage party.

It is very apparent at this point that two extremes were a characteristic pattern of Elric's reaction under pressure of affectionally frustrating circumstances. While driven by a pervading need to seek out the "ideal mother" in his heterosexual contacts, he was likewise propelled by the threatening aspects of his sexual relationships to prove his worth to younger males whose recognition he craved as a competent and self-sufficient person.

Since he, like Delbert and others of his emotional calibre, have tended to operate on a demanding, "all or none" level in the affectional sphere, the current problem would appear to be one of resolving these behavioral extremes through a more sensitive awareness, and a more refined application, of the "shades of gray" which lie in between.

At the time of his return to the sex crimes facility as a parole violator, Elric was greatly troubled over the possibility that he and the mother of seven children, with whom he had been living in a common-law relationship, might be denied correspondence during the period of his confinement. He sobbed like a child during two or three interviews following his return to the institution, thereby exhibiting an emotional involvement never before apparent in any of his many therapeutic sessions.

It appears that Elric, more than anything else, feared the rejecting consequences of his emotional involvement. The lifelong conflict between his intense dependency needs and the desire to establish himself as a responsible marital partner came to a head in this last heterosexual relationship, thereby precipitating the incidents which followed. These experiences were, in a sense, an emotional rehearsal of intellectualized insights which he had gleaned through 14 years of confinement, and which he finally had the opportunity to test out in the last of four successive parole releases.

In view of this man's very superior mental capacity and intensive exposure to the treatment program over a prolonged period, there would seem to be, surfacewise at least, little that he had gained from all of this effort in his behalf. Upon closer observation of his case, however, as well as those of the other two group members who failed to keep their parole, there had been a definite alleviation of the viciously compulsive elements which may describe a man as "dangerous."

From the standpoint of public policy, of course, there was a pattern of repetitively regressive and potentially dangerous behavior in an individual of superior intelligence who did not appear to be profiting from his past mistakes. Were we, however, to focus on these external circumstances for the "protection of society" to the exclusion of the more subjective evidence of individual gains in emotional adjustment, we would very effectively destroy the offender's own hopes and incentives for further gains, as well as those of us who have invested so much in his emotional growth.

Elric Jungfeld was an outstanding example of unrealized potential in a superior mentality which had gone virtually untapped because of recurrent problems centering in an overwhelming sense of rejection. The morbid anticipation of failure, in spite of the obvious insights which he had gained, had continued to undermine his self-confidence. And, as we know, the mental power behind the defensive needs in one of superior endowment may be a detriment rather than an asset in the orderly discharge of frustrated emotions.

It would, therefore, be entirely wrong to base anticipated progress on an intellectualized awareness of past mistakes which assumes that the offender might be thereby driven to take advantage of available opportunities in accordance with his superior potential. It is equally wrong to discount small advances in emotional control and extra-institutional adjustment because of the overwhelming evidence of recidivistic trends.

We are, much too often, inclined to project our own drives and ambitions into the rationale of behavioral difficulties as presented to us by our most unpredictable and socially withdrawn clients. Acting on our own freedom from paralyzing emotional involvement, and the psychotherapist's sometimes overly reactive need for establishing an insightful pattern, we inadvertently dampen their ardor with the intensity of expectations beyond their emotional capacity to fulfill.

Actually, it is the therapist's problem, first of all, to recognize the deep-seated nature of his client's emotional difficulties. He must then allow credit for whatever effort and application this chronic offender is able to make toward a more adult expression of his feelings, no matter how slow or painful this may be.

As it developed, Elric became involved once again in a newly formed group of chronic offenders, all of whom were parole violators like himself. Under the guidance of a new therapist with a new approach, they began reevaluating similar experiences in the light of their past intellectualized insights. They were now in a position to recognize the inadequacy of these insights from the new perspective of emotional pressures which each had encountered in a free setting.

In line with current thinking, the therapeutic emphasis turned sharply away from psychoanalytic theory, and, once more, the tangible "security" of objective data assumed primary importance in both the diagnostic and rehabilitative efforts of the Clinical Services unit. A newly expanded staff of consulting and research psychologists, psychological technicians, and student trainees focused on the psychometric, social, and medical evidence of environmental versus "brain damaged," nonadaptive functions, while devising institutionally unique situations and techniques for applying the behaviorist's emphasis on "operant conditioning" and learning theory to criminal behavior.[7, 33, 34]

Staff conferences with resident and consulting psychiatrists devoted considerable time to the analysis of pertinent family and social data, the extent and character of the criminal record, and other historical data suggestive of pathological trends. The medical indications of neurological changes, inherited biological traits, and even chromosomal eccentricities were given considerable weight in the staff discussions.

The Special Review Board, during this period and despite an otherwise favorable psychiatric report, found the statistical indications of a repetitive pattern of sexual assault or viciously aggressive behavior as almost exclusively discouraging. The continued drive toward any real change in the thrice repeating, assaultive offender was most certainly restricted, despite the "faint light in the shades of gray," as an almost hopeless gesture in terms of any new trial on parole.

From the standpoint of a continuing application and a consolidation of gains he had already made, Elric was, however, permitted to carry on a correspondence with the divorced woman in whose life he had become so emotionally involved during the period of his last release. Concurrent with his most recent psychotherapeutic exposure, he was engaged in regular counseling sessions with her as a realistic extension of tape recorded group therapy meetings revolving around a mutual exchange of tapes with a group of both normal and emotionally disturbed females.

The intensified pressure on new learning through ingeniously devised, conditioning procedures required the introduction of expensive new equipment. This included a pupilograph and polygraph machine as "necessary" adjuncts to elaborately sensitive psychometric and visual motor aids, and by means of which otherwise undetectable organic, as well as functional, abnormalities might be ascertained. An appropriately styled movie projector and a closed circuit television had already been acquired, and these, in turn, called for related technological assistants and interested research personnel.

This impressive display, and multiple focus of individual attention on an otherwise vastly impersonal medical plane, will hopefully shed light on behavioral problems as yet not apparent. It, nonetheless, poses a multitude of unanswered questions which threaten to confuse the overall issues on crime to a still greater degree.

One of the most elusive issues with regard to the behaviorist's "conditioning" of the criminal offender sparks a question as to the extent to which these, and other "reinforcement" oriented, "computerized" techniques,[7, 33, 99] may detract from the offender's all-important acceptance of personal responsibility for his behavior. Expressed in another way, to what degree may individual initiative and effort in the direction of personal achievement regress for want of exercise in an ultimate "depersonalization" of future adjustment problems?*

With Elric, the problem continues to be one of adequate preparation for a much more self-assured and stable relationship in the sexual area of his existence when he is again released on his own responsibility.

But, because of the fact that his association with a sexually experienced and considerably older divorcee with seven children is not only condoned but encouraged in accordance with the emotional involvement which each has invested in the other, Elric's chances for a successful adjustment on his fifth parole would now appear to be more nearly on a par with those of Pete Pamperson who had successfully consumated a similar marital relationship.

VENTED HOSTILITIES MAKE ROOM FOR NEW LIVES IN TWO OUT OF FIVE

For those of us who are most intimately involved in the abortive struggles of the chronic offender, it becomes increasingly obvious that tremendous pressures are clamoring for release. The sensitive edges of conflicting feelings are frayed against the erratic demands of a confused identity, and an inflamed emotional sore swells and festers. In the midst of all of this unreasoning turmoil, the therapist attempts to maintain his own integrity and sincerity of purpose, around which the hostile reactions of his clients might eventually be rallied.

*The dangers, as well as the overall ineffectiveness, of behavioral conditioning procedures, have been realistically expressed by Dr. Carl R. Rogers in *On Becoming A Person*,[93] and later by Dr. Seymour L. Halleck in *Psychiatry And The Dilemmas Of Crime*.[56] It is interesting to note that recent books dealing with *Reality Therapy*,[45] *I'M OK—YOU'RE OK, A Practical Guide To Transactional Analysis*,[60] *Gestalt Therapy Verbatim*,[86] and *Psycho-cybernetics & Self-fulfillment*,[72] all emphasize the acceptance of personal responsibility as an integrative function emanating from an increased sense of personal worth which tends to overshadow negative feelings. There is also, the obvious influence of the therapist, himself, as a sincerely dynamic and integrated personality. This influence is interestingly portrayed in *Carl Rogers On Encounter Groups*,[94] and in *The Psychology Of Self-Esteem* and *Breaking Free*, by Nathaniel Branden.[18, 19]

Although the therapist must not fear an honest exposure of his own intense feelings, he cannot allow them to be fed into the same interacting, therapeutic "grist mill" without a strong sense of trust in the hidden values and ultimate worth of his client. He must also have a profound sensitivity, along with patience, tolerance, and a capacity for understanding, as well as unshakable convictions of his own.

One of the convictions which grows on him with each soul-shaking session is that which makes any form of personal renumeration a consideration of secondary importance. For he knows, with each genuine release of otherwise inescapable inner tension, that he has pushed a step closer to the emergence of a more productive emotional life. Herein awaits a form of reward which must be experienced in order to be appreciated.

An individually acute and overriding emotional problem, then, becomes a primary focus. The therapist becomes increasingly aware, also, of the fact that his clients, no matter how confused about their own place in the scheme of things, are highly attuned to any break in the therapist's emotional armor which might justify their charges of "phoniness" in the authoritative approach.

At the same time, while in the midst of a heated emotional exchange, the psychologist knows, almost instinctively, that if it were possible to correct or to help in the correction of just two chronic offenders, his salary, as well as that of a social worker and at least one consulting psychiatrist over the course of a year, would be more than repaid.

Pete Pamperson had led the way in what appeared to be an honestly acceptant attitude. His changed outlook and renewed incentives were fortified by a matching chain of circumstances tuned to his needs at the time of his release to a free setting. By contrast, the last of the five, whom we will recall as Mark Stout, appeared to have generated the necessary inner motivation for formulating his own set of favorable circumstances.

Group Member Five: Our last glimpse of Mark was one in which he had been provoked into an intense emotional upheaval following his fourth successive rejection by all three members of the Special Review Board. At that time, his sullen resistance and vehement projection of blame had incited a sharply critical response from the other group members, the harassing emotional effects of which provided a new perspective concerning a commonly shared blind spot (see pp. 111-113).

As a result of Mark's intensely negative reaction, each had for the first time realized, on a rarely exposed feeling level, that one who is self-rejecting is already rejected by the others. Mark was especially made aware at that time of the fact that the Special Review Board's rejection of him was actually a reflection of his own deeply ingrained rejecting attitudes.

Not long after this outwardly hostile, but inwardly purging emotional experience, Mark was transferred to a nearby medium security institution as one who had achieved a maximum benefit from whatever the prison had to offer. A staff conference of psychiatrists, psychologists, and social workers, at this time, concluded that he was ready for the type of coordinated academic and vocational training which would prepare him for eventual release.

He was, at this point, described in a final psychiatric report as one "whose capacity for adjustment should be tested in the more relaxed atmosphere, and less structured setting, of a social and vocational situation more nearly geared to that in which he would be ultimately returned."

Following his transfer, and in the face of serious doubts with respect to the strength of his motivation toward a particular goal, Mark was for the first time demonstrating his capacity for a full exercise of his innate potential. In marked contrast to his indifferent application in the environment of the state prison, he was reported as an excellent student with a high average rating as an apprentice bricklayer. In an astonishing short space of time, he had completed a course of study in the academic phase of this school related program, earning a high school diploma, as well as an A rating in his performance.

At the time of his release on parole, he had shown evidence of consistent interests in his chosen vocational field, together with an unqualified rating of excellence in effort and application with respect to both the spiritual and recreational areas of his life. Contrary to the recorded negatives which appeared in all prior progress reports, he was now regarded as an exceptional inmate in both behavior and interpersonal relationships. Also highly significant of his changed outlook was his volunteered activity as a speaker on the benefits of the institution vocational program whenever he was offered an opportunity for regularly spaced contacts with visiting personnel.

One might add that the final touches to his changed approach were evidenced in his voluntary refusal of the Special Review Board's apparent willingness to release him at this time. He showed unexpected purpose and consistency of outlook in a current self-presentation as one who realized his aims and limitations as a man who still had much to learn. He simply stated that he was happy with a teaching instructor and shop foreman whom he described as matching all of the ideals he had ever hoped for in an understanding father.

He indicated, furthermore, that one of the things he had learned, over and above everything else, was the joy in having achieved something on his own power.

Within another six months, Mark was unanimously granted the green light of a speedy release. As a result of prior preparations with an understanding employer who recognized his talents, he made a very favorable and productive transition to a free society. It should be noted that his employer, far from any solicitous concern for the free world handicaps of a multiple recidivist with the fatalistic "three strikes against me" philosophy of a potential "four-time loser," saw in this man a productively valuable employe with a rejuvenated integrity which was "good for the company," and well worth the time and energy spent in his behalf.

Mark Stout's "ups and downs," with a strong emphasis on the "downs" of a postadolescent, as well as those of his adolescent and preadolescent period, comprise material for a personal success story that is too rarely told. That is because we as a people, and not excluding institutional personnel, are much too inclined to brand spirited hostilities, and all of the more obviously associated surface negatives which threaten our own "secure" position, as irreversible.

In the news media, we are so much in the shadow of the overwhelming violence and perverted thrills which activate a spotlight on sensational crime that we fail to see the "light under the bushel" of many who have suffered untold mental and emotional agonies, but who are today much better citizens because of their suffering.

There are those who would argue from a purely situational standpoint that the passage of time is the only effective form of treatment. In Mark's case, one might contend that he was aided principally by the final dissolution of his questionable marriage. Or, one might add that the demise of his neurotic mother, and the enfeebled needs of his aging father, had a most decisive effect on his ultimate adjustment capabilities. One might draw a much more obvious conclusion to the effect that he, himself, had graduated from the tension tormented uncertainties of his unstable twenties, that he now felt needed, and that time had filled the vacuum of a now ineffective and "burned-out" psychopathy with a more settled outlook.

We know, of course, that a criminal offender of superior mentality and a long-standing recidivistic background can, unquestionably, become most adept in the art of manipulation for personal gain against what he perceives as the ever-encroaching restraints of authoritative controls over his personal freedom. Like the chronic forger, confidence man, or accomplished safebreaker, this may be an inherent "aptitude"; the main key to his identity as a man capable of "deceiving an otherwise hypocritical and deceptive society."

If this were the case with Mark Stout, however, we should have to admit that he had learned to manipulate for personal advantage in a very unusual and constructive way. He had learned to apply his sociopathic defense system in a manner which had earned him the descriptive designation of "a warm and pleasing personality," and which had caused his peers to feel comfortably at ease and hopefully aware of his presence. No matter what the source of the layman's rationalizations, or what the more authoritative professional conclusions may be, he had learned to manipulate his life so as to get along with all manner of people, and with authoritarian figures in particular.

Any lurking ulterior objectives, under these circumstances and in the broad framework of effective social interaction, would appear to be the superfluous manifestations of purely theoretical considerations.

One might, at this time, consider the poignant holiday messages, and voluntary verbal reminders, from a released offender to his former therapist which unexpectedly come through on the spontaneous wings of a freed spirit. These unsolicited, simply worded communications attest to a changed attitude associated with a healthy peer camaraderie wherein shared fears and anxieties had been dramatically unleashed in an atmosphere free of arbitrarily condoned condemnation and ridicule. They reflect an honestly sincere and profoundly acquired gratitude for an inner sense of well-being and self-respect which they had never had the opportunity to realize in the horrible emotional turmoil of their growing years.

There are very few "graduates" of the many intense hours of group psychotherapy who would not, at this stage, admit long-repressed hostilities, the subversive and potentially violent impact of which had, through patience and tolerance born of a recognized need, been tempered against the sensitive "anvils" of understanding ears. It is obvious that much of this shared mental anguish and emotional catharsis has had an unrecorded, but overwhelming effect on the natural capacity of each ultimately discharged offender to withstand frustration and to meet the problems of life in a more acceptable manner.

Chapter 9

THE DRIVING FORCE BEHIND THE INNER NEED FOR VIOLENCE

THE expression of violent thoughts, for most of us, is synonomous with the potential for murder, and we entertain the mistaken belief that those offenders who are committed to prison on life sentences head the list of our most vicious criminal offenders. This may be true of an asocial minority who have killed policemen and other authoritarian figures while in the act of a premeditated assault, robbery, or burglary. It may be true of the mentally disturbed sadist, or a few "cold-blooded" killers who thrive on discontent, and who act on an intensely obsessive need to revolutionize their surroundings.

An inherently vicious nature, in our experience, is certainly not prevalent in a majority of first degree murder offenders serving life sentences on a first offense of extreme violence. In many of these offenders, a viciously assaultive act against persons, usually within the home environment of "loved ones," reflects an explosive release of emotional pressures which had been allowed to accumulate in intolerable proportions during the most trying period of their young adult years.

The most vicious offender may be described as one who is coldly calculating, and whose projective and clinical evaluations show no evidence of emotional warmth or capacity for empathy in his human relationships. He often has an early record of temper outbursts, and a rather subtle history of sadistically toned behavioral reactions may be uncovered during the course of staff conferences and routine psychotherapeutic interviews. Coupled with the historical evidence of violent potential is an absence of remorse, a detached manner of approach, or an otherwise unfeeling quality in his response pattern.*

Despite the subjective and apparently unpredictable nature of violent behavior, we do have the psychological tools for evaluating elements of sadistic, suicidal, or homicidal phantasy ideation in terms of the quality, intensity, and degree of control which may be projected in the test content reflecting this form of preoccupation. In many instances, however, any real acceptance of the deeply entrenched, underlying causes of violent behavior is blocked by solicitous parents, rejected by guilt-ridden marital partners, or fearfully denied by other close family members. The danger signals of a protective need to provide emotional shelter, while minimizing an unchanged pattern of juvenile irresponsibility, are blindly glossed over, painfully rationalized away, or hopefully postponed for a more thorough consideration on a "brighter" day.

The offender most threatening to the lives of law abiding persons frequently has a record of antisocial behavior which follows the progressively amoral pattern of a superciliously withdrawn, or blandly indifferent person, with a socially warped outlook. Unless his past history is frighteningly vicious or obviously threatening, however, the "soft signs" of inappropriate behavior and dangerously assaultive tendencies are, for the most part, apathetically ignored. One of our most coldly noncommittal, inherently vicious prison commitments, who later renounced his American citizenship for the sadistically motivated "glory" of Cuban "justice" as a Castro executioner, had been given a mandatory discharge after serving the maximum of a four-year-sentence on a rape offense which had been technically reduced to "Carnal Knowledge And Abuse."

Most of our "lifers," on the other hand, have demonstrated a capacity for both exemplary prison records and congenial interpersonal relationships. Except for those with prior records of mental

---

*Halleck points to "the presence of violent motivations which are deeply repressed or denied," as "an ominous indicator of potential dangerousness." He says that "the person who denies all unpleasant impulses is more of a threat than the person who is troubled with conscious aggressive thoughts."[56] Wolfgang notes that nearly two-thirds of those who commit violent crimes had a previous arrest record,[123] and Palmer offers evidence of a "high incidence of physical and emotional frustrations in those who commit violent offenses."[85] Macdonald adds to the total picture with his own profound observations of the subtle threat in homicidal and suicidal phantasies, along with evidence as to the reluctance of both the aggressor and his frequently masochistic victim to seek help against the threat of personal injury.[70, 71]

instability or antisocial behavior, only a few have revealed an incapacity for adequate adjustment in a free setting after the mandatory 11 or more years which precedes their eligibility for parole.

Despite the close security stipulations of his life sentence, he has proven himself over the years as one who has the necessary motivation for readjustment. He has shown himself as one who is resigned to the fact that he has much time to serve, and that he must, consequently, make the best of available opportunities to keep himself mentally alert and physically occupied.

He is, in other words, not confused by controversial dogma which, in so many instances, does not allow the inmate offender the security of knowing just how he stands with authoritative controls. He knows he is in for life, and that he must, short of an extremely doubtful commutation of sentence through executive clemancy, serve out a mandatory segment of his most productive years. This knowledge, in itself, forces a hard look at the facts of his current adjustment needs. It should be remembered, also, that this type of offender is filled with remorse, and, in his case, a minimum of 11 years may be a necessary time interval for an alleviation of the guilt feelings with which he is imbued.

MOTIVATION OF A REMORSEFUL "LIFER"

The innate, good qualities of this type of offender are dramatically revealed in the early family history and subsequent reactions of an emotionally traumatized colored man. He had shot and killed his attractive, but sexually promiscuous colored wife, thereby lining his own prison of remorse with the inescapable awareness of having, for all practical purposes, orphaned his seven small children.

The prosecuting attorney won a first degree murder conviction against the defendant because of amply substantiated evidence to the effect that he had previously threatened to kill his wife, and because he was carrying a fully loaded pistol concealed on his person at the time of the murder. But the real circumstances of his intense, compensatory need to bolster an insidiously deteriorated ego in the only manner he knew were legally restricted as irrelevant and inadmissible during the course of the court proceedings.*

---

*Actually, these circumstances were tremendously relevant, and from a clinical standpoint, they were intensely consequential and materially significant as well. It will be recalled that the Wisconsin Psychiatric Field Services did, at one time, have a

From a purely clinical standpoint, this colored offender whom we shall identify as Spike, was actually a victim of emotional and situational pressures beyond his capacity to control. A group analysis of his situation later revealed him as one who had been victimized by his wife, the legal victim, long before he was propelled into a violent removal of her aggravating influence through an impulsively overwhelming discharge of fatal shots against her person.

He became particularly incensed over what he described as police intervention which tended to ridicule his responsibilities as a husband and father, while accepting his wife's insinuations as a true account of everything which had transpired between them. It was his contention that because of unwarranted police harassment and the deceptive "good-acting" qualities of his wife which seemed to be emotionally more convincing than anything he could offer, he got so that he apathetically agreed with everything the police were saying about him.

He perceived the whole thing as futile, insofar as his own defense was concerned, and he masochistically resigned himself to what he had come to regard as racist, authoritative manipulations for the purpose of depriving him of his manhood.

Later, in a group interaction which focused on the aggressively unpredictable behavior of each group member, he was able to see his situation from a new, heretofore unrecognized point of view. He saw himself as needing his wife so badly that he had to overlook her infidelity and abide by her periodic rejection of him at the expense of his own integrity and capacity for making a decision on his own power.

He said that he had been brought up to regard women as morally inviolable, and that a minister had drilled him on the importance of keeping the family relationship intact, even to the point of "turning the other cheek" whenever he saw that he was being wronged. He, nonetheless, succumbed to violent arguments with his wife on the

team of psychiatrists who were free to consult locally on the Courts' periodic requests for clinical advice (see pp. 23-25). Practically the entire staff of five correctionally experienced psychiatrists were, however, unceremoniously removed in the late thirties so as to conform with a new governor's ideas of government economy and efficiency of operation. The taxpayer has unknowingly paid dearly in both materialistic gains and moral incentives as a consequence of this egocentric narrowing of the rights of the individual to make himself understood for the type of person that he really is.

question of money, of which he was apparently never able to produce enough to satisfy her much more affluent needs.

Spike's face blanched, and he became visibly shaken and almost incoherent as he attempted to clarify the very embarrassing circumstances involving his questionable paternal responsibilities for a brood of hungry children whose mother controlled the family purse strings. This, in itself, might have been tolerable had she not cleaned out his pockets while he slept, and without explanation called for his check at his place of employment. These incidents put a psychic crimp in his love life, and money for him became the symbol of a pervading impotence in his marital relationship of which his wife was consistently and relentlessly depriving him.

Once the traumatic circumstances relating to his marital experience were uncovered, he was able to talk more freely about his early home life with a mother who babied him because of rickets and braces on his legs. But this handicap, as he described it, later became the reason why he was kept inside to do the housework while his two older sisters were freed of these menial chores in order that they might indulge their romantic interests with boyfriends at any time that they pleased.

Spike wiped his glistening forehead while trying to find words for the painfully echoing memory of his mother's shrill-voiced admonition that he couldn't do this and that he shouldn't do that. He haltingly told of his later accidental discovery of the fact that he was not only capable of walking without braces, but that he could participate in many of the things that she had kept assuring him he could not do. Thereafter, he rebelled violently against her attempts to control him, and eventually, against any woman who tried to force him into this very incapacitating, dependency role.

He went on to explain how his mother had degraded his father, who showed more interest in the vice of gambling than he did in her need for regular church attendance. Here, too, he had become convinced that these "negative" qualities were at least out in the open, and therefore not nearly as bad as his mother's deceptive hold on his right to a self-sufficient existence through normal peer relationships.

To this day, Spike admitted, he couldn't help feeling an unreasoning resentment toward anyone who spontaneously offered him "a pat on the back." He somewhat defiantly confessed that any form of praise tended to anger him, since it was associated in his mind with the kind of "phoniness" and confining deceit which his mother had used in order to gain his favor for services and some measure of the personal attentiveness which was denied to her by his father.

It was at this point that several other group members extended their emotional support by stating, quite emphatically, that the same difficulty, the true circumstances of which none of them had felt free to voice previously, had been experienced by them.

When asked to compare an early sense of masculine deprivation at the hands of his mother with that later experienced through the equally deceptive manipulations of his promiscuous wife, Spike at first belligerently refused to entertain even the possibility of any existent similarity. Gradually, however, as his self-concept was advanced through the genuinely spontaneous support of the other group members, he was able to concede a similarity in the sense that his wife had also left him alone with the housework and with the responsibility of caring for the children.

He had serious doubts as to which, or how many, of these children were really his own, and a confirmation of his unacceptable suspicions blasted his long-repressed hostility through the weakened barrier of ineffectual surface controls at the time that he discovered his wife had been spending her late evening hours with another man. At this time, however, he had stopped short of murder by beating her up and threatening her life if she ever saw this man again.

Then, after he and his wife had separated, she used his court stipulated support payments for her personal needs, which included a furtherance of her illicit relationship with a boyfriend. Spike was even denied the privilege of taking his oldest son to the movies, since his wife was worried over the possibility that he might thereby check on the fact that his payments were not being properly allocated to take care of household bills and other essentials of which the children were very much in need. Her tearful complaints to the police, however, were solicitously sustained on the basis of previous threats which her husband had made against her.

Through all of this authoritative condonation of a tense emotional situation which was otherwise legally intact, Spike became more and more disturbed over the fact that his wife continued to exercise a dominating influence on his emotional life. At this time, as well as during the course of previous separations, she taunted him by seeking him out to the point of getting him to come to bed with her, and then ignoring him for another man as soon as they started living together again. It was at this point that long-frustrated feelings were loosed in a violent and final termination of his wife's insidious hold.

Despite his life sentence and a nightmare of guilt, Spike obviously welcomed his forced removal from the unbearable tensions of his marital relationship. And, in view of the fact that he was diagnosed as a man of normal intelligence who was practically illiterate at the time of his commitment, he was encouraged to attend the institution school. This he did with an enthusiasm and motivation for personal achievement which earned him the equivalent of an eighth grade education in less than five years. He was subsequently transferred to a medium security institution geared toward fulfilling his social and vocational needs in a personally satisfying manner similar to that experienced by Mark Stout (see pp. 132-136).

This man, with understanding psychotherapy and subsequent consolidation of a renewed self-concept through an individually oriented vocational guidance program, has all of the inner fortification necessary for a successful adjustment in a free setting. In spite of an excellent adjustment and a good prognosis, however, he still has to hurdle the punitive demands of a biased public which knows him only as a potential threat to human life.

He is also faced with the unpredictable results of an intervening time span which, at best, has taken his "fatherless" children through all of the self-doubts and trials of an inescapable rejection over more than a decade of their most formative years. A succession of positive clinical evaluations, in conjunction with family counseling, "study-release," "work-release," and "halfway house" planning, will certainly help Spike to get out sooner than might otherwise have been possible. In the final analysis, however, "public policy" will dictate the time and conditions of the parole board's ultimate decision as a most important and primary consideration.

ACUTE FRUSTRATIONS NARROW "FREEDOM OF CHOICE" TO ONE ALTERNATIVE

Most murder offenses are committed under intense emotional pressure which has been building up over a period of many years.

The offender finds himself in a quandary wherein he seeks this violent outlet as the only possible form of release. The precipitating causes for a first offense involving first degree murder, however, rarely appear again, and a crime of this nature is seldom repeated.

In most cases, after the minimal 11 or more years preceding parole release, the need for violence is replaced by more diffuse interests, the constructive utilization of which parallels an advance in the offender's self-concept in association with his peers. That is to say, he has begun to see himself as a more competent person in a free world of people.

It is paradoxical, but nonetheless true, that the remorseful, self-condemning emotions of a "lifer" may be more conducive to an expansion of his true potential in the narrow confines of a prison than they are in the more normal, but confused selectivity, of a free setting. Spike's experience certainly attests to a form of self-realization which would never have been possible in the competitive tensions of the conflicting cultures from which he was removed.

THE NEED FOR NONCONFORMITY

Spike's refreshing example of self-sustaining achievement contrasts markedly with the indifferent, superficially conforming reactions of nearly 50 percent of our prison population. These are offenders who repeatedly commit crimes of forgery, larceny, burglary, robbery, and other property offenses because of a deeply ingrained emotional need to retain the identity of the social outcast or underdog. They thrive on a self-perpetuated form of "authoritative rejection and abuse" which serves to justify a chronically unchanged pattern of criminal behavior.

Actually, for this type of offender, the pressures of a competitive existence hold the unnamed dread of a rejected and lonely nonentity. He is repelled by the deflating mental image of a day-by-day lunch bucket routine, the signing of a weekly check which is less than might be realized on a family welfare dole, and the monotony of a socially exacting self-discipline which includes all of the "thanklessly boring" self-sacrifice of a "namby-pamby family man."

The excitement of crime, especially while in the company of another "underdog," provides a form of ego identification which is emotionally gratifying. It carries over in a mutually sensed bond of authoritative protestation which draws its strength from a common awareness of the fact that vital energies are helplessly trapped within the otherwise secure boundaries of their prison "home." Under these circumstances, it is no exaggeration to assume that our prisons provide an emotional solace between the gravitating extremes of a solicitous dependency fulfillment, on the one hand, and the time-avenging, crime-stimulating proclivities of many of our hoodwinking, chronic offenders, on the other.

The readjustment possibilities of a sizeable group of criminal offenders, therefore, remains unchanged because of the emotional satisfactions of a criminal culture which overshadow or outweigh the incentives toward the more demanding requirements of a socially conforming approach.

It is these "socially nonconforming prison conformists" who pressure other inmates with a contemptuous, "all-state" label for conscientious effort, and who utilize other indirect and underhanded ways of discrediting established procedures. They retain their criminal patterns because they have become most adept at convincing persons in authoritative positions of their desire for change, while at the same time offering every conceivable reason why the "system" has made it impossible for them to achieve this goal.

Most of these chronic offenders, although unwilling to adjust to the demands of a free society, are not dangerous in a deliberately harmful manner. That is, they usually find their emotional release in property offenses which tend to avoid any assaultive confrontation with people. The truly assaultive offenders, apart from the situational involvement of those convicted of first degree murder, have an underlying sadistic quality, the social and psychological roots of which are deeply enmeshed in the personality.

CONCLUSIONS

A comparison of those who are inclined to violent behavior points up a personality composition which is characterized by an interlocking or overlapping combination of the following traits:

1. To begin with, each shows evidence of rigid intellectual defenses, together with contrastingly immature emotions, which make for a markedly wide gap between the levels of intellectual and emotional growth. Whereas the offender's intellectual faculties may remain keenly intact, the quality of his judgment or reasoning powers under stress may be subject to the dictates of his grossly immature emotions.

2. Concurrent with this wide discrepancy between reasoning power and feeling level are the emotional frustrations resulting from the intellectual awareness of an unrealized potential, both academically and vocationally.

3. There is a tendency to withdraw, to bottle up feelings, and to permit only a cold, rationalistic approach to the more obvious circumstances surrounding the offense. The real reason, or the true emotional basis for the crime, is jealously guarded because of the unacceptable nature of the emotionally traumatic circumstances which precipitated the act.

The above qualities, of course, could apply to most any criminal offender in the average to superior brackets of intellectual abilities. It is the intensity of the frustration and the path taken by the hostility which makes the difference. There are, however, certain specific circumstances which appear to be most strongly associated with the need for a violent discharge of hostile feelings against another.

4. At the top of the list, we find that in practically every case there is a history of an affectionally indifferent and hostile father. He is often alcoholic, and inclined to severe measures of discipline, beginning frequently with harsh, derogatory attempts at curbing an enuretic condition in his son. These punitive tactics have fearful implications because of barbaric threats which can only add to the boy's inner tensions and consequent incapacity for voluntary control.

Along with this forced repression of a natural function, and with which the father himself may have had reason to be preoccupied in his growing years, is the need to belittle his son's masculine traits. At the same time, his neurotic mother strives to ease this deeply sensitive and verbally inexpressible hurt in a most aggravatingly deceptive and overly solicitous manner. The father seeks to assert his slipping authority in angry denunciations and further punitive controls, all of which add fuel to the triangular, father-mother-son conflagration, and effectively destroy any real relationship with his family.*

*These observations are the result of a long and painstaking review of the social and family backgrounds of a wide range of our most assaultive criminal offenders, most of whom had participated in both group and individual psychotherapy at the Wisconsin State Prison. The traumatic backgrounds and emotional needs of many of our most serious offenders were noted during the course of early diagnostic evaluations (see pp. 21-30), and the potentially explosive quality of these observations received more specific attention during the increasingly controversial years following the start of our group therapy experiment in 1951 (see pp. 67-90).

5. As a consequence of a confused identification, the boy grows up feeling deeply inadequate in his heterosexual contacts. He is often subject to homosexual panic reactions as a consequence of his prison confinement in close association with other emotionally disturbed, or socially distorted offenders.

6. A paranoid defense system is gradually inculcated in his make-up, and a hostile projection of blame thereby saves him from an intolerably deflating, face-to-face confrontation with his own hateful bundle of contradictions.

7. During the course of psychotherapy, one very personal fact is finally extracted with the painful reluctance of an abscessed molar. There is, in practically every instance, an early traumatic emotional experience—one which is usually laden with shocking sexual implications.

This fact emerges with the startling impact of an anxiety drenched revelation on the part of the offender as one who had himself been victimized in his early years. At first noncommittal, rejecting, and projective of blame, he is suddenly given a first vague look at himself as one who was compulsively driven toward a reversal of roles which made him the aggressor and another the victim. It is highly significant of the insidious emotional pressures with which he is faced, that his first victim is often one of an age level comparable with that he himself had reached at the time of his first serious emotional trauma.

8. He is inclined to react violently against anyone whose attitude and reaction tends to inflame his already frayed inferiority feelings with questions of doubt as to his personal integrity. His intense emotional reaction against this "underhanded" attempt to "cut him down" is a reflection of an ingrained sensitivity calling for a projection of accumulative feeling as a consequence of the absence of integrity in authoritative figures who took advantage of him in his preadolescent years.

It appears quite obvious from the foregoing, whether or not violent behavior is associated with a sex offense, that the tendency toward violence is inseparably linked with unacceptable sex problems. This does not mean, of course, that sex offenders are necessarily violent or vicious. There are those who, in a futile search for their lost identities, more or less compulsively follow a mild, nuisance form of sexual deviation. What it does mean, however, is that practically all of our most abhorrent and most bizarre capital offenses are committed by those with inherently conflicting, and persistently rejecting, problems in the sexual areas of their existence.

In the following chapter, we shall offer documentary evidence of this indignantly denied, and therefore generally unrecognized, core of violent and uncontrolled emotions. A true account of the painfully resistant and lengthy uncovering process experienced in a representative case history may provide clues as to the manner in which inherently vicious tendencies might be rechanneled into a more normally productive and self-satisfying existence.

Chapter 10

"I **MUST** TAKE THAT WHICH HAS NEVER BEEN MINE TO GIVE"

The power to give is one of those self-sustaining intangibles which make a man psychically secure in the lifelong battle to maintain emotional control and mastery over his own destiny. This is particularly true of his capacity to give love, the early deprivation of which can paralyze his function for a mutually satisfying heterosexual relationship.[6, 58, 59]

The resultant frustrations, when perpetuated by the deceptive manipulations of a vain, but authoritatively protected female, can create a vicious circle of repression following each new buildup of accumulative hostility. The pressure of this hostility, with all of the normal outlets plugged, first by the emotionally debilitating object of his affections, and then by the self-serving interests of authoritarian controls, must eventually explode into some form of violently unpredictable behavior.

Few people are aware of the compulsive needs of the rapist whose apparently vicious attacks may be the product of an undefined, deeply disturbing fear of rejection which he attempts to relive at an earlier, unresolved period of his emotional growth. Since his entire life has been geared to a need for repressing intense feelings, no one could know of the inner turmoil prompting him to seek mastery of himself in a situation which revives the unhealed hurts of his earlier years.

We repeatedly introject our own rationale into what we perceive as a sadistic and intolerable assault, assuming that this "predatory animal" is fully responsible for his behavior. We call him insensitive and animalistic, and once it has been shown that he knows the difference between right and wrong we tend to see him as a criminal who deliberately chose this mode of attack in order to satisfy an inherently perverse desire for sexual gratification.

This false perception is accentuated by the cool, almost serene countenance, and apparently remorseless disposition of the defendant in court. While stimulating a punitive, authoritarian reaction, it completely overlooks the fact that the offender has at this point a dire need to maintain his personal integrity with a callous outer veneer which belies the turbulent feelings underneath. Were it possible at this time to push him into a repentant admission of guilt, it is quite likely that his brittle characterological structure would shatter, and that the only alternative to a cool head and a massive denial of feeling would be one of total insanity.

There are also those who are deceptively cooperative, and whose subservient, almost grovelling concern over the atrocious nature of the offenses committed by them wins them a special recognition while obscuring the need for syphoning off the pervading hostility which poisons their emotional response to the opposite sex. This type of offender, to begin with, may show little in the way of personal initiative. He tends to adopt a passive, noncommittal approach to his problems, relying heavily on external facts and circumstances as an explanation of his difficulties.

Despite the vicious nature of his offense and the confused objectives which he displays, it is this latter offender who tends to be the best motivated of those whose inner conflicts and false fronts call for some form of psychotherapy. He is most receptive to a changed approach primarily because he has the strongest need to reach out for warmth and acceptance in his fellow man. He might also, however, be most difficult in terms of conflicting drives and a bland denial of hateful feelings. He is motivated in the sense that he appears to be sensitive to human needs and frailties, but equally difficult from the standpoint of his intense need to tighten the lid on a seething reservoir of hostility each time a test of his affectional resources fires up the "hot spots" in his makeup.

The extremely complicated and long-drawn process in reconciling these opposite poles in the offender's makeup are best demonstrated in the emotionally involved experiences of a chronic rapist. We may find in his repetitive offenses, under almost identical circumstances, both the early beginnings and the later need for a periodic discharge of violence in the form of his behavior disorder.

Joe Marvel was a light complectioned, handsome young man of 25 with wide-spaced blue eyes. He had a ready smile which curled the corners of his sensitive mouth into a dimpled expression of innocent good will. His mild manners and captivating smile conveyed an air of good-natured conformity which was very deceiving, and certainly out of context with the assaultive offenses of which he had been convicted. Although the court testimony and weight of evidence against him was indisputable, it was hard to believe that he was capable of rape, least of all the deliberate, stalking game which he played with helpless females whom he had observed from his car.

His method followed a set pattern, usually at midnight or in the early morning hours. He would spot a woman alone in her car while driving to her home in the suburbs of a large city after a late evening with relatives or friends. At this time of the night, of course, traffic was minimal, and unless there were obvious signs of trouble, no one was likely to stop to investigate a couple of parked cars at the side of the road. Joe had apparently developed the fine art of simulating the conscientious concern of a police official in plainclothes who just happened to notice something odd in the behavior of the car he was following.

Having spotted his quarry, he would wheel up behind the car with its lone passenger, blinking his lights rapidly, and then cutting around to the left side and waving the woman driver over to the shoulder of the highway. Then, on the pretense that she had a wobbly wheel, a sagging spring, or a loose tail pipe, he would direct her attention to the rear of the car, after which he would take her by the arm and assist her into his own car.

He would do this, presumably, for the purpose of taking her to a service station for help. Instead, he would drive quickly up a side road and force her to disrobe after parking in a secluded spot. Thereafter, he appeared to take great pleasure in ordering her every move in minute and sensuous detail, and in accordance with his wishes and desires of the moment.

He found something very stimulating about her cringing, fear-wrenched reaction. He somehow found himself to be much more potent, as well as much more relaxed, after forcing his emotionally paralyzed and numbly resistant victim into an act of sexual intercourse under threat of sudden death in the event that she did not comply. It was a glorious interlude, not because of any particular sexual gratification, but because his act was a sign to all womankind that he was the master. Somehow he had shown them all what it really meant to be "taken."

He slept soundly that night, but the next day a great fear crowded out these omnipotent feelings, and he found himself being goaded mercilessly into an aimless flight from prosecution. An overwhelming emotional reaction took possession of him, and in the midst of his disorganized thinking he left a clearly definable trail which led to his speedy apprehension.

Joe had a history of prior arrest on a burglary charge for which he had served a two-year probation term between the ages of 20 and 22. He also had a record of juvenile offenses, but, as frequently occurs with many other young offenders, the real motive underlying his delinquency was not probed beyond the surface indications of "proper" custodial care. This was especially true so long as he had shown himself capable of conforming to the imposed supervisory restraints of his probationary period.

A year after his last release from probation, he was arrested on what would appear to be a rehearsal of the type of offense which later resulted in his conviction under the sex crimes law. On this occasion, he accosted a woman in the early morning hours by blinking his lights in the manner described above. This was something of a trial run of later events in that he led the woman to believe that her car was in need of repair, and that he would assist her to a service station.

When she refused to join him in his car, he played a cat and mouse game for a time, returning twice within the next half hour after an apparently futile attempt at finding the help he had promised. He experienced a vicarious pleasure in finally persuading her to follow him slowly in her own car, even though she eluded him by turning in at the first service station where she quickly discovered that he had been deliberately misleading her.

He related this incident in the frank, but smugly self-satisfied manner of one who knew that he had given the woman little cause for any legal complaint. He had afforded her every opportunity to obtain his license number, and when arrested shortly thereafter, he was able to relate a convincing story of his own apparent misinformation and unsuccessful efforts to be of some help in a situation which "she appeared to have misinterpreted."

Joe was, in fact, a very convincing person, and he capitalized on this superficial, but highly advantageous quality to a degree which hardened his defenses against any actual penetration to the real person underneath. Whereas the particular charge against him was speedily dismissed, he had set the stage for his approach in the subsequent offense which was to become an established pattern of personal gratification against the unsuspecting female.

One might, however, question why he had again made the mistake of giving the woman an opportunity to memorize his license number, thereby providing law enforcing officials with an obvious lead to his arrest and ultimate conviction. But, at this point, one might also inquire into the strange mental gyrations and emotional needs of a highly narcissistic individual who actually phantasied his women victims as enjoying this type of forceful participation in the sex act.

Had the woman not reported him, he would have been convinced that she had obtained a certain perverted satisfaction from his aggressive assault. Even so, there was a strong element of doubt in his mind as to whether or not she was driven to report him out of a fear of pregnancy. And who could say that she was not reacting to a defensive need to protect herself against her own unconscious desires and "animalistic impulses?" His egocentric makeup would not, at this stage, permit a recognition of the essential qualities of warmth and understanding in the sexual union before any genuine response on the part of the female might be anticipated.

As it was, none of the more basically egocentric and hostile impulses against the female were admitted by Joe during the first year of his confinement under the treatment program. He had, in fact, persisted over a period of six months with a fabricated story about having recognized what he thought was an old friend in the car he was following. Upon realizing his mistake, according to the story which he had related at that time, it became necessary for him to explain his actions in a manner which would justify this type of behavior. So he "lied" to the woman about emergency repairs for her car; then found himself in the grips of an unspeakable anger toward her when she seemed to outwit him with a brand of deceptive resistance which revived the intensely hostile feelings long dormant in his makeup.

The fact that he had a mental capacity of better than average calibre did not promote a more rapid understanding, nor an increased awareness, of the true nature of his problems. Judging from the superficial quality of his self-evaluation, and the external pressures to which he attributed his impulsively aggressive acts, it would appear that quite the contrary was true.

He had previously spent many hours defending his position on the basis of a back injury which he said had conditioned him to assume a passive role in his marital relationship. It was his contention that he had thereby been deprived of a normally responsive attitude toward sex. He, however, enlarged on this passive relationship to a degree which emphasized an as yet unrecognized interest in the feminine role as a function of his own makeup.

He otherwise perceived his marital relationship as being constantly threatened by a dominating sister-in-law who exercised a great deal more influence over his wife than he himself was able to muster. Over a prolonged period, he attempted to maintain his rigid emotional controls by projecting his own deceptive nature into what he perceived as the hypocritical machinations of his wife and in-laws. Since it was not possible for him to admit the pressure of an accumulative hostility over which he feared a complete loss of control, he directed all of his energies into the maintenance of a personable veneer of congeniality and social conformity.

His subtle flatteries and practiced manipulations for personal advantage had the desired effect, as they had on innumerable occasions when he assumed the role of the underdog. He, thereby, "merited" the attention of those at whose hands he was again suffering an intense affectional deprivation. In all aspects of the treatment program, he gave the impression of being fully cooperative and acceptant of his psychotherapeutic needs. His keen "intellectual understanding" of his own shortcomings, and his apparent willingness to concede his mistakes, overshadowed the underlying ugliness of his feelings to the extent of promoting his release on parole within a period of two years and seven months.

One might list the gains which he had made prior to his first release in the following order:

1. He had shown himself to be extremely well motivated in the direction of verbalizing his difficulties in both individual and group therapy sessions.

2. There was persistent evidence of a keen "intellectual insight" with respect to both his own problems and those of others with whom he had been interacting in the group therapy sessions.

3. He had at all times shown himself to be a skillful and dependable worker in the institution metal industry, and there were consistent indications of his willingness to help others in their vocational endeavors.

4. He appeared to be capable of realistic parole planning, and his expressed intentions with respect to both his interpersonal and family relationships suggested an attitude in marked contrast to the earlier psychosomatic complaints which tended to disguise his true feelings.

THE FIRST CONFRONTATION OF NEGATIVES BEHIND A "POSITIVE" FRONT

Despite all of his "commendable" motivation and conforming performance within the confines of the institution, Joe's violent reversion to sexually deviated behavior within less than six months of his parole release provided equally strong evidence of the fact that the inner core of feeling responsible for his vicious assault had actually never been penetrated. The first psychiatric review following his return to the sex crimes treatment facility pointed up "a strong capability for acting out under pressure of significant stress situations despite an increased self-understanding and more appropriate ways of coping with emotional problems."

Three months later, after the initial shock of his recommitment had worn off and Joe was again seriously involved in the treatment program, a new psychiatric evaluation by another psychiatric consultant focused on the "pseudo-psychiatric schizophrenic" reaction which this man presented in times of stress. This, as well as the earlier psychiatric appraisal, had described the offender as one who presented the intellectual and psychological potential for significant progress, but whose conflicting feelings in the sexual area had obviously not been worked through.

A consensus of opinion in the most recent staffing evaluation concluded with a recommendation that the offender be confronted more directly with the self-defeating nature of his manipulative tendencies, and that he be made to realize the futility of his otherwise bland emotional response. The primary goal at this time was one of "provoking whatever evidence of depression, anxiety, or hostility might be made manifest in this individual, pending a more advanced level of personality integration and control."

He subsequently became intensively involved in two therapy groups, one of which retained his original therapist, while the other introduced a dual therapeutic role which forced his attention on both the positive and the negative aspects of his group participation. It is significant that the independent evaluations of his response to each therapeutic situation after a two year interval suggested some very meaningful changes in terms of a more profound emotional awareness, and a much more honest appraisal of his own feelings.

Faced as he was with the negative aspects of each "positive" attempt at winning acceptance for his "unusual insights" and outwardly conforming nature, he had gradually become less verbal, and, likewise, much more uncomfortable in his reaction. He finally reached a point wherein he was able to concede, or at least consider the likelihood, of what the psychiatrist had termed "an amazing capacity for seductiveness and manipulation of others." By his own admission, he had for the first time become aware of the self-defeating manner in which his own emotionally insincere and deceptive nature "might have been projected" against his wife and in-laws.

On the heels of this much more intimate concern with his own feelings also came the recognition of his underlying passivity and fears of aggression at the hands of others. This new awareness, in turn, served to dissipate the smoke screen behind which he had concealed a hated self-concept of diminutiveness, along with frightful homoerotic phantasies, a loss of virility in his heterosexual contacts, and a pervading sense of failure.

Up to this point, insight and understanding as one normally perceives this development in the psychotherapeutic process had actually never penetrated the tough shell of a seductively pleasing and outwardly conforming disposition. Underneath his mild mannered, deceptively cooperative veneer was the emotional buildup of an intensely hostile counterreaction to an otherwise strongly defended, but unacceptable passive-dependent need.

Joe had, of course, offered hints of these conflicts at the very beginning when he described the panic reactions which he had experienced because of "hospital smells" to which he was subjected when confined with a back injury and the prospect of major surgery. But it wasn't until his second commitment under the sex crimes law that he was able to admit the true nature of the panic he had experienced while confined as a hospital patient. There was genuine tension and anxiety in his initial attempts at letting go of this vital segment of feeling.

It began with his request for a special individual session for the purpose of discussing a matter of grave importance to him. Even after this preliminary admonishment of something which he could not bring out during the course of the group discussions, Joe continued to stall until just before the end of the hour. Then, hesitantly, and after a painful circumvention of this mountainous problem, he told how he had suffered a rupture at age 16 while trying to convince his foreman that he was capable of doing a man's work.

As he explained it, a section of his intestines had dropped down into the space occupied by one of his testicles. He went on to tell how his intense self-consciousness about this occurrence had caused him to hide his discomfiture to the extent of avoiding medical attention for the ensuing three or four years. At age 19, a painful infection finally forced him to seek medical advice, and when admitted to a veteran's hospital he was subjected to surgical removal of the infected testicle which doctors feared might develop into a cancerous growth.

At the hospital ward which he occupied with several older patients, he said that he was teased by nurses and patients alike as "One Hung Lo." He admitted to having left the hospital three days after surgery as a result of this teasing, and he contended that upon his return home, his father, aunt, and uncle continued to tease him in the same manner. He said that he refused to go back to a doctor for further observation, and even removed the surgical stitches himself. He then returned to work much earlier than medical advice would dictate, and with the resultant debilitative effects on his physical and emotional well-being.

It is very significant of the traumatic aspects of this hospital experience that an entire year had elapsed since his recommitment on a new sex offense before Joe was able to talk about his surgery. In view of his prior extensive psychotherapeutic exposure, and what appeared to be an honest attempt at resolving his difficulties, his bland avoidance of the emotional implications of an operation which he had earlier vaguely dismissed as a back injury was quite inexplicable.

That is to say, that he, himself, was unable to offer any reason as to why he had kept this climacteric event hidden from his therapists. His intense blocking in this area did, however, emphasize the acute nature of the castration fears and associated masculine insufficiency to which he was subject. It became quite evident, also, that his quick smile and generally pleasant, subservient demeanor camouflaged a great deal of tightly controlled hostility of which even his most intimate family members were unaware.

The rigid moral expectations and deceptive interactions of an emotionally inhibited family relationship may, in fact, be as conducive to the development of a false front as they are repressive of any genuine expression of feeling. That is why it is so important for the therapist not only to tolerate but to encourage the expression of otherwise hatefully avoided negative feelings. These feelings, in other words, must be spasmodically, and in most cases unpleasantly, unleashed in a controlled, clinical setting before any positive reconstitution of the personality can take place.

The first real measure of progress in the offender under treatment is in the strength of his need to share the weight of his tremendous emotional burden with his therapist. At this point he has obviously developed some degree of trust in his own inner resources and capacity for acceptable behavior. For some, this initial extension of trust never materializes. For many others, however, the first impetus in the direction of self-confidence and a relaxation of tension emanates from the warm atmosphere of unexpected tolerance and understanding helpfulness in which the offender's defensive manipulations are viewed by his therapist.

This avenue of approach, for the reason that it avoids any authoritative condemnation in favor of an unbridled group interaction, tends to encourage and applaud a verbally spontaneous release of feeling as an end in itself. At the same time, it does not deny a man his right to silence or withdrawal pending a future more timely, or more appropriate, encounter of his own choosing. In any event, a later release of emotionally charged, "top-secret" material must run the gauntlet of mood swings and behavioral reactions in which the offender is often calling for help in a weak, almost inaudible voice, while at the same time seemingly smothering this call in a brash, strident bid for rejection.

Chapter 11

A BRIMMING WELL OF HOSTILITY SUBSIDES
IN HONESTLY SHARED FEELINGS

IF THE offender's experimental attempts at fitting himself to a more acceptable role are to survive, his conflicting feelings and irritating moods must be recognized for what they are in the cathartic framework of a necessary emotional release. It is a time when the therapist's own frustration tolerance meets its greatest test, since all of the offender's negative feelings may, for a time, be focused against him. It is during these periods of apparent nonconformity, involving depressed moods and a sullen, self-defeating hostility, that the therapist must be on the alert for that fleetingly minute, but positive need which is looking for room in which to grow.

Let us trace the development of this muffled and emotionally distant cry for help, beginning with our ambivalent offender's totally manipulative reaction at the time of his recommitment. He, at first, voiced a disinterest in the treatment program as in any way beneficial to him, since he contended that any and all incentives which he might have toward uncovering and reviewing previously unacceptable emotional needs were being neutralized by the repressive prison milieu to which he was being subjected.

He, furthermore, stated that it should be obvious to everyone that his earlier release had been poorly timed, and that his return to an area where his marital conflicts were reinforced to an intolerable degree was evidence of poor judgment on the part of the parole planning staff. At the same time, he did not deny his own insistent clamoring for release at the earliest possible moment, and to a place which would enable him to prove his worth to his ex-wife and minor children.

His admitted recognition of the contradictory nature of these statements, however, did not lessen the bitterness of his attack against the prison as a treatment milieu. But the martyred intensity of his arguments, together with a certain polite subservience in his tone, commanded an impressive audience. It is significant that, despite a second premeditated assault against helpless females, he had the committing judge, as well as the district attorney and his defense lawyer, all involved in a futile search for alternative treatment commitments in a state hospital environment prior to his final return to the only available treatment facility for sex offenders in a prison setting.

For the first few months following his return, Joe continued to reject personal responsibility by emphasizing adverse environmental pressures as precipitating causes for his reversion to deviated criminal behavior. At the same time, he saw himself as one who was once again being deprived of an intense need for individual attention in a relaxed hospital atmosphere. This "ideal" therapeutic milieu he perceived as the antithesis of that in which he was presently confined. He, nonetheless, made regular requests for individual sessions, and when offered the opportunity for a new, and perhaps younger therapist, he somewhat anxiously hinted that there were personal matters which he would prefer to discuss with someone like myself who was already familiar with his sordid background.

Gradually, the pressure of external circumstances was replaced by a new set of values which took cognizance of the far-reaching effects of his internal conflicts. He began expressing a great deal of concern for a new girlfriend whose acquaintance he had made during the eight-month-period of his release to a free setting. He admitted being very much shaken up over the sentiments expressed in valentines which he received, especially since it didn't seem logical to him that the girl and her family should be so considerate of his welfare in view of what had happened.

It was then that he recognized the true circumstances of the "Dr. Jekyll and Mr. Hyde" existence which he had been leading. He saw how he had been placing the girlfriend on a pedestal as one who was untouchable, while at the same time giving vent to aggressively debased and sexually degrading behavior against what he perceived as intolerably sophisticated and promiscuous females.

At this point, Joe was asked whether or not he wasn't again seeking a haven from unbearable tensions and frustrations which he had encountered in a free setting. He had indicated earlier that the act of driving an automobile alone and over long distances was in itself relaxing to him, but that he had no longer found himself able to dissipate the wrenching emotional effects of repressed marital tensions in this manner.

He saw some pathological significance in the fact that, just prior to marriage, he had had sexual intercourse with his wife in her car, and that she had thereafter used sex as a weapon to manipulate and to control him in accordance with her personal needs. He was, at the same time, torn by a sense of loyalty and obligation toward an "ideal" father-in-law, who, because of his own passively inadequate role in the marital relationship, appeared to be quite sympathetic and understanding of his son-in-law's predicament.

Despite what he regarded as a profound intellectual insight into his emotional problems, Joe was beginning to recognize how the confused marital picture and multiple choice situation with which he was confronted had interfered with the proper application of his new awareness in a free setting.

There was at this point, also, a glimmering of insight into his pervading lack of self-confidence and nonacceptance of personal responsibility in the role of a husband and a father. There was even some fleeting recognition of an inner driving force—a function of his own makeup—which had been propelling him into the much more secure, but dependent role of a social outcast in a noncompetitive prison environment.

In contrast to his habitually bland and seductively amiable manner of response, Joe had begun to show evidence of feeling, the hostile implications of which had heretofore been completely foreign to the "milksop" character which he had presented to the outer world. It became very apparent that there were certain aspects of his feeling which he had never been able to express, and that he had actually been attempting to convey what his subservient early conditioning had told him was the anticipated response. His intense need for acceptance behind a mild mannered exterior would allow for no show of the depraved abnormality which he feared that others might sense in the turbulent feelings to which he was subject.

He, for example, perceived himself as so "far out" in his feelings compared with those of the average person that he spent a great deal of time and energy attempting to adapt his rape offense so as to conform with a sexual gratification motive which was nonexistent in terms of any real stimulation. Actually, he was experiencing a degree of tension which had much more far-reaching effects, and which was centered primarily in his intense feelings of rejection by members of the opposite sex. While admitting that his reasoning had been faulty, he could not divorce himself from the feeling that close contact with women made him vulnerable to a deceptive form of feminine manipulation at the expense of his own capacity for self-assertion and control over his impulses.

Once the importance of this concept was given the emotional consideration it deserved, the focus on repressed angry feelings became much more pertinent. He gave a dramatic account of the bind in which he had found himself as a consequence of his wife's "insidious" manipulation of his inherent passivity to the advantage of his in-laws. He told how he was being "used" under threat of having his sexual needs rejected by his wife in the event that he did not comply. His paunchy, and otherwise medically restricted brother-in-law had only to put on a "big brother" act with his own family, and Joe's inadequate emotions would be wrung dry with the need for supplying this parasitical relative with the benefit of his services.

Joe's lifelong conflict, which one might generalize as an intense need for dependency gratification as opposed to incompatible masculine strivings, was demonstrated time after time in the frustrating circumstances of his family contacts and interpersonal relationships. On one occasion, his wife's brother, instead of appealing to him directly, asked his sister to persuade her husband of her family's need for someone to advise them about a new roof which they were planning to put on their home over the weekend. Joe had made plans for a long anticipated hunting trip at this particular time, but because of his wife's pleas, and because he felt guilty for not responding to what appeared to be a genuine need, he finally agreed to renounce these "selfish" interests in order to help his brother-in-law.

As it developed, however, Joe arrived at his in-laws' house on the following morning to discover that no one was up, and since the shingles were available, he began doing the job himself. Later, members of the family called him in for a cup of coffee, at which time his brother-in-law yawningly admitted to having bet his brother that he could get his sister to talk Joe into helping him out.

At this point, Joe explained how his smoldering anger had brimmed over. He told of a nauseatingly hot, prickly sensation on his face and down the back of his neck, followed by a stabbing pain at the base of his spine. He admitted that, instead of "telling them off" and getting rid of his feelings directly, he had squirmed painfully out of his chair and leaned speechless for a moment with hands clutching the edge of the table. He related how his in-laws hovered around offering advice and support which he as quickly refused with a shake of his head. Then, with all of their belated sympathies and solicitous apologies following him out of the door, he described how he had tucked his drooping form behind the wheel of his car and drove home.

Now, in a quiet rage over his wife's cool reaction to his whipped appearance, he found himself in petulant agreement with her practical suggestion that he remain home with the children while she did the family shopping. Meanwhile, his seething hostility was being fanned to a white heat with the realization that he had not only forfeited his cherished hunting plans, but had made himself an unacceptable husband as well as a spineless fool in the eyes of his wife and her family.

At the time, he was completely unaware of his obsessive need to relive a life of early affectional deprivation in the role of a neglected and abused child. In this role, and throughout his formative years, he had become very adept in the art of counteracting deception with his own brand of wide-eyed innocence and deceptive good will. It was only when the authenticity of this unnatural cover was challenged by his fellow inmates—rape offenders like himself—that the volcanic sore spot in his makeup began to erupt with a more genuine expression of feeling.

It emerged in response to a simple question from another parole violator toward the close of a group session in which Joe had been particularly proficient in the exercise of his intellectually descriptive powers. Joe was asked to state honestly and truthfully whether he was really sincere or whether he had practiced some form of deception to make himself look so good at the time of his last parole release.

The question left Joe speechless and completely noncommittal behind the blandly innocuous and innocent smile which had become something of a trademark with him in similar touchy situations. It, nonetheless, carried a tremendous emotional impact, since a few days later he was forced by sleepless nights to request a special individual session in an attempt at resolving the gnawing anxiety which this breakdown in his lifelong defense system had created.

THE LAST DECEPTIVE BARRIER SUCCUMBS TO A RECEPTIVE AUDIENCE

The doubts which other group members had entertained with respect to Joe's sincerity were freely aired in subsequent sessions, and faced as he was with a need to regain acceptance from an entirely different point of view he began to unlock the nightmarish corridors of memories which until this moment had effectively blocked an expression of his true self.

This soul-shaking effort had all the agonies of a purge, and before he had finished he had soaked the faded seams of his khaki shirt several times with the dammed up feelings of his boyhood years. He first told of the emphasis which had been placed on sex by his three athletic brothers, four to eight years older than himself. The three stood apart from Joe in both age and temperament, and he recalled the diabolical finesse with which they had introduced him to the "masculine need for sexual potency and conquest" in their dealings with the female.

As is frequently the case, the gravity of the emotional conflict which Joe developed in the sexual area of his existence was greatly accentuated by the provocative attitudes of a younger sister in contrast to the prohibitive reaction of his puritanical mother. He spent hours straining against the verbal expression of these intense feelings before he finally revealed the traumatic incidents associated with elements of incestuous guilt and high potency needs in the role of a virile and dominant male.

It was like a child touching a hot stove, the frightened withdrawal from which called for consolation and reassurance at the emotional level from which it originated. The other group members, all of whom had become increasingly aware of the need for releasing their own childish emotions, sensed the tumultuous feeling against which Joe was laboring, and patiently allowed him the time and understanding which had never been his during his formative years.

The feeling poured out in clipped, disorganized phrases between spurts of tears and defiant, self-castigating attempts at recovering his composure. It caused eyes to glisten with the reflected intensity of a growing avalanche of feeling—the honest expression of which had until this moment been sidetracked to the dark, cobwebby reaches of his hated past.

In tremulously short, disjointed sentences, Joe told of his futile attempts at matching up to his father's expectations of a man with the physical strength and muscular coordination of his three older brothers. He felt somehow shortchanged, since they were all built like his father, whereas he had inherited the delicate features and soft-toned physique of his mother.

The older boys seemed to enjoy his frightened reaction to their brash demands, and there were times, Joe apprehensively admitted, when they forced him into a type of "sex education" which they said he needed in order to become a "man of the world." This "sex education" involved all of the forms of homosexual involvement which the imagination could conjure, followed by a visit to a house of prostitution at the age of 15 when he found himself, and what he had been taught to regard as a most vital organ, paralyzed with fear.

Later, after he had enlisted in the Marine Corps and again visited a house of prostitution while on a home furlough, the woman who examined him callously referred to the missing testicle as "half a man is better than no man at all." Shaking with emotion, Joe recalled his sudden relapse into an uncontrollable rage which prompted him to beat the woman unmercifully until she was lying on the bed bleeding and unconscious. He then threw all of the money he had in his wallet, about 60 dollars in bills, onto the bed beside her and left without checking to see how badly she may have been hurt.

The next morning, Joe slept late after a sleepless night waking up to find that his mother had taken his rumpled clothes down to the basement to be laundered. Later that day, he returned to his room to discover that she had extracted a pack of condoms from his pocket, separating them one by one from their wrappings, and severing each through the middle with a scissors. He found them arranged in an orderly row, with the matching cuts like pieces of a jigsaw puzzle, on the snow-white cover of his neatly made bed.

Not one word, he said, was ever spoken by his mother regarding this incident, and to this day he is not aware as to whether or not she had informed his father. He had, however, from that moment been continually aware of an insatible rage, the intensity of which he also realized that he must never allow to get out of control with "decent" women, including his mother, whose love he needed and cherished.

So, beginning with his mother and ending with his wife, he could never permit himself anything but an expression of the passive conforming qualities which were so foreign to his inner nature, but at the same time so necessary to the retention of his affectional needs. As it was, he experienced unbearable tensions of an intensely fearful nature whenever he came close to revealing the violent quality of his overwhelming anger.

At this point, Joe was able to talk freely of a pet collie which had accompanied him on his solitary walks in the woods, and with which he had apparently identified in terms of an unusually sensitive but otherwise helplessly dependent and subservient nature during his preadolescent years. It pleased him and gave him strength to realize that the dog dutifully obeyed all of his changing moods; that it kept following him about no matter how angry or rejecting he would sometimes become in an apparent rehearsal of things he would like to do to members of his family who had hurt him so much.

Throughout his early adolescent years, there was a camaraderie with this animal which he could never match with any of the more "communicable" members of his family. There was something in the dog's alert manner and blind obedience to his commands which took much of the pain and suffering out of the guilty relationship which he had experienced with his sensuous older brothers, a deceptively flirtatious younger sister, and a castrating mother whose witch-like qualities he sought to control in the passive-dependent manner of a whipped child.

These were tender years, but he vividly recalls standing just outside the kitchen window at age 13 and listening to his father's complaints to his mother about the extra cost of keeping the dog. He was speaking sharply of the need for ridding themselves of this extra care, as well as bringing Joe to a realization of his responsibilities about the house.

Listening with his cheek pressed hard against the outer wall, Joe heard his father condemn the long walks which he had been taking in the woods, belittling him as a weakling and a sissy who could never do anything right, and who would never grow up with the "he-man" qualities of his three older brothers. Then, with poignant clarity, he heard his father's voice rise with the finality of his decision to sell Joe's pet collie to a visiting cattle buyer who was looking for "a real working dog."

His mother protested mildly, but without conviction, and with the obvious fear of provoking his father's hair trigger temper on the touchy question of her youngest son's affectional needs. Even in the anxiety and confusion of his thoughts at that moment, Joe knew that his mother could never appreciate the intensity of his yearning for love and understanding as a boy who so much wanted to be recognized with the qualities of a man like his father and three older brothers.

Later that day, after his father had returned to work on farm machinery with which he would never trust his young son in the field, Joe's mother indulgently, and as he perceived it, somewhat guiltily, slipped him an extra piece of his favorite blueberry pie. She patted his head and added a dip of homemade ice cream, all of which he bolted with the ravenous appetite of one who was making a desperate, but futile attempt to fill the aching hollow in his stomach.

Finally, in a blind wordless rage, the self-destructive aspects of which he was at that time completely unaware, Joe took his pet far into the woods and commanded him to assume an attitude of pensive supplication with his head between his soft, white tipped paws. It was an old act in a familiar setting—one which he had performed many times before.

Only this time his feelings were much more painfully intense, and goaded by his inner revolt against a picture of helpless dependence he impulsively swung his boy scout hatchet in a blow which split the animal's skull into a writhing mass of matted flesh and bone. At that moment, deprived of his only friend and boyhood companion, he compressed all of his anger, along with his intense affectional needs, into the warped mold of a boy who felt irrevocably betrayed by his loved ones in a hostile, adult world.

It was here that he first learned to match betrayal with betrayal, telling his father that the dog had run away while relishing an inward satisfaction in the knowledge that, since he was not permitted to have the pleasure of the dog's company, no one else would have it either.

A reversal of roles developed with an unconscious but insidious certainly throughout his formative years, and to a point wherein he eventually perceived his wife, and finally his respected father-in-law, as deceptively manipulative of his energies for the purpose of advancing their own personal advantage. Because he could not tolerate the consequences of his intense anger toward those who were closest to him, he struck out blindly against strange women whose self-sufficient manner and "dominating emotional controls" he had an obsessive need to reduce to the sexually degrading and subservient level of his boyhood phantasies.

His awareness of these phantasies as an integral part of his adult life provided the emotional perspective he needed for a more self-confident and realistic control over his impulses. Before this goal could be reached, however, it was necessary for him to peel off layer after layer of deceptive conformity, each section of which exposed a well of hostility and counteracting submissiveness with which he attempted to salve his flayed emotions. He did this through many ups and downs of discouragingly unpredictable moods, all of which were weathered in the receptive climate of emotionally interacting peers who had, as a consequence, become more and more excitingly aware of similar problems in their own frustrating experiences.

Finally, after the last hostile artesian had been tapped, all the way from his castrating hospital experience to the death agonies of his earliest and most prized affectional source, Joe was able to relax in the tender awareness of a genuine sincerity which obtained its strength from his recognition and eventual acceptance of his lifelong veil of pretense. He now had a firm grip on a form of emotional reconditioning through which he might acquire and offer a measure of love which he had previously felt an overwhelming compulsion to wrench from his victims.

CONCLUSIONS

On the basis of many similar examples of violent criminal behavior, it would appear that all have a common bond in personality characteristics which at this time might be highlighted as follows:

1. Each is subject to an early instilled sensitivity to ridicule, and to a deeply ingrained need for the violent expulsion of an uncom-

fortably prolonged sense of inferiority. As a result of this deeply entrenched sensitivity, and because of the early feelings of rejection which the juvenile offender has suffered at the hands of his father, or father substitute, his own defensive need to reject becomes more intense.

The underlying dynamics responsible for the violent discharge of an accumulative hatred build up gradually until they reach explosive proportions toward all men who pose a threat to the offender's identity as a competent person.

2. There are indications in each offender of morbidly regressive oral preoccupations hinging on a sense of emptiness as a consequence of an early instilled affectional deprivation in his preadolescent period. Unresolved dependency strivings are, therefore, an integral part of his emotional life, as is also the underlying, and often perverted need for a maternally protective spouse. The clinging circumstances of this otherwise psychoanalytically abused maternal fixation concept are obviously incompatible with a heterosexually satisfying experience.

3. For many criminal offenders who have committed vicious acts against their fellow man, there is a contrastingly sentimental attachment for dogs and other sensually receptive and faithfully submissive animal pets. This may be because of the passive dependent identification which this otherwise affectionately compliant creature provides in the midst of a lonely and isolated existence.

4. In practically all cases, there is a deep-seated fear of authoritarian figures because of some unnamed, insidious threat originating in early, painfully repressed, childhood experiences. There is a marked tendency, then, to gravitate toward peer associations with mutual feelings of rejection, bitterness, and loneliness. The defensive resistance against authoritative controls is thereby strengthened by this common need for sharing a hostile, criminal identity.

5. Underlying all hostile, criminal behavior is a paranoid projection of deceptive attitudes which tend to be exaggerated and continually fortified by a negative transference of similar situations and experiences. The deceptive attitudes of authoritarian figures, especially those which are first encountered in the conflicting, self-serving devices of incompatible parents, may be regarded as the earliest implanted emotional seeds of violence.

6. The continued emphasis on a form of prison security which

denies or represses the criminal offender's need for a substitute release of his violent feelings operates on the same principle as the earlier, abusive restraints of a rejecting father. An emotionally restrictive and dependency fostering prison is, in fact, a massive, socially acceptable enlargement of the father prototype, wherein the father was driven to further rejection of his son because of the boy's dependency upon the overly protective attentions of a masculine depriving mother. The prison, thereby, rejects the very problem which it has, through gross misunderstanding, worked so hard to create.

We must, of course, bear in mind the fact that the foregoing six points involve the "constants" in a wide band of subjective psychological evaluations, intermingled with an extensive but otherwise select array of objective observations. These conclusions can be realistically substantiated only through a patiently knowledgeable and painstaking research procedure. They represent what would appear to be pertinent overall generalizations which may or may not apply to the complex personal histories, ever changing circumstances, and intricate emotional pressures inherent in certain individual cases. The illustrated facts, conclusions, and generalizations herein stated, however, may hopefully provide a working hypothesis for the eventual resolution of many unknowns in criminal conduct. They may be particularly helpful as a starting point in the constructive exposure of that subtly concealed, underlying drive which precipitates viciously unpredictable criminal acts.

At this point, correctionally informed thinking people realize that unless the rigid disciplinary requirements of authoritarian controls can be reconciled with a genuinely human, emotional "safety valve" for the harmless release of "bad" feelings, a vicious cycle of hostile, criminal behavior is likely to continue in an ever widening and unpredictable manner. The solution, of course, is one wherein both clinical and custodial personnel are able to agree on ways of halting the chain reaction of a punishing form of rejection, the coldly aloof, rule-centered aspect of which has been erroneously appraised as a most effective measure in the "deterrence of crime."

This punitive rejection implicitly denies any innate good or basic competence behind the overt expression of hostile feelings. As it is, it can only stimulate more subtle ways of expressing more intense forms of rejection on the part of the criminal offender, and once again, more authoritative demands for controls under which he is to be still more rigidly enjoined.

If criminal behavior is to diminsh in the forcefulness of its ever present potential for a violent release of feeling, punitive controls, as we know them, must give way to a coordinated awareness of the offender's dire need for a self-elevating, counteracting form of emotional release. Only then will he be enabled to advance toward a full realization of his true potential, and a consequent lessening of his need to rebel in the form of criminal behavior.

Chapter 12

THE EMERGENCE OF A WHOLE MAN

THE start of a new decade, with growing indications of prison uprisings and riots culminating in horrifying spectacles of violence, first at San Quentin, California (August 21, 1971), and then at Attica, New York (September 13, 1971), have brought the myopic ineffectiveness of our rehabilitative structure into an agonizingly indefensible focus. There are many questions in regard to prison custodial problems alone for which we have nothing but highly controversial answers.

By what desperate need, for example, might the rebel inmates at Attica have been motivated to face a violent death, or at best a more drastic tightening of security controls, after refusing concessions which granted 28 and denied only two of their most unrealistic and unreasonable demands? What was lacking after every effort to negotiate a reasonable solution for the safe release of hostages had failed?

Why, after four days of conflicting feelings and accumulated tensions in the stalemated, inmate-custodial confrontation at Attica, did the final, apparently indiscriminate shooting which resulted in the deaths of ten hostages and 29 inmates become necessary? Three inmate victims, whose bodies exhibited the vicious, multiple stabbings of an apparent psychopathic killer, were earlier discovered outside the inmate controlled cell block area. Did the horror of this situation precipitate exaggerated reports of castration mutilations and throat slashings resulting in the subsequent incitement to a violent termination of the ordeal? What effect did the "observers'" emotional appeal for amnesty and a "third-world" safe passage to a "nonimperialistic country" have on the psychopathic leadership then in control of the inmate revolt? Was the armed assault by law enforcing authority carried out too early or too late, and what might have prevented the buildup of this explosive situation in the first place?

These questions, as well as those involving many other related issues, have no easy answers. All that we know for certain is transfixed in the hindsight of widely diverse alternatives, any one of which we might select as better than that which was followed. In the comfortable seclusion of our own thoughts, we "know" what might have been the "best" alternative, since we were in a position to view from afar the tragic results of unreasoning tensions in the grip of a venomous emotional upheaval. We know because we saw both the urgency and the tragedy of the authoritative need which took the lives of "helpless" individuals, while the reputation and respect of a necessarily secure corrections system was at stake.

We know, too, that a costly riot, like a series of fatal highway accidents at a particular location (and with many times the emotional impact), is the most frequent precipitating circumstance, or final impetus, to a radically revised approach. Any tragic happening, the hazardous, but seemingly preventable circumstances of which are, thereby, readily observable, tends to solidify the forces of conflict and controversy into a unified demand for corrective measures.

As in most prisons at one time or another, we may draw, by way of illustration, a significantly analogous situation from the annals of our own familiar correctional setting. The Wisconsin State Prison riot of January, 1944, for example, brought a discreet exposure, and a sudden halt, to underlying corrupt practices in which special favoritism had become rampant. Several of the more sophisticated, highly intelligent institution-wise inmates had been assigned to key positions and internally manipulative clerical functions in exchange for a "smooth-operating" institution. This practice, of course, invited hatefully condoned, stool-pigeon tactics and the perverted vices of those who knew how, when, and where emotional pressures might be utilized to the best advantage, and in accordance with their own egocentric needs.

It was not at all unusual for a political hierarchy to have developed among the inmate body at this time which encouraged deceptive manipulation, on the one hand, and total submissiveness, or a spiritless conformity, on the other.

The riot changed all of this so that the ringleaders were exhaustively screened and segregated. Individual privileges were subsequently curbed or rigidly regulated, the prison magazine as a vehicle of inmate expression was thrown out, and a new prison security system based on the findings of a classification board with respect to maximum, close, medium, or minimum custodial needs was devised. The far-reaching, but highly manipulative inmate grievance committee, for which the uninformed, but idealistically motivated businessman director of the state welfare department had had high hopes, was completely wiped out (see pp. 24-25). Each individual offender was now, supposedly, in a position to voice his own special needs, and to stand "straight and tall" on his own two feet.

As it developed, however, individual hopes for a true expression of their inmate needs in a prison environment were now repressed more than ever. Instead of meriting any of the rioting demands for bargaining privileges on an inmate's most vital questions relating to food, clothing, medical attention, visiting rights, working conditions, and parole "discrimination," they were now restricted more than ever.

For many years to come, individual needs were, on the whole, subordinated to the custodial requirements of the institution which emphasized the sharp-eyed, mistrustfully alert guard status in an amply justified, protective authoritarian role. Individually meaningful hobby outlets and consequent independent, mind stimulating activity was generally denied as too threatening to the primary function of protection and security for which the warden took credit as the "staunch captain" of a "tight ship."

Gradually, however, following this initial punitive reaction, came the swing to a more enlightened approach which paralleled the expansion of probation and parole services to include many for whom prison would have been the only alternative. It accompanied a much more dynamic reorganization of the overall public welfare function into separate divisions for which a progressive administration appointed several young and enthusiastically capable administrative heads.

Spurred by a new flexibility in this coordinated attempt at alleviating a rigidly entrenched penal system, the new head of the corrections division emphasized the need for more highly trained custodial officers. At the same time, he strove for more practical ways of offering necessary academic and vocational training to the inmate population.

In the aftermath of the 1944 riot, an attempt was made to assimilate the overall needs of the institution with those of the offender. The new warden, former head of the probation and parole services, was nearing retirement. He functioned as a temporary replacement for the regular warden who was on leave with the armed forces of World War II. The former had, for personal reasons, and in accordance with the individualistic incentives of all new administrative heads, a need to institute noticeable elements of change in the relatively short space of time alloted to him.

On the unusually profound assumption that we tended to be victims of a fad with the pendulum swinging to the far right or to the left depending on which rehabilitative approach happened to be in vogue, he considered the entire matter as one of a global need which should embrace the positive qualities of both extremes.

THE MISSING SUPPORT IN A THREE-LEGGED REHABILITATIVE PLATFORM

The new warden introduced the analogy of the "three-legged stool," each leg representing the educational-vocational, clinical-social, and moral-religious legs of a program which he concluded should be emphasized simultaneously. He perceived the inmate as responding to each of these three phases of his program in a manner which would give him at least a minimum basis for adjustment in a free setting.

The institution school had, of course, been in operation for the benefit of interested persons on a limited basis over a period of many years. The need for work, likewise, and despite the fact that it was geared to the needs of the institution rather than to those of the individual, had long been recognized as a necessary fulfillment for idle minds and languishing bodies. Spiritual needs, also, were given over to a part time chaplain and visiting priest upon request, and in accordance with the inmates' "free worshipping" incentives during the long weekends.

The clinical phase, because of early recognized diagnostic needs, had been in operation on a routine level over a period of more than 20 years. The "three-legged stool" concept, however, introduced an "equal" emphasis in each of these areas. It was new in the sense that it attempted to make these three functions a matter of administrative policy which the offender was *expected* to follow in the event that he was to show "improvement," or the necessary rehabilitative progress to warrant his release to a free environment.

This "new" policy, like many other similar innovations, tended to overlook a very necessary fourth leg, without which none of the other three legs could effectively support their own weight. This fourth leg, to continue the analogy, is based on the offender's own self-evaluation; the extent of his self-respect and sense of personal achievement as opposed to his, much more often defeatist attitude and gross anticipation of failure.

It was an attitude strongly associated with the identity which he had established for himself in relation to his family and to his peers. Were it possible to establish this identity in each individual as a competent and worthwhile person, the other needs relating to self-confidence, concentrated interest, and consequent motivation toward self-improvement would be consistently fulfilled as a matter of course.

It is the fulfillment of this elusive need which has been the bane of clinical services and administrative personnel since the date of the "three-legged stool" concept, or, for that matter, since a clinical approach was first introduced into penal procedures. It continues to merit top priority up to the present time. The big question, stated in another way, revolves around the stimulation of motives or incentives in the direction of constructive, self-lifting, and socially acceptable behavior.

What is it that continues to provide an allure for the stimulating effects of criminal behavior in spite of the myriad opportunities for a changed approach which are dangled within reach of the convicted offender? What is it that causes him to revert at a time when the family relationship appears to be intact, when his job situation is at its best, and when all of his parole requirements have been fulfilled? What is lacking in the personality composition of almost half of our prison commitments who continue to commit criminal acts during our most affluent periods?

There was a time, especially during the depression years and in that very unsettled period which had plunged us into World War II, when economic pressures, "4-F" classifications, and the family disruptions caused by the war itself, offered what might be regarded as ample justification for situational or circumstantial pressures responsible for criminal behavior. It has, however, been demonstrated quite conclusively over the years that crime tends to be accentuated in both number and severity of offenses during the most affluent periods of our national life.

In the fourth United Nations Congress on Prevention of Crime and Treatment of Offenders in which 80 countries were represented (Kyoto, Japan, August, 1970), there was a consensus of opinion on the high correlation between economic progress and the incidence of crime. The UN Undersecretary General for Economic and Social Affairs, furthermore, warned of a generalized breakdown of order which was robbing a democratic society of its openness and mobility, and pushing governments in the direction of "terrifying new instruments of surveillance." Earlier associations of crime with evidence of an impoverished economy, and the supposedly demoralizing effects of slum conditions, appear to have been largely unfounded, or at least secondary to much more pertinent causes.

We might, perhaps, be closer to the truth were we to give more serious consideration to the identity problem, and to the need for antisocial stimulation as described in Robert Ardrey's book *The Social Contract.*[6] In any event, we must look toward a defect in the personality itself for a true explanation, and for the means of controlling the need for criminal behavior.

In this arduous search for the truth behind criminal incentives, we must not be discouraged by the fact that only a relatively few of our most dangerous offenders are apprehended and brought to justice. We must operate on the assumption that the correction of one criminal can conceivably snowball into a contagious release of the inherent criminal pressures responsible for the criminal acts of many others.

"CORRECTIONS" IMPLIES A CORRECTIVE WILLINGNESS FOR CHANGE

The title of this book, which implies that the events of the past four decades have been a corrective experience for the correctional psychologist, as well as being in many ways productive in terms of emotional fulfillment for the criminal offender, also suggests that a certain correctional awareness and solidity of effort in the treatment process has been achieved.

We are, in fact, on the threshold of some very pertinent and realistic conclusions which cannot be avoided if the treatment process, as such, is to have any real meaning.

1. First of all, it is important to recognize that an adequate screening process in our dealings with the criminal offender is one of paramount importance. To begin with, it is no exaggeration to say that half of our institutionalized offenders could be separated from the others as minimum risks deserving of an objectively oriented approach in accordance with their special interests and vocational aptitudes. This group would, however, require separation from the others on an incentive basis which would allow for a rewarding expression of their special skills without the deadening influence of those who set the pace for work slowdowns with an "all state" rebellion against conscientious effort.

This latter element should also be screened from the others on the basis of a fatalistic, defeatist attitude which serves the personally degrading ulterior purpose of shifting responsibility away from themselves in a projection of blame onto external causes and circumstances. This type of offender consistently blinds himself to any awareness of his own capacity for resolving his difficulties. He tends to close the door on necessary insight and understanding which even the most effectively trained psychiatrist is incapable of unlocking without his help.

2. One of the least understood of the self-punishing incentives with which most of our recidivistic prison commitments are faced is the drive toward a martyred, "underdog" form of identity. The rewards of this "authoritatively abused, underprivileged" offender are great, in that he, thereby, achieves a status which he recognizes as impossible for one of his mediocre achievements in an otherwise "normal" existence.

For these persons, punishment relieves the anxiety which is precipitated by their concept of praise, the phony nature of which is accentuated by a deeply ingrained feeling that they are undeserving of this form of attention. What they really want is a direct and honest confrontation, and a *just* punishment for their wrongdoing. These are qualities which they, themselves, would tend to deny since each had experienced a dearth of this moral exercise throughout their formative years with indifferent or overly solicitous parents.

They are, nonetheless, ambivalently moved to search for firm boundaries outside of themselves in a last ditch attempt at controlling a form of behavior which they, themselves, do not understand. It is the reason why a disciplinary infraction is frequently followed by a more serious rules violation simply because the original rebellion was "insultingly" overlooked or "unjustly" excused.

It is also the reason why, on the verge of parole and what would appear to be a deserving break, the inmate will "senselessly" take "unofficial leave" of his trusty location, or perhaps propel himself into some uncompromising position which merits the purging recognition of solitary confinement. He fears the world of personal responsibility, and most of all, the uneasy anger which is awakened within him by the praise of those who reason, quite erroneously, that this is psychologically the one quality of which the offender has the greatest need.

The inmate offender dreads, and desperately strives to cover up, the anxiety laden, inner turmoil, and associated "masculine weakness," which begins to show when condescending praise of his efforts tells him that he is being moved by the insincere, authoritarian ego like a pawn on a chessboard. He wants the security of clearly defined "boundaries," a more realistic confrontation, less ideational hypocrisy, and less of the gently belittling and otherwise meaningless admonition that he "keep up the good work," or "we know you can do it" forms of "encouragement."

No one is more keenly aware than he is of the fact that he cannot, except through many ups and downs and a long, hard pull of his own uphill effort, make it on his own power. He sees those who are in control of his destiny as expecting too much, and offering too little in the way of any genuine interest or empathic concern, in order that they might, thereby, further their own self-centered needs.

3. Any form of training in a prison environment must take into consideration the security requirements of the institution as related to the custodial needs of both chronic, institution-wise commitments, and the more amenable, situational offender. The good intentions of the latter may be hampered by the ulterior motives of the former, since the security needs of the best are unavoidably governed by those of the worst with whom he is associated.

Then, too, whatever training may be specifically geared to the needs of the individual is continually overshadowed by the much more pressing need to produce tangible results. There is, in other words, a price tag on the training program itself which calls for a justification of its worth in terms of the self-supporting qualities of a tax supported, public welfare facility. Money savings must be somehow objectively demonstrated in a rehabilitative world of over-riding, subjective needs.

This tendency has been alleviated in recent years through the increased emphasis on medium security institutions focusing on "work release," "study release," and general vocational training needs more nearly commensurate with those found in a free setting.* Minimum security designations, however, often apply to the passively dependent, institutionalized recidivist as well as to first offenders who are sincerely motivated and who operate on a much higher level of personal responsibility. The need for effective screening, therefore, continues to be an urgent one, since potentially capable and well-motivated inmates are easily confused with the much more immature, but often likeable manipulations of the skilled sociopath.

As opposed to one of purely manipulative interests, an offender with ambition and drive toward social and vocational adjustment at a higher level is also a minimum risk by virtue of his effort and the consistency of his aims. He might, however, for that very reason be shifted to a farm or to a "key" position in the institution for the "good" of the administrative function, and at the expense of his own academic or vocational needs (see pp. 43-44).

This has happened over and over again. It was the primary cause for the failure of a job analysis and vocational aptitude testing program which was assiduously followed in Wisconsin adult correctional institutions over a two-year period following World War II (see pp. 36-40). Although the basic aptitudes were there, comparable to any which might be found in a free setting, the adverse pressures of morally perverse, authoritatively resistive, institution-wise inmates presented a stronger influence.

Then there was the ever pressing need, as well as the opportunity, for the best motivated offender to take advantage of available minimum security designations. These were often highly subservient, trusty assignments which did little to facilitate any form of personal initiative or training skills (see p. 43).

Under pressure of the sociopathic manipulations of the attention

---

*"Work release" is a 1965 legislative authorization and extension of a program patterned after Wisconsin's pioneering 1913 Huber Law that allowed convicted persons (originally restricted to misdemeanants) to hold outside jobs.

grabbing institution-wise inmate, a trusty placement was sometimes the "best" way out of an intolerable emotional situation. At the same time, it effectively sabotaged the growth of personal integrity, along with the offender's more realistic interests and training incentives which might otherwise have paved the way to a successful post-institutional adjustment.

4. The spirit of the committed offender should be retained at all costs, since all of his rehabilitative incentives hinge on his inner drive toward the assimilation of an initially mistrustful and slowly accepted sense of personal achievement. A consequent buildup of self-confidence depends on the self-respect which he is able to acquire in place of long accustomed dependency gratification. It must be of sufficient strength and tenacity to replace a tentatively exciting, but frustratingly inadequate behavior pattern.

As opposed to the disciplinary need for quelling the rebellious spirit which is searching for a recognized identity, we should be seeking ways of encouraging spirited behavior as a measure of integrated ego strength. In the hands of a competent clinical psychologist, the quality of this integrated aggressiveness might be readily discernible through a projective evaluation of the individual personality structure.

By the same token, we need to discourage the passively conforming behavior of the socially withdrawn person who complies with all of the institution rules without question, and without any evidence of personal initiative or capacity for independent thinking. He does all of this only to violate his supposedly "well-earned" parole within a year or less following his release as a "model prisoner."

5. It is extremely important that the basic requirements of each individual be determined on a clinically devised scale of priorities wherein primary needs are continually reviewed at regularly spaced intervals through a staff consensus of professionally trained personnel. The offender's most intense and frequently unspoken needs vary in accordance with the severity of inner pressures generated by a frustrating awareness of his inadequate functioning in relation to his true potential. It is a grossly misconstrued fact of prison life that the necessary utilization of his meagre emotional assets is sometimes irrevocably lost in a pervading sense of failure. The framework of this debilitating shell of criminal rehabilitative objectives is, more often

than not, erected along the authoritatively well-intentioned, but self-demeaning route to "intellectual fulfillment."

It should be apparent, under these circumstances, that the offender's functioning is, for the most part, governed by the conflicting qualities of his self-defeating emotional drives. The nature of these drives must, therefore, be sensitively appraised in the light of his family and interpersonal relationships. At the same time, they must be *consistently* evaluated against a balancing scale of *coordinated* test results, school and work progress reports, long range planning ability, spiritual outlook, and the frequently overshadowing incidence of disciplinary infractions.

The extent and character of the offender's inner resources, as well as the level of his emotional growth and associated capacity for empathic warmth and insight into human relations, must all be taken into consideration. Then the first and most pressing need should be isolated in each case as one which requires the combined attention of all with whom the offender is involved in the treatment program. He should not, for example, be subjected to vocational aptitude analysis, and a frequently inaccurate follow up of this need, before indicated emotional conflicts are sufficiently resolved so as to allow for the necessary release of his inner capacity for sustained interest and concentrated effort.

As indicated earlier, one priority which should be reversed is that which inadvertently gives first consideration to the chronic agitator and psychopathic complainer (see pp. 27-28). The otherwise well behaved, but much too quiet and socially withdrawn inmate should be brought into the psychotherapeutic and institution training arena whenever and wherever possible. It is quite possible that he may not only be most in need of help, but, once he is aware that someone is sincerely interested in his welfare, he may be better capable of aligning his inner resources toward the fulfillment of more constructive goals.

Finally, it is imperative that these privately guarded, cleverly disguised personal needs are recognized for what they are in a coordinated approach which promotes rather than conflicts with the institution security requirements.

6. Individual offenders must be trained in the direction of vocational skills, indicated academic needs, and related interpersonal adjust-

ments with the single idea of increasing the capacity of each for self-fulfillment through an elevation of his *personal* sense of achievement. It would be possible, thereby, to offer comparable incentives to the perverse stimulation of ego inflating, criminal behavior. This would involve the establishment of long neglected, competitive goals which, far from the self-demeaning penalties meted out for minor authoritative infractions, would actually condone the emotional catharsis of a frank and open authoritative evaluation.

We should, perhaps, test our own adaptability on the assumption that if we have nothing to hide we will have nothing to fear in an open discussion of authoritative vulnerability. We must strive more realistically for a frank expression of our own feelings as related to those of inmate offenders whom we hope to treat. Let us, then, permit ourselves the benefits of an honestly sincere appraisal as it appears from the point of view of those whom we hope to eventually reconcile with our own way of thinking and acting in a free world.

7. Group psychotherapy has done much to fulfill this need, but not to the extent that it is recognized and accepted for what it really seeks to accomplish in terms of individual initiative and acceptance of personal responsibilities. As presently conceived in a traditional, punitive framework, it is often threatening to the jealously guarded automony of an administrative authority which is primarily geared toward effective custodial controls.

Group psychotherapy has, nonetheless, taken a long step in the direction of providing the necessary atmosphere for developing an essential quality of self-respect in the criminal offender. An integrated awareness of this very important, but intangible need might be further advanced through staff oriented, sensitivity training sessions which require periodic participation on these controversial issues by all who are involved in correctional procedures.

8. Perhaps the greatest advancement in psychotherapeutic procedures with the criminal offender, next to group psychotherapy, is a relatively recent refinement of counseling sessions to include the wife (or girlfriend), parents, and/or siblings, in frank discussions of emotional insights which the offender has gleaned from his individual and group therapy sessions. The various family members are, thereby, placed under the spotlight of an emotional involvement on personal problems which each had, heretofore, been fearful of bringing out into the open.

The therapist, as an outsider who has a controlling influence with respect to the offender's effective utilization of dormant emotional assets, must first isolate these previously undisclosed emotional needs in appropriately spaced individual and group therapy sessions. Then, if he is sincerely interested in his client's future emotional welfare and adjustment potential in a free setting, he will insist on an airing of significant feelings in relation to those of the offender's family members. This is particularly true of those with whom the offender may be intimately associated at the time of his release.

FAMILY THERAPY NARROWS THE READJUSTMENT GAP

A most revealing example of the far-reaching gains resulting from prerelease family counseling sessions is that of a young couple with three small children. The 27-year-old father had been committed under the Wisconsin Sex Crimes Law for the rape of a nine-year-old girl. His pretty wife, also 27, had married her husband with a full awareness of his earlier involvement in forgery and burglary offenses, as well as the fact that he had philandering interests similar to those which had been demonstrated over the years by his own father.

The need to escape an underlying feminine identification, along with his futile attempts at matching up to the "potency" level of his "enviable" father, was recognized and thoroughly explored over a three-year-period of intensive group psychotherapy.

Throughout this period, his outwardly refined and obviously attractive young wife had never wavered in her loyalty toward him. She visited him at regular intervals at the prison despite the need to arrange for baby-sitters on her day off from a regular job through which she conscientiously sought to supplement the needs of her family.

During the period that her husband was confined, she was tormented by the overly attentive attitude of her supposedly sympathetic and helpful father-in-law. She later revealed that his proffered assistance had at times involved apparent attempts on his part to seduce her. She also admitted that, during the course of lonely weekends with her hard-to-manage family, she was under constant pressure to submit to adulterous behavior with former "friends" of the couple.

All of this she frankly discussed with her husband at the time of her regularly scheduled visits with him. Very much shaken over a chain of events in regard to which he was able to do nothing, the husband, in turn, sought advice and reassurance from his therapist. As a result, the wife and her husband's parents were individually interviewed, and once an understanding had been reached the entire family ultimately became involved in semimonthly counseling sessions.

Regular sessions, apart from their usual visiting time, continued with the inmate husband and his wife over a period of 18 months. These meetings were interspersed with Special Review Board appearances. The agonizing tensions of repeated denials on his application for parole precipitated a therapeutically valuable, but characteristically morose and sullenly hostile reaction on the part of the inmate offender.

Following the very discouraging news of his latest and third successive rejection by the Special Review Board, his distraught wife was propelled by a need to make a personal confession. For the first time, she revealed a cruel and painfully recalled segment of her own early behavior in which she had, as a child, pulled off the legs of frogs, and impaled other helpless creatures on the end of a sharp pointed stick.

She ultimately admitted guilt feelings over what she now recognized as a sadistic handling of her husband's most vital emotional needs. She confessed to using sex as a weapon against him, hoping, thereby, to prove to him how much he really needed her.

As it developed during the course of succeeding discussions, she had come to rely on deceitfully refined methods of dealing with her husband's gravitation to other sex partners. She now talked excitedly, since she suddenly realized that his need for new sex experiences was actually a form of retaliation against her own futile mismanagement of dominating controls. She told how she would, in those frustrating years of emotional distance and associated marital misunderstanding, entice him with every sexually provocative trick she knew, and then as quickly refuse him at the moment when she knew he was sexually worked up.

She admitted to using these tactics several times during the course of one evening. Then, when she finally relented and poutingly offered herself to him, he as suddenly lost his desire and refused to indulge in her own intense needs of the moment.

This was something that her husband's distorted moral concepts, enveloped as they were in an aura of untouchable motherhood, would never permit him to reveal on his own power. Whereas he had given some hint as to his generalized revulsion against sex as "dirty," and therefore incompatible with the sanctity of a "perfect" marriage, he had never at any time admitted anything which might in any way reflect against his wife or mother.

Under group pressure, however, he did confess his own inadequacy in the sense that he had always felt frustrated and never quite satisfied in the sex act with his wife. Whereas he was able to give a vague description of his confused feelings and associated psychic impotence, he never found words for the intense frustrations and unresolved anger which he must have experienced deep within himself as a consequence of his wife's tightening control over his most potent needs.

Once these intimately involved emotional problems were finally aired as a consequence of his wife's own unbearable sense of guilt, other personally traumatic incidents were discussed much more freely. Both parents admitted an intense concern over their son's masturbatory practices which they perceived as a genetic counterpart of the same painfully recalled experiences of the father. The father had, furthermore been quick to attribute his deviated behavior to the "perverted taint" which he saw foreshadowed in his own early masturbatory excesses.

At this stage, the parents responded eagerly to a form of enlightenment which served to shift their attention to a less emotional and more rational solution of their son's difficulties. They were now able to see the real evil in a *punitive handling* of the boy's masturbatory compulsions, and both were greatly relieved when they discovered that their most intense fears in this area had been greatly exaggerated.

The wife was subsequently brought to a realization of stern disciplinary measures with regard to her son's masturbatory practices as injurious to the boy's emotional growth. But, much more important at this point was her concomitant awareness of the manner in which her sadistic manipulation of her husband's sexual needs had tended to fortify his fearfully inadequate and warped concept of sex.

Once his wife had made a genuine emotional concession and admission of her own faults with respect to her husband's deviations, he, on his part, felt free to reveal heretofore undisclosed incestuous drives toward a younger sister. He haltingly told how he had attempted to rape her when he was 15, and when, as he now suddenly realized, she was at an age level identical to that of his victim in the current offense.

The intensely frustrated emotional needs of both husband and wife were consequently brought together in a manner which would never have been possible without the sensitive understanding of commonly shared psychotherapeutic sessions in a whole family context.

How can we measure the far-reaching effects of this family understanding on intimate emotional problems, the repercussions of which extend over two, and perhaps three, generations? This man has never again come to the attention of law enforcing authority, and we can only assume that he is leading an emotionally much more secure and increasingly stable existence with his much more understanding wife. But we have in this case, as in innumerable others, examples of positive changes which go unrecognized, simply because they no longer evoke the threatening spector of a crime ravaging emotional problem.

PUBLIC IMPATIENCE GIVES A NEGATIVE PUSH TO A POSITIVE NEED

As it is, we smother the quietly hopeful, but unheralded positives under the weight of our complaints against an "unjust" system of criminal controls. With all of our strength, if not with our apathy, we continue to see, feel, and live the negatives! We repeatedly tussle with them in chronically unchanged form because public protection demands that we direct at least 90 percent of our energies in this direction. Perhaps, if we devoted more time toward finding out who can, and who has been able to overcome serious criminal tendencies, we would know more about dealing with those who continue to repeat.

Most of those who have been able to make the adjustment to a more responsible and emotionally satisfying existence, however, do not want the publicity of any rehabilitative example which they might be able to offer through an unpleasant revival of their earlier conflicts. They could be of an immense help to other, less fortunate offenders. But, except in certain instances of volunteered services which are often anonymous, we are at a loss to know in what manner, or under what conditions, this example of rejuvenated strength against criminal patterns of behavior might best be presented as a helpful guide to others.*

One might suggest that there is a definite rehabilitative incentive in the knowledge that one is needed, and that he is able to exercise some measure of responsibility toward fulfilling the needs of his fellow inmates. It would, unquestionably, be helpful to the offender, as well as to parole releasing authority, if an obligatory return to the institution following a year of adjustment in a free setting were to be made a condition of his parole. This plan might, however, experience difficulties in terms of legal technicalities or "legal rights issues."

It would appear, therefore, that the voluntary concerns of an otherwise select group of former inmates would still be the main criteria for a hoped-for return in order that a therapeutic review of the "positives" in a released offender's adjustment experience might be offered.

In the meantime, we are confronted with the discouraging impact of the three out of five who continue to be the recidivistic forerunners of a chronically maladjusted criminal population. As a consequence, even the therapist has had to face the adverse conditioning of a negative point of view.

We are forced to devote prime consideration, for example, to an attempted control of the unpredictably dangerous, sadistic offender whom we know as a threat to law abiding citizens everywhere. Actually, about two-thirds of our prison commitments are for offenses other than those involving homicide, rape, robbery, and other forms of violence against persons. Among the potentially violent one-third, moreover, no more than 5 percent might be realistically appraised as inherently vicious, or deliberately antisocial, in their criminal tendencies.

It is the threat of this 5 percent criminal minority, however, which drags perhaps 95 percent of our rehabilitative energies under

*One of three federal grants which have for the first time been approved by the Wisconsin Council on Criminal Justice for the ten-year-old medium security Wisconsin Correctional Institution at Fox Lake, provides for the use of ex-offenders as group counselors. Since this was not made possible until mid-1971, it is still in an experimental stage, and subject to the usual restrictions of prison security and administrative controls. Under the plan being tried, however, at least four carefully selected ex-offenders who have succeeded on parole are invited to return for the purpose of conducting weekly group counseling sessions at the institution.

the pall of its negative influence. Nevertheless, because of our prolonged conditioning within the narrow range of this negative focus, we do have the raw materials for drawing together a composite picture of the unpredictably violent criminal offender. It can be safely assumed that we do know something of his personality composition, and what appears to be a coldly calculating and callous emotional reaction.

We know him, for example, as one who is motivated by a need to strike out with lethal weapons in a compulsively violent effort to rid himself of his own hateful inner turmoil. We know him, also, as one who has suffered the most from an insidious rejection of loved ones in his formative years. A review of the life histories and hidden backgrounds of practically all of the young male offenders who have committed sensationally vicious crimes in recent years will reveal a common affectional deprivation under the most intensely frustrating and intolerably rejecting circumstances imaginable.*

In practically every instance, as experience has shown, the potentially dangerous offender, or one who has already committed a criminally vicious or violent act against a person or persons, is the son of an unknown or affectionally indifferent father. When the father is known, he is often an affluent, authoritatively exacting, prestige conscious, and punitively rejecting person whose life interest is measured primarily in terms of material losses and gains.

The mother, on the other hand, is a seductively cruel affectional source; one who indirectly blames her son for "her ulcer" or her

*Five psychologists reporting in Washington, D. C. before the September, 1967 American Psychological Association convention with regard to their specialized studies on "the final act of alienation," arrived at some very significant conclusions. Their reports included the studies of Edwin I. Megargee of Florida State University,[76] and those of George R. Bach of Beverly Hills, California, Institute for Group Psychotherapy. They found that about 38 percent of all homicides in this country are committed within the family, and that about 40 percent occur among friends. Many murders within families were reported as having been committed by persons who were described as "chronically overcontrolled." Other descriptive phrases referred to the "deliberate, and relatively unemotional attitude" of the murderer toward what was "the most emotionally expressive act of his life." The murderers were otherwise described as "super coverts, or persons who suppressed aggressive instincts." These qualities "outnumbered those of persons who showed aggression by more than three to one." On the whole, the killers were described as "very nice guys," who were vulnerable to abusive undercurrents of "secrecy and deception." They were, consequently, strongly motivated to "use the punishment of death to take out their frustrations in the act of trying to love or to be loved."

"heart condition" while smothering him with kisses and special affectional nuances for which the father "does not have the time." She undermines his emotional capacity for self-sufficiency and self-assertiveness, while at the same time leading him to believe that she needs him to replace her apparently philandering, cruelly neglecting, and often abusively rejecting husband.

It is a viciously frustrating bind which calls for a vicious release of feeling, and which, barring any clinically available outlet, is projected against the person who revives this conflict in its most aggravated form.

THEY NEED MORE THAN PROFESSIONAL SKILL OR THE LIFT OF A NEW IDEA

We know that there are many facets to the emergence of a "whole man" during the highly controversial and generally uncertain course of a psychotherapeutic approach to his criminal behavior. But then there are other more tangible, and much more readily observable, forms of treatment. Work release programs, incentive pay scales, prerelease centers, halfway houses, and academically coordinated vocational training geared to the actual needs of the "institutionalized" offender in a free setting, are all slow, but sure-footed steps in a realistic, self-sustaining form of achievement.

Current recommendations in the direction of a more profound consideration for the *normal* needs of the individual offender reflect the enlightened hopefulness of long experience tempered by the tragic events of a failing prison system. The overall rehabilitative need is now visualized in the shape of community based treatment centers which might eventually eliminate prisons as we know them, or at least reduce the prison population to a more cohesive and individualized treatment unit.

Before this might become a reality, however, radical changes in public concepts of rehabilitation as *opposed* to punishment are an essential first step. Then the second most important step toward a more coordinated awareness of the top priorities in treatment versus security needs would become possible, and an integrated approach to the entire problem of criminal behavior would automatically follow.

As it is, we continue to find in all of our most "enlightened" proposals an absorbing interest in one area of treatment at the expense of another. We find ourselves in the center of a critical evaluation which stresses the inadequate or "unjust" handling of prisoners without regard for the necessary funding or material wherewithal for change. We perceive, with grave misgivings as to the sincerity, empathy, or understanding of wordy government officials, that they are often the showy harbingers of a rigidly narrow and one-sided point of view. We are frequently disillusioned by the discovery that these officials are flexible only in the sense that they bend in the heat of strategically well-timed political maneuvering under pressure of a publically inflamed emotional appeal.

If our present shallow tirade against "social ills" carries the weight of an excuse for revolutionary tactics which would tend to relieve the criminal offender of a personal accounting for his acts, who is to instill him with a normal sense of responsibility in our free society? How can he be both a victim and a defender of our continued hypocrisy, brash inconsistencies, and consequent "injustices" when we finally release him to his own "self-sufficient" devices? On what grounds can we say that, once he has been led to believe that "the end justifies the means," he is not again likely to rebel in the form of even more violent criminal behavior?

The unalterable truth continues to point the way to the criminal offender's whole-hearted motivation in the solution of problems which, in turn, require the consistency of our own deep understanding and faith in his capabilities as a person in his own right. Inmate self-governing units with an emphasis on personal responsibility, as well as responsible groups of ex-inmates in extra-institutional settings, must all prepare programs with individualized motivational goals as a topmost consideration in any positive controls over criminal patterns of behavior.*

*Since the tragedy at Attica, we have had gratifying news at both geographical extremes of our nation with respect to the self-determined beginnings of a much more responsive and responsibility minded offender. There is, for example, the "Fortune Society" composed of a group of ex-prisoners in New York who got their start in 1967 as a result of the self-elevating incentives which they found in a Broadway play. The aim of this organization is one of creating a public awareness through so-called reality sessions guided by an ex-offender in company with a correctional officer. Although prison wardens are understandably cautious and somewhat resistive to this form of "intrusion," the experiment has helped to fulfill a very vital need. The "activists" in this society contend that it "cuts down on unrest in an institution through an offer of hope and a form of *personal identity.*" It is, furthermore, presented as an example of positive rehabilitation which begins from the date of entrance into a penal institution, and which promotes, not "model prisoners, but

Not one program, no matter how cleverly designed, can result in any lasting benefit for the individual offender unless it is effectively coordinated with a changed self-concept. This calls for an increased sense of personal worth, and a new spur to motivational stimulation which must first be generated through related individual and group psychotherapeutic intervention. Group psychotherapy over a period of almost 20 years in Wisconsin Correctional settings has, in fact, proven its effectiveness in both institutional disciplinary controls, and in the otherwise submerged and seldom voiced positives which unquestionably exist in the extrainstitutional adjustment capabilities of the treated offender[114,115] (see pp. 68 and 85-90).

BUT, THEN COMES A NEW SWING ON THE OLD REHABILITATIVE "FULCRUM"

In this fast changing, "throw-away" world, we must forever discard the old and try something new! Except for the negatively critical and consequently threatening effect which it has on the stability of traditionally entrenched penal practices, this flexibility in our clinical approach might be regarded as most essential to progress in human behavioral controls.

In recent years, however, these changes have occurred much too frequently under pressure of an erudite impatience in the learning needs of academically oriented treatment personnel. At the expense of any truly integrated, or time-tested rehabilitative assimilation of plus or minus indices of success, enthusiastically proposed changes have often become lost in undercurrents of resistance and controversial uncertainty. The main difficulty is that many of the new approaches, by their very nature, tend to be clinically biased, professionally aloof, and academically transitory in the quality of their appeal. It stands to reason, then, that the long-standing supportive "security" upon which a new approach to the criminal offender's treatment needs must operate will tend to plug up the chinks in its

model citizens" upon release to a much more acceptant society. At Walla Walla, Washington, another group of prison inmates known as "The Family" operate on three major, self-determined rules: "no drugs or alcohol, no violence, and no apathy." They have the privilege of deciding the family's membership, as well as the power for the necessary expulsion of any of its members who cannot, or will not, adhere to its self-made conditions. A "spin off organization" of the original "Family" is a second group known as "The Community," members of which are pledged to condition themselves to extra-institutional functioning, including the realistic acceptance of personal responsibility and self-control in a free environment.

armor covering an otherwise subversively immobile and repressive force.

Currently, the treatment pendulum is describing a new arc. In the midst of the conflicting concerns for authoritative "respect," on the one hand, and the self-respecting needs of the criminal offender, on the other, a somewhat frightening focus on behavioristic techniques has developed. The continuing controversy and underlying confusion as to the most effective means of treatment again tends to favor the more statistically concise, tangible results, as a most desirable objective.*

In harmony with this forcefully expressed need is the cumulative evidence over the past decade of a form of densensitization, in combination with relaxation, aversive, or approach-avoidance techniques, designed to extinguish undesirable patterns of behavior while fortifying other more desirable adjustment goals. So-called counterconditioning, extinction, operant conditioning, and modeling procedures, based on four principles of learning, have been successfully pursued in the laboratory and in other isolated experimental situations. These experiments presuppose that criminal behavior might be similarily extinguished, while other more purposeful behaviors are positively reinforced through properly conducted behavioristic techniques.[7]

These findings, however, open up serious doubts as to the ultimate effects of this behavioristic conditioning process on the total personality and the necessary freedom of the individual's capacity for social adaptability.

One is made aware at this point of a potent question, originally posed in the thoroughly enlightened and thought-provoking works of Dr. Seymour L. Halleck.[56] He points out the limitations and fallacies involved in the attempted correction of criminal behavior through the removal of an "antisocial symptom," and asks: "Is it really in the

*In a 1971 book by B. F. Skinner, *Beyond Freedom and Dignity*,[99] there is considerable emphasis on a "technology of behavior" which assumes that each of us is a "unique bundle of behavior determined solely by a host of environmental influences." Skinner assumes that man has never been free in the traditional, humanistic sense; that he has never possessed an inner autonomy. He emphasizes the rewards of "positive reinforcers," which he contends are more effective than punishment. Although he concedes that behavior technology can be misused to the extent that it might result in regimentation and despotism, he maintains that we desperately need the "cultural design" of an advanced technology toward a better system of control through the behavioristic sciences.

patient's best interest to extinguish maladaptive behavior if nothing is done to alleviate the other stresses of his existence?"

Expressed in another way, Dr. Halleck questions the advisability of taking away, through specially designed behavior therapies, something which is not only maladaptively useful, but vital to the offender's current adjustment needs. Are we in a position to offer any new found inner incentives or strengths of purpose to put in the place of the specific asocial focus, or negative reaction to stress, which in an experimentally mechanized and generally unfeeling fashion we are so insistently anxious to remove?

We are then obliged to ask ourselves this question: Are we, with all of the energetic twists and turns of our most hopefully beneficial treatment procedures, really seeking to advance the potential strength of the individual offender, and thereby increase his sense of personal responsibility? Or, are we simply narrowing the intensity of our efforts in a search for a new level of mass security through the authoritarian will? Are we, in effect, adding a new form of passive conformity to the already dependent attitudes of a large segment of our chronically incarcerated criminal offenders?

No matter how purposefully therapeutic the aim may be, we need a consensus of opinion on the ultimate goal as one which places the driving power with respect to his own destiny in the hands of the individual himself. Any approach, no matter how diversified, defeats its own purpose unless it maintains the concept of individual initiative and flexibility of movement in our free society.

This can be no less true of the criminal offender than it is of any other human being. It is our professional duty, as clinical workers in the correctional field, to open up new avenues to a full expression of these all important, self-sustaining needs. A fully rehabilitated criminal offender, thereby, becomes one who has found an avenue through which the constructive awareness of personal achievement has been inwardly generated.

External pressures within the institution itself are presently encouraging the extremes of increased visiting privileges which invite a clamor for specially arranged conjugal relationships on regularly spaced occasions. Naturally, the overriding majority are single, or legally separated offenders, who are demanding this privilege along with the married ones whose family relationships are still intact.

This self-gratifying need, as in all of the more immature, attention-seeking agitations, is spearheaded by the egocentric urgings of an irresponsible minority who have many otherwise passively dependent, and highly suggestible followers. Only a few of the more responsible inmate offenders have given any thought to the more pressing need for a psychic understanding, and the mutual respect which is implied in any satisfying sexual union. Intimate physical contacts without this understanding present an almost impossible and potentially explosive situation within the shadow of prison walls. It is a privilege which must be earned, and gradually indoctrinated in the group psychotherapeutic and general rehabilitative process.*

A newly established prison magazine, revived at the Wisconsin State Prison after an interval of 26 years, has provided a needed verbal medium of authoritative expression on the part of many who are urgently in need of this form of emotional release. But, while this outlet has been expanded with obvious benefits to the otherwise repressed inmate, group therapy is in danger of taking on the more shallow and generalized characteristics of discussion groups with rather questionable goals.

This may be in part due to the fact that the earlier clinical incentives, which were associated with a mandatory sex crimes treatment program, have now been "hospitalized" in a more relaxed and less challenging mental hygiene setting (see p. 77). Or, it may be a defensive reaction against the more intensely objective "prison reform" and prisoner's legal rights issues now pending under pressure of suddenly increased investigative interests on the part of the Governor's Task Force and the House Judiciary Subcommittee on Penology.

The clinical shift in group psychotherapeutic depth might be more realistically explained in its overall context, however, as a waning of the essential enthusiasm through which all innovations in therapeutic endeavor achieve their initial success. It is a lesson in the much more pressing need for recapturing this enthusiasm through the innate flexibility and contagiously dynamic interests of the therapist himself.

*A measure which was approved in April, 1971 by the Wisconsin Board of Health and Social Services provides for an Adult Furlough Law which would permit the Department to establish regulations under which adults could be released from an institution for up to 30 days for purposes such as family visits during emergencies, funerals, contacts with respective employers, or for purposes of release planning.

Clinical research has, nonetheless, been inexorably advanced, and a variety of stimulating professional papers based on more than a decade of exploratory psychological and psychiatric experience in correctional settings, speak eloquently of the creative thought and constructive effort which is being expended.*

There is, nonetheless, a trend in corrections everywhere to emphasize what we might call a "fad" in the application of psychotherapeutic techniques which often obscures what should be a more global viewpoint in our dealings with the criminal offender. Despite the often rewarding reaction of prison inmates to uniquely different, or previously untried, treatment innovations, the underlying need must resolve itself in a patiently sincere and confident elevation of the self-concept of the individual offender. Only then can any durable alteration in his asocial characteristics and antisocial pattern of behavior be realistically anticipated.

CONCLUSIONS

Despite every available opportunity for self-improvement, we know that it is not possible for the offender to respond under pressure of unresolved fears, anxieties, emotional depression, or deeply repressed hates, with anything but a small and ineffective part of his inwardly creative or constructive potential. We know, also, that this potential tends to be destroyed through punitive measures which deny a man his right to express his true feelings.

These feelings cannot be unlocked unless a man has some measure of trust in the fact that they will be accepted in an understanding light. This, in turn, depends on authoritative recognition of the importance of self-respect in each individual offender before he can be expected to show respect toward others.

*It should be noted in the interest of Wisconsin Corrections, that the significant research efforts of Asher R. Pacht, Ph. D, Director of the Bureau of Clinical Services have been recognized at the August, 1971 meeting of the American Association of Correctional Psychologists in an award for "Outstanding Achievement in Correctional Psychology." The impact of what Dr. Pacht regards as the combined efforts of an enthusiastic and dedicated staff, is most appreciated in the overall perspective of the 101st Annual Congress of Corrections meeting at Miami Beach, Florida. Here, Sanger B. Powers, Administrator of Wisconsin's Division of Corrections was presented with the Edward R. Cass Award, the highest that the American Correctional Association has to offer in recognition of leadership and achievement in the corrections field.

When a man is able to appreciate the worth of his own intense feelings in a wholesome interaction with those of others, he comes very close to being a well-integrated and enthusiastically motivated person. That is because he is able to tolerate the other as a *genuine* person with his own brand of imperfections which might, thereby, be accepted for the "normally" human qualities which they are.

He becomes increasingly more tolerant because of the understanding tolerance which others are able to extend to him. He, therefore, emerges a whole man because he no longer needs to consume all of his psychic energy and skill in a perpetually frustrating cover-up of childish threats and fears against the smothering contempt of authoritative condemnation and ridicule. He now has both the inner strength and the purposeful incentive for a constructive release of his most satisfying ambitions and drives.

BIBLIOGRAPHY

1. Abrahamsen, D.: *Crime and the Human Mind.* New York, Columbia University Press, 1944.
2. Abrahamsen, D.: *Who are the Guilty?* New York, Rinehart, 1952.
3. Abrahamsen, D.: *The Psychology of Crime.* New York, Columbia University Press, 1960.
4. Ackerman, N. W.: *The Psychodynamics of Family Life.* New York, Basic Books, 1958.
5. Albert, L. H.: Prisoners, family life, and prisons. *Correctional Psychologist, 3*:15, 1967.
6. Ardrey, R.: *The Social Contract.* New York, Atheneum, 1970.
7. Bachrach, A. J.: Some applications of operant conditioning to behavior therapy. In Wolpe, J., *et al.* (Eds.): *The Conditioning Therapies.* New York, Holt, Rinehart & Winston, 1964.
8. Bandura, A., and Walters, R. H.: Dependency conflicts in aggressive delinquents. *J Social Issues, 14*:52-65, 1958.
9. Bell, P.: Psychiatric Field Service, sixth biennial report. *Report of the Wisconsin State Board of Control,* July, 1934-1936.
10. Bender, L.: Psychopathic disorders in children. In Lindner, R. (Ed.): *Handbook of Correctional Psychology.* New York, Philosophical Library, 1947, p. 360.
11. Bennett, J. V.: A cool look at 'the crime crisis.' In special supplement on crime and punishment. *Harper's Magazine,* April, 1964, pp. 122-187.
12. Bennett, J. V.: *I Chose Prison.* New York, Alfred A. Knopf, 1970.
13. Bergler, E.: *The Basic Neurosis: Oral Aggression and Psychic Masochism.* New York, Grune & Stratton, 1949.
14. Berkowitz, L.: *Aggression: A Social Psychological Analysis.* New York, McGraw-Hill, 1962.
15. Berne, E.: *Group Treatment.* New York, Grove Press, 1966.
16. Bieber, I., *et al.*: *Homosexuality: A Psychoanalytic Study of Male Homosexuals.* New York, Basic Books, 1962.
17. Boszormenyi-Nagy and Framo, J. L. (Eds.): *Intensive Family Therapy.* New York, Hoeber-Harper, 1965.
18. Branden, N.: *The Psychology of Self-Esteem.* Los Angeles, Nash Publishing, 1969.
19. Branden, N.: *Breaking Free.* Los Angeles, Nash Publishing, 1970.
20. Bromberg, W.: *The Mold of Murder.* New York, Grune & Stratton, 1961.

21. Burke, J. C.: Prisons are not made to punish. *Federal Probation, 4*:30-35, May, 1940.
22. Caldwell, G.: *Criminology.* New York, Ronald Press, 1956.
23. Clark, R.: *Crime in America.* New York, Simon & Schuster, 1970.
24. Cleckley, H. M.: *The Mask of Sanity,* 3rd ed. St. Louis, C. V. Mosby, 1955.
25. Clinard, M. B.: Criminal behavior is human behavior. *Federal Probation, 13*:21-27, March, 1949.
26. Coogan, M.: Wisconsin's experience in treating psychiatrically deviated sex offenders. *J Social Therapy, 3*:6, 1955.
27. Corsini, R. J., and Uehling, H. F.: A cross validation of Davidson's Rorschach adjustment scale. *J Consulting Psychology, 18*:277-279, 1954.
28. Corsini, R. J., Severson, W. E., Tunney, T. E., and Uehling, H. F.: The separation capacity of the Rorschach. *J Consulting Psychology, 19*:194-196, 1955.
29. Cottle, C. R.: Group therapy in prisons. *Correctional Psychologist, 3*:7-12, 1967.
30. Cressy, D.: Limitation on the organization of treatment in the modern prison. In *Theoretical Studies of Social Organization of the Prison.* New York Social Science Research Council, 1960, pp. 78-110.
31. Ellis, A., and Brancale, R.: *The Psychology of Sex Offenders.* Springfield, Thomas, 1956.
32. Ellis, A.: The sex offender and his treatment. In Toch, H. (Ed.): *Legal and Criminal Psychology.* New York, Holt, Rinehart & Winston, 1961, pp. 400-416.
33. Eysenck, H. S.: *Behavior Therapy and the Neuroses.* New York, Pergamon Press, 1960.
34. Eysenck, H. S.: *Crime and Personality.* Boston, Houghton Mifflin, 1964.
35. Fenton, N.: The prison as a therapeutic community. *Federal Probation, 20*:26-29, 1956.
36. Fine, R.: Psychoanalytic theory of sexuality. In Slovenko, R. (Ed.): *Sexual Behavior and the Law.* Springfield, Thomas, 1965, pp. 147-167.
37. Fink, A. E.: *Causes of Crime,* Perpetua Edition. New York, Barnes, A. S., 1962.
38. Fox, V.: *Violence Behind Bars.* New York, Vantage Press, 1956.
39. Fox, V.: Why prisoners riot. *Federal Probation, 35*:9-14, 1971.
40. Freud, S.: Some character types met with in psychoanalytic work, the criminal out of a sense of guilt. In *Collected Papers,* Vol. 4. London, Hogarth Press, 1959.
41. Freud, S.: Inhibition, symptoms, and anxiety. In Strachey, J. (Ed.): *The Standard Edition of the Complete Psychological Works of Sigmund Freud,* Vol. 20. London, Hogarth Press, 1959.
42. Fromm-Reichmann, F.: *Principles of Intensive Psychotherapy.* Chicago, University of Chicago Press, 1950.

43. Gibbons, D. C.: Who knows about corrections? *Crime and Delinquency, 9*:137-144, 1963.
44. Glaser, D.: Criminality theories and behavioral images. *Am J Soc, 61*:433-445, 1956.
45. Glasser, W.: *Reality Therapy.* New York, Simon & Schuster, 1970.
46. Glover, E.: *The Roots of Crime.* New York, International Universities Press, 1960.
47. Glueck, S., and Glueck, E.: *Predicting Delinquency and Crime.* Cambridge, Harvard University Press, 1959.
48. Guttmacher, M. S.: *The Mind of the Murderer.* New York, Farrar, Straus & Cudahy, 1960.
49. Haley, J.: *Strategies of Psychotherapy.* New York, Grune & Stratton, 1963.
50. Halleck, S. L.: The criminal's problem with psychiatry. *Psychiatry, 23*:409-412, November, 1960.
51. Halleck, S. L., and Pacht, A. R.: Current status of the Wisconsin sex crimes law. *Wisconsin Bar Bulletin,* December, 1960.
52. Halleck, S. L.: The initial interview with the offender. *Federal Probation, 25*:23-27, 1961.
53. Halleck, S. L.: The impact of professional dishonesty on behavior of disturbed adolescents. *Social Work, 8*:48-53, 1963.
54. Halleck, S. L.: American psychiatry and the criminal: A historical review. *Am J Psychiatry, 121* (Suppl):1-21, 1965.
55. Halleck, S. L.: Emotional effects of victimization. In Slovenko, R. (Ed.): *Sexual Behavior and the Law.* Springfield, Thomas, 1965, pp. 673-686.
56. Halleck, S. L.: *Psychiatry and the Dilemmas of Crime.* New York, Harper & Row, 1967.
57. Harlow, H., Uehling, H., and Maslow, A.: Comparative behavior of primates. 1. Delayed reaction tests on primates. *J Comparative Psychology, 13*:313-343, 1932.
58. Harlow, H. F.: The nature of love, *Am Psychol, 13*:673-685, 1958.
59. Harlow, H. F.: Social deprivation in monkeys. *Scientific American,* November, 1962, pp. 1-11.
60. Harris, T.A.: *I'm OK—You're OK. A Practical Guide to Transactional Analysis.* New York, Harper & Row, 1969.
61. Johnson, E. H.: A basic error: Dealing with inmates as though they were abnormal. *Federal Probation, 35*:39-44, 1971.
62. Johnson, J. A.: *Group Therapy, a Practical Approach.* New York, McGraw-Hill, 1963.
63. Karpman, B.: *The Sexual Offender and His Offenses.* New York, Julian Press, 1954.
64. Karpman, B.: Criminal psychodynamics: a platform. *J Criminal Psychodynamics, 1*:1-96, 1955.

65. Kinsey, A. C., *et al.* Institute for Sex Research, Inc.: *Sex Offenders.* New York, Harper & Row and Paul B. Hoeber, 1965.
66. Lesse, S.: *An Evaluation of the Results of the Psychotherapies.* Springfield, Thomas, 1968.
67. Lorenz, K.: *On Aggression.* London, Methuen, 1966.
68. Ludwig, A.: *The Importance of Lying.* Springfield, Thomas, 1965.
69. Lyle, W. H.: The psychopathic offender: Issues in treatment. *Correctional Psychologist, 3:3-8, 1968.*
70. MacDonald, J. M.: *The Murderer and His Victim.* Springfield, Thomas, 1961.
71. MacDonald, J. M.: *Homicidal Threats.* Springfield, Thomas, 1968.
72. Maltz, M.: *Psychogybernetics and Self-fulfillment.* New York, Grosset & Dunlap, 1970.
73. McClintock, F. H.: *Crimes of Violence, an Enquiry by the Cambridge Institute of Criminology.* London, Macmillan, 1963.
74. McCord, W., McCord, J., and Zola, I.: *Origins of Crime.* New York, Columbia University Press, 1959.
75. McCorkle, L. W.: The present status of group therapy in United States correctional institutions. *International Journal of Group Psychotherapy, 3:85, 1953.*
76. Megargee, E. I., and Hokanson, J. E.: *The Dynamics of Aggression.* New York, Harper & Row, 1970.
77. Menninger, K. A.: *Theory of Psychoanalytic Technique.* New York, Basic Books, 1955.
78. Menninger, K. A.: Verdict guilty, now what? *Harper's Magazine,* August, 1959.
79. Menninger, K. A.: *The Vital Balance.* New York, Viking Press, 1963.
80. Menninger, K. A.: *The Crime of Punishment.* New York, Viking Press, 1966.
81. Morris, A.: What do administrative and professional staffs think about their correctional systems? *Correctional Research, 2:1-28, 1968.*
82. Pacht, A. R., Halleck, S. L., and Ehrmann, J. C.: Diagnosis and treatment of the sex offender, a nine year study. *Am J Psychiatry, 118:802-808, 1962.*
83. Pacht, A. R., and Halleck, S. L.: Development of mental health programs in correction. *Crime and Delinquency, 12:1-8, 1966.*
84. Pacht, A. R., and Roberts, L. M.: Factors related to parole experience of the deviated sex offender. *J Correctional Psychology, 3:8-11, 1968.*
85. Palmer, S.: *A Study of Murder.* New York, Thomas Crowell, 1960.
86. Perls, F. S.: John O. Stevens (Ed.): *Gestalt Therapy Verbatim.* Real People Press, 1969.
87. Phillips, L., and Smith, J. G.: *Rorschach Interpretation: Advanced Technique.* New York, Grune & Stratton, 1953.

88. Richmond, F. C.: Psychiatric Field Service, fifth biennial report. *Report of the Wisconsin State Board of Control.* July, 1932-1934.
89. Richmond, F. C.: Prison of the future—suggestion no. 5. *News Bulletin, The Osborne Association, Inc.,* 5:5, 1934.
90. Roberts, L. M., and Pacht, A. R.: Termination of inpatient treatment for sex deviates: Psychiatric social and legal factors. *Am J Psychiatry, 121*:873-880, 1965.
91. Roche, P.: *The Criminal Mind.* New York, Farrar, Straus & Cudahy, 1958.
92. Roebuck, J. B.: *Criminal Typology.* Springfield, Thomas, 1967.
93. Rogers, C.: *On Becoming a Person.* Sentry edition, Boston, Houghton Mifflin, 1961.
94. Rogers, C.: *On Encounter Groups.* New York, Harper & Row, 1970.
95. Rosenbaum, M.: Group psychotherapy and psychodrama. In Wolman, B. (Ed.): *Handbook of Clinical Psychology.* New York, McGraw-Hill, 1965, pp. 1254-1273.
96. Rothstein, J.: Corrections is based on the dignity of man. *Federal Probation, 34*:38-40, 1970.
97. Shapiro, L. N.: Psychiatry in the correctional process. *Crime and Delinquency, 12*:9-16, 1966.
98. Shultz, G. D.: *How Many More Victims?* Philadelphia, New York, J. B. Lippincott, 1965.
99. Skinner, B. F.: *Beyond Freedom and Dignity.* New York, Alfred A. Knopf, Inc., 1971.
100. Slavson, S. R.: *A Textbook in Analytic Group Psychotherapy.* New York, International Universities Press, 1964.
101. Slovenko, R.: *Crime, Law and Corrections.* Springfield, Thomas, 1966.
102. Slovenko, R.: *Psychotherapy, Confidentiality, and Privileged Communication.* Springfield, Thomas, 1966.
103. Stratton, J.: Prisoner rehabilitation-confluence or conflict, *Correctional Psychologist, 3*:8-12, 1967.
104. Szasz, T.: Criminal responsibility and psychiatry. In Toch, H. (Ed.): *Legal and Criminal Psychology.* New York, Holt, Rinehart & Winston, 1961, pp. 146-168.
105. Terman, L. M., and Merrill, M. A.: *Measuring Intelligence.* Boston, The Riverside Press Cambridge, Houghton Mifflin, 1937.
106. Thurrell, R. J., Everett, H. C., Uehling, H. F., and Gray, D. E.: Didactic supplementation of psychiatric treatment programs. In Masserman, J. H. (Ed.): *Current Psychiatric Therapies, Vol. 5.* New York, Grune & Stratton, 1965, pp. 150-156.
107. Thurrell, R. J., Halleck, S. L., and Johnson, A. F.: Psychosis in prison. *J Criminal Law, Criminology and Police Science. 56*:271-276, 1965.
108. Uehling, H. F.: Comments on a suggested revision of the Woodworth psychoneurotic inventory. *J Abnormal and Social Psychology, 28*:462-467, 1934.

109. Uehling, H. F.: Psychological testing of delinquents in Wisconsin. *Sixth Biennial Report of the Wisconsin State Board of Control,* 1934-1936.
110. Uehling, H. F.: Interpretation of intelligence test results. *The Rebuilder, State Board of Control of Wisconsin,* 1:83-85, 1937.
111. Uehling, H. F.: Place of psychological tests in penal classification. *Public Welfare, Wisconsin State Department of Public Welfare,* 1:18-20, 1945.
112. Uehling, H. F.: Rorschach "shock" for two special populations. *J Consulting Psychology,* 16:224-225, 1952.
113. Uehling, H. F.: The inner man steps out. *Creative Wisconsin.* Spring, 1960, pp. 9-13.
114. Uehling, H. F.: Group therapy turns repression into expression for prison inmates. *Federal Probation,* 26:43-49, 1962.
115. Uehling, H. F.: Crime breeds on smothered feelings. *Federal Probation,* 30:11-17, 1966.
116. Vedder, C. B., and Kay, B. A.: *Penology.* Springfield, Thomas, 1969.
117. Watkins, J. G.: Psychotherapeutic methods. In Wolman, B. (Ed.): *Handbook of Clinical Psychology.* New York, McGraw-Hill, 1965, pp. 1143-1167.
118. Wattenberg, W. W.: Psychologists and juvenile delinquency. In Toch, H. (Ed.): *Legal and Criminal Psychology.* New York, Holt, Rinehart & Winston, 1961, pp. 243-270.
119. Wechsler, D.: *Measurement of Adult Intelligence,* 3rd ed. Baltimore, Williams & Wilkins, 1944.
120. Wertham, F.: *The Show of Violence.* New York, Doubleday & Co., 1949.
121. Wilson, D. P.: *My Six Convicts.* New York, Rinehart & Co., 1951.
122. Wilson, J. C., and Pescor, M. J.: *Problems in Prison Psychiatry.* Caldwell, Idaho, Paxton Printers, 1939.
123. Wolfgang, M.: A sociological analysis of criminal homicide. *Federal Probation,* 25:48-55, 1961.
124. Yablonsky, L.: *Synanon: The Tunnel Back.* Baltimore, Penguin Books, 1965.

INDEX